DATE DUE

TEACHERS' PROFESSIONAL DEVELOPMENT AND THE ELEMENTARY MATHEMATICS CLASSROOM

Bringing Understandings to Light

STUDIES IN MATHEMATICAL THINKING AND LEARNING
Alan H. Schoenfeld, Series Editor

TEACHERS' PROFESSIONAL DEVELOPMENT AND THE ELEMENTARY MATHEMATICS CLASSROOM

Bringing Understandings to Light

Sophia Cohen

LEA LAWRENCE ERLBAUM ASSOCIATES, PUBLISHERS
2004   Mahwah, New Jersey   London

The research for this book was primarily supported by a joint grant to the author from John D. and Catherine T. MacArthur Foundation and Spencer Foundation under the Professional Development Research and Documentation Program. In its earliest stages, the author's research for this book was supported by grant number ESI - 9254393 awarded by the National Science Foundation to Deborah Schifter, Virginia Bastable, and Susan Jo Russell. The author conducted the research for this book while an employee of the Education Development Center, Inc., which also provided support to the author in her publication of this book. Any opinions, findings, conclusions, or recommendations expressed in the book are those of the author and do not necessarily reflect those of the funders.

Lawrence Erlbaum Associates, Inc., Publishers
10 Industrial Avenue
Mahwah, New Jersey 07430

Library of Congress Cataloging-in-Publication Data

Cohen, Sophia R.
   Teachers' professional development and the elementary mathematics classroom : bringing understandings to light / by Sophia R. Cohen
      p. cm.—(Studies in mathematical thinking and learning)
   Includes bibliographical references and index.
   ISBN 0-8058-4287-X (c. : alk. paper)   ISBN 0-8058-4288-8 (p. : alk. paper)
   1. Mathematics—Study and teaching (Elementary). 2. Mathematics teachers—Training of. I. Title. II. Series.

QA135.6.C64   2004
372.7—dc22   2003049453
                                                                                      CIP

Books published by Lawrence Erlbaum Associates are printed on acid-free paper, and their bindings are chosen for strength and durability.

Printed in the United States of America
10 9 8 7 6 5 4 3 2 1

For Maia and Nina, my daughters,
with whom I've come to many new understandings.

And for all of the other great teachers—
both in and out of classrooms—
with whom I've had the pleasure of learning.

Contents

Foreword

Suzanne M. Wilson
Michigan State University

A handful of truisms about professional development currently curry favor among teachers and policymakers. Professional development should be long term, giving teachers a chance to go in and out of their classrooms, try things out with their students, and subsequently reflect on what they have learned. Professional development should focus on the concrete products of student work, grounding teachers' work in that of their students. Professional development should pay equal attention to developing teachers' content and pedagogical knowledge. These seem such sensible assertions. Although there is some research that supports these claims, scholarship in teacher learning is characterized by more rhetoric than empiricism.

With this extended and finely detailed description of and reflection on the work of teachers in Developing Mathematical Ideas seminars, Sophia Cohen makes an important contribution to our empirical and conceptual understanding of teacher learning. While reinforcing many contemporary truisms, Cohen does so much more: Taking us inside of those seminars and inside of the participants' classrooms, she shows us the complexities inherent in teachers' attempts to learn about mathematics, about students, about teaching, and about changing their teaching. Her thick descriptions of teacher learning allow us to understand both the teachers' perspectives and the internal workings of professional development. By bringing teachers' understandings to light, she helps us learn about teacher learning. Let us consider some of the lessons readers might take from this sojourn.

One lesson involves the courage it takes to engage in genuine professional development—that is, in professional development intended to

fundamentally influence one's knowledge and practice. Learning—not
picking up helpful tips, but learning mathematics and learning about children and how they think—is hard, like all intellectual work. In a conversation I had with a mathematician colleague recently, he spoke of the role of
despair in his own learning: He has never had a mathematical insight, he
claimed, that was not preceded by a long period of personal and intellectual despair. Long-term, ongoing professional development asks teachers
to learn, to recognize their own limitations, and to strive to alter those limitations. It is painful and frustrating, as Ella, one of the DMI participants
says, "It is thinking that you know so much and realizing that you know
so little. . . . It was an eye-opener . . . I wondered, 'Gee whiz, should I even
be teaching?' " Sticking with DMI once one realizes, as Ella said, how little
one knows takes courage.

A second lesson involves understanding the difference between recognizing a problem with one's teaching and having the skills and knowledge to work on or remedy that problem. For instance, it is one thing to realize how little one understands mathematics or how little one knows
about what students understand. It is another thing to move beyond that
problem identification or recognition to new practice. As readers see in
this book, one of the DMI participants, Abby, recognized that she needed
to hear more from students. So she changed her practice; she started asking more questions. But questions are not created equally, and the whole-
sale adoption of asking questions is neither sound pedagogically nor efficient. Thus, over time, Abby learns to rethink her "understanding" of
what are good times to ask students questions and what questions make
the most pedagogical sense.

Third, this work—moving from rhetoric ("I should learn more about
student learning") or realization ("I don't know enough about mathematics") to a reformed practice and deepened knowledge and skill—takes
time and practice. It also entails making mistakes, telling others about
those mistakes, and using those mistakes as opportunities to learn.
George Bernard Shaw is reputed as having said, "A life spent making mistakes is not only more honorable but more useful than a life spent doing
nothing." Learning how to put ideas into practice requires practice as well
as the unavoidable mistakes that come with that practice. This is a problem faced by all professions. Gawande's (2002) description of learning to
become a surgeon is a poignant reminder of how hard this process is.
"Mine were not experienced hands" (p. 12), he noted. "In surgery, as in
anything else, skill and confidence are learned through experience—haltingly and humiliatingly" (p. 18). As readers come to see, errors—both
mathematical errors and teaching errors—play a major role in professional learning. This is also true of all professional work, as was so thor-
oughly described and analyzed in Bosk's (1979) classic sociology of man-

aging medical error; teachers, like doctors, need to learn to "forgive and remember" as they learn from their mistakes.

A fourth lesson involves the need for community and peer review. "Learning communities" is a popular slogan in education reform, suffering like most slogans from overuse and misunderstanding. Cohen's careful portrait of the DMI seminars, and how the participants and facilitators gradually created for themselves a public forum for peer critique, sheds light on when such learning communities might be helpful and why. DMI participants felt supported and known; they learned to trust the other participants and have faith that everyone had something to learn. It would be a mistake to stop at trust, presuming that that is the single critical feature of these communities. Trust was just the beginning. The real educative impact of the seminars was from the developing capacity of the participants to make their thinking (even flawed) public, to invite criticism, and to learn how to be critical of their own teaching. We see here that, using that trust as foundation, the seminars because public forums for surfacing, testing, questioning, and critiquing teachers' ideas. Teaching too often is a private affair; it is a profession characterized by what Shulman (1993) called a "pedagogical solitude." By creating communities of teachers who brought concrete work to share with one another and learned to critically look at each other's teaching, these teachers broke through that solitude and began to require a more public accountability for their instructional choices and the conclusions they drew about their experiences.

That professional learning takes courage; that it takes time, starting with the recognition of a need to change and moving "haltingly and humiliatingly" toward a new practice; that professional learning needs to acknowledge and learn from error; and that communities of learning teachers are effective when they lead to a discourse of peer review critique are but four of the many lessons readers will take from this careful and respectful study of experienced teachers deepening their knowledge of mathematics, of children, of learning, and of teaching. Samuel Smiles, the Scottish political reformer and moralist, once wrote: "Practical wisdom is only to be learned in the school of experience. Precepts and instruction are useful so far as they go, but, without the discipline of real life, they remain of the nature of theory only." The power of the stories offered here is that they teach us about how our favorite professional development truisms play out in "the school of experience." It is the practical wisdom that these stories represent that is Sophia Cohen's major contribution to our work as professional development leaders, teacher educators, scholars, and policymakers. I am a wider scholar of teacher learning for having shared the experiences of these DMI participants. I hope too that I am a wiser teacher.

REFERENCES

Bosk, C. L. (1979). *Forgive and remember: Managing medical failure.* Chicago: University of Chicago Press.

Gawande, A. (2002). *Complications: A surgeon's notes on an imperfect science.* New York: Picador.

Shulman, L. S. (1993). Teaching as community property: Putting an end to pedagogical solitude. *Change, 25*(6), 6–7.

Acknowledgments

This book, and my thinking about teaching and learning, owes much to 4 years of rich collaboration with colleagues from Education Development Center, TERC, SummerMath for Teachers, and 40 talented and dedicated elementary teachers from across Massachusetts. It was this group that worked together at understanding and further developing the teaching practices of the 40 participating teachers, and eventually, it was this group that designed and wrote the first two modules of the DMI seminar materials.

I am particularly grateful to Deborah Schifter, a colleague from Education Development Center, who introduced me to the work of elementary mathematics teacher education, who showed, by example, some of the powerful uses of narrative cases in exploring the intricacies of teaching, and who has remained a valuable critic as I have sent her drafts of chapters for comment. I am also grateful to Susan Jo Russell and Lisa Yaffee at TERC, and Virginia Bastable and Jill Lester at SummerMath for Teachers, with whom, over the course of our work together on DMI, I learned enormously.

The research that this book reports on was made possible by the Spencer and MacArthur Foundation's Professional Development Research and Documentation Program. I would like to thank both Peggy Mueller and Mark Rigdon (who administered the Professional Development Research and Documentation Program at the Spencer Foundation) for their support along the way.

To all of the teachers who so generously and courageously allowed me in to watch their professional development work and to watch them in their classrooms, I am enormously grateful. It was in the seminars and elementary classrooms that this book took shape, and it would have been impossible to write without the willing cooperation and engagement of the teachers and seminar facilitators. Although I cannot thank them here by name because of confidentiality agreements, all were extraordinarily generous with their time and with their thoughts. Their colleagueship along the way taught me so much and made the journey so interesting. I am also thankful to the many children and school communities who made this work possible.

Education Development Center (EDC), where I worked from 1991 to 1999, provided a stimulating and supportive home for this book's research. I am very grateful to Barbara Scott Nelson for her support—both intellectually and institutionally—and to Tony Artuso for his patience and persistence as we worked to find the right publisher. EDC colleagues Deborah Schifter, Ilene Kantrov, and Barbara Scott Nelson have all offered comments on various drafts of this work. The book has improved considerably from their thoughtful criticism.

This book has also been shaped in many ways by my training as a developmental psychologist. It is my intellectual debt to Annette Karmiloff-Smith (from whom I learned a great deal both when I was her student in Geneva and in the years since) that is most obvious to me in the pages of this book. Her work has always been an inspiration.

I am thankful to Miriam Gamoran Sherin for her comments and suggestions in a thoughtful and thought-provoking review of an early draft, as well as for her continued availability and valuable input near the end of the writing.

Naomi Silverman, the acquisitions editor at Lawrence Erlbaum, and Heather Jefferson, the production editor, have been wonderfully patient and helpful. It is thanks to their help that this manuscript has made its way through all of the various stages of production.

I am especially grateful to Alan Schoenfeld and Suzanne Wilson. Each has improved the quality of this book enormously, reading and re-reading chapters, generously and tirelessly offering insightful criticism as well as encouragement. It was a joy to learn from them. I could not have asked for more.

Finally, I would like to thank my family and friends for their support and encouragement, for reading sections of the manuscript, and for remaining (or at least seeming to remain) genuinely interested over the years of this project. In the final weeks, each of my daughters took on a different, but equally helpful, role. Maia, thank you for your editorial solutions to some of my last dilemmas. Nina, the challenge of your smiling skepticism that I would *ever* put this manuscript in the mail—"I'll believe it when I see it!"—was a wonderful kick in the pants. Thank you!

Preface

This is a book about bringing students' and teachers' thoughts and ideas out into the open. It is about making classrooms the kinds of places where these thoughts and ideas are welcome and, more than that, where they are considered and explored. It is a book about the kind of journey it takes for a teacher to make her classroom one in which children's ideas take center stage. It is a book about the kind of journey it takes for a teacher to balance her attention to her own understanding of an idea with her attention to her students' understanding, using both in pursuit of strong subject matter knowledge. It is a book about the potential value of such a journey.

But there is no getting around the fact that there is a journey involved in creating classrooms and teaching practices of this kind. For while we all have thoughts and ideas, they can be fleeting, invisible, momentary events. Our own ideas can slip away. Those of others can be difficult to grasp. Even if we manage to hold onto them, they can remain vague and ill-formed. Bringing ideas to light—carefully considering a thought's potential—takes a strong focus, a concerted effort, and, initially I will claim here, a mentor who models and supports such work.

For our children in their classrooms, this mentor can be the teacher. However, the kind of teaching practice I focus on here and the subject matter knowledge it requires are far from common. For our children to have teachers who are mentors in this way, our teachers also need mentors—people who can guide and support them as they pursue and acquire solid subject matter knowledge and learn to teach in ways that enable the exploration of seminal ideas.

This book is built of stories about what happens when teachers have such a mentor and engage in serious study of their own and of children's mathematical conceptions. The stories illustrate the journeys of elementary school teachers across 1 year's time as they participated in a teacher development seminar focused on mathematics and changed their beliefs, their knowledge, and their practices.

Two story lines run through the book and are central to each of the individual stories told. One story line concerns psychological and social changes: teachers and students coming to listen to their own and to others' ideas in ways they had not previously done, creating the kind of classroom community in which individuals treat themselves, their colleagues, and the ideas that each expresses with careful consideration. These changes relate to the quality and nature of interpersonal relationships within the classroom, including the manner in which members of a classroom community express, attend to, and grapple with one another's thoughts and ideas.

The second story line concerns changes in mathematical thinking among children and teachers as they learn to make mathematical conjectures, to represent them, to argue for or against them in substantive, mathematically valid ways, and to join together in considering the conjectures and arguments as they build stronger understandings of topics in elementary mathematics. Throughout this book, we see examples of elementary school teachers in the process of learning that this kind of rigorous mathematical thinking exists, learning how to engage in it themselves, and learning to notice when children engage in it. In the last chapters, we see some of the ways that teachers' classrooms change as they build this mathematical competence, and we see some evidence that their students, in turn, begin to work with more mathematical substance and rigor.

These two story lines—the psychosocial and the mathematical—are intimately related. Collectively exploring ideas in meaningful ways requires a strong, safe, respectful community. It requires trusting relationships, for who would share a thought about which he or she felt uncertain with others from whom he or she expected disrespect or even disinterest? At the same time, constructing new thoughts together is one way that bonds and trust are built; going deeply into ideas together is a way to build community. Just as a strong intellectual community can help build ideas, the building of ideas is a way to build community. Supporting children as they immerse themselves in one another's ideas requires a teacher who is able socially and emotionally, and one who is strong enough in the subject matter, mathematics in this case, to enable productive exploration. This is a tall order.

This book provides images of teachers working to fill this tall order. The stories emerge from a 2-year study of teacher learning that I conducted. The study focuses on the learning of participants in a mathematics teacher development seminar for elementary school teachers. The seminar, Developing Mathematical Ideas ([DMI] Schifter et al., 1999a, 1999b, 1999c, 1999d), is one example of intensive, domain-specific professional development: the kind of professional development so often called for by educators. DMI is a published, nationally available teacher development curriculum in which teachers (a) study elementary mathematics to deepen their own understanding of it, (b) study the development of mathematical ideas in children, and (c) experience a teaching and learning environment focused on the joint exploration of ideas.

I was particularly interested in what teachers in this seminar learned because I had helped design and write these seminar materials. Although as a team those of us who worked on building DMI knew what we hoped the seminar might accomplish, I wanted to look carefully at the issues that actually arose for teachers taking the seminar. Further, because the DMI seminar is an example of a kind of professional development that reformers across disciplines are calling for, it seemed to me that the stories of teacher learning I was collecting and analyzing might serve as a case that would be of interest to a broad group of educators.

The study of teacher learning that gives rise to this book followed two DMI seminars and the classroom practices of seminar participants. It involved both teachers' own reports of what they were learning and direct observations of participants' classroom practices. The data include rich cases or stories about individuals as well as check backs to data from the whole group for some sense of the representativeness of each story. The stories are used to define and illustrate three strands of teacher learning. Each of these strands relates to both of the two story lines that run through this book, although each of the strands highlights a different aspect of the story lines. Together the strands portray the work involved for teachers who are transforming their practices. Bringing these strands to life is a central mission of this book, and the lion's share of the text is devoted to exploring that work.

Although this book focuses on elementary mathematics and the DMI seminar, the issues it examines could be considered with respect to changing teaching practices at any grade level or content area. This book is addressed to multiple audiences: researchers and teacher educators within universities, as well as those people in every community who have responsibility for making decisions about how teacher development time and money are spent. For all readers, this book offers an opportunity to examine—at close range—the kinds of changes in focus, knowledge, teaching practice, and opportunities for children that resulted from the work of teachers over the course of 1 year. For all readers the stories provide an opportunity to envision the teaching and learning toward which they would like their communities to build. However, because different readers will come to this book with different concerns, I address a few words, separately, to different groups of readers.

To teachers:

The stories in this book are stories of your colleagues in the midst of working at strengthening their teaching practices. They are working simultaneously to understand more mathematics for themselves, to better understand their students' expressions of mathematical ideas, and to develop teaching practices that help children understand more mathematics. Because the DMI seminar work aims at illuminating core mathematical ideas and their development in children, the work we see the teachers doing in the stories is pertinent to elementary mathematics teaching no matter which curricular materials you use. As we read about teachers doing this work, at times we see their worry and frustration. At times we see their joy, excitement, and pride. Their work is both rich and difficult.

Some issues these teachers encounter may be ones you have faced. Other issues may be new to you. Either way, I hope that the stories and the analysis these pages hold are helpful to you as daily you reenvision the kind of mathematics teacher that you'd like to be and the kinds of experiences that might support your growth and your school community's growth in that direction. I hope this travelogue—describing the long journey toward more powerful teaching practices—helps teachers and their communities develop the knowledge and patience to see this process through.

To mathematics-education researchers, professional developers, and administrators:

This is a book about teacher change. The stories offer rich detail about the process of reform—about the learning that takes place when we offer teachers professional development that is subject matter intensive, long term, and rooted in the study of student work. The stories offer an existence of proof that this kind of professional development is possible, as well as shedding some light on the work it takes. They also allow us to explore the impact this professional development has on a teacher's ability to support herself and her students, intellectually and emotionally, as they struggle with ideas.

Some of the stories in this book look at changes in belief and knowledge. Some take us on forays into classrooms where we can see how teachers' practices shift as they come to know more about the subject matter and as they come to face the ideas of the subject matter more directly themselves and with their students. These demonstrations come from full-time public school teachers engaged in a professional development seminar offered by skilled and knowledgeable teacher leaders in their own school districts: a model for professional development that is becoming more and more common.

I hope, as readers, you will join with me in exploring the stories of this book for what they can teach us about the learning that takes a teacher from a more traditional teaching practice to one that has begun to focus on important mathematical ideas. I use the stories as a means to understand both the changes themselves, and the potential of teacher seminars as vehicles for change.

This book is written in the hope that the stories of professional development and teacher learning it contains, and the strands of teacher learning that these stories illustrate, will be helpful to you as you consider, craft, offer, and evaluate the professional development experiences with which you work.

The teacher changes described in this book are deeply rooted, but they are also slow and gradual. It is not a process that takes only days, weeks, or months—although any of these will get the process started—for learning about mathematics and children could be a lifetime's work. Thus, having begun is just the beginning. The year's work that is described in the stories of this book is such a beginning.

To mathematicians:

This is a book about teachers grappling with mathematics. I hope the stories it contains offer mathematicians an opportunity to grapple with envisioning new generations of professional development that will excite and nurture teachers as they learn more mathematics and consider how and what to teach children.

Throughout the book, you will see teachers coming to view mathematics as a field of highly interconnected meanings—meanings that both teachers and children are able to construct. You will see teachers pursuing mathematical knowledge through valid argument and proof. Finally, you will see teachers offer their students, our children, opportunities to enter into this more rigorous, meaningful mathematical world.

Although mathematics holds a central place in this book, it does so alongside concerns about teaching and learning. What is it that teachers need to understand about mathematics, *and* about how people make mathematical sense, in order to engage children in rich and productive mathematical study?

Both adults and children portrayed in this book at times explain and justify their mathematical ideas with reference to the physical world that mathematics can model. You will see both teachers and children making sense of the formal elements of the mathematical system by connecting them with the physical world they know well. This work can be difficult, complex, and slow. Yet this work is a prelude to meaningfully reasoning within the formal system itself. It is this kind of richly connected and meaning-filled knowledge base that will later support strong mathematical thinking when the entities are more abstract.

For some of you, your own mathematical thinking may reside primarily within the realm of formal mathematics. That is, as you work to justify a mathematical proposition or an algorithm to yourself, you might appeal only to elements of the formal mathematical system. For others, I imagine that the process of grounding mathematical reasoning in knowledge and intuition about the physical world might be a familiar part of making mathematical sense. For all of you, I hope that the stories you read here invite you to think about the role played by what we know well in building mathematical knowledge that is new to us.

Finally, and importantly, the teachers whose work is at the heart of this book showed enormous bravery and trust by allowing me to observe their ongoing professional development work. As professionals, it was not easy for them to make their own intellectual struggles public—to open them to study and commentary. I hope that all readers will offer, in return, the same respect for the teachers' developing ideas that the teachers are learning to offer when they encounter ideas—their own or students'. We will gain most from a reading of the teachers' work that takes the stance of trying to understand what the teacher grasps and what he or she is working at understanding or creating. The picture that emerges will inform us about the current state of teachers' relationships to mathematics, and to teaching and learning. It will inform us about the potential of teacher seminars as vehicles for change. It will inform us about the route ahead if the national visions for education are to come to life in classrooms across the country.

1

Setting the Stage

In truth, I am eager to begin with chapter 2 and the telling of the stories of teacher learning that are at the heart of this book. Yet there are many preliminaries and I would be remiss in ignoring them. It is the work of this first chapter then to set the stage for the stories and analyses that follow.

This is a chapter in four main parts. The first part places the teacher seminar from which the stories grow—the Developing Mathematical Ideas (DMI) seminar—in the context of national visions for elementary classroom teaching and teachers' professional development. The second part describes the DMI seminar in some detail—its content, pedagogy, and rationale for these. The research project that gave rise to this book is briefly described in the third section. The fourth and final section provides an overview of the book: introducing the three strands of teacher learning that emerged from the study and that structure the remaining chapters.

PART 1: SHAPING PROFESSIONAL DEVELOPMENT, SHAPING TEACHING

Let's begin by situating this exploration of teacher learning—learning among DMI seminar participants—in the broader context of the national conversation about elementary education, and especially about teacher education that leads to improved instruction.

Over the past 15 years or so, a chorus of voices has been raised in support of new teaching practices—not just in one subject matter, but across the board. That chorus includes national standards projects, new curricula, new assessment tools, and myriad other voices. Some themes are heard again and again: preparing our children for their lives in the 21st century, offering equal access to quality education for all children, and creating classrooms in which children work to build deep understandings of subject matters—taking on the work of scientist, historian, mathematician, or writer.

Together these themes point to teaching practices that ask more from children than memorization and recitation. They point to teaching practices that support, in all of our children, the ability and proclivity to make sense, solve problems, and answer questions by serious explorations of their own and others' understanding. As a nation, we are looking for teaching practices that—in their focus on ideas and on students making meaning—enhance the rigor and solidity of children's subject matter knowledge, including the knowledge of how to investigate new topics in a domain.

There is widespread agreement that supporting the growth of these new teaching practices both calls for and depends on new kinds of teacher development work. In making choices about the nature of teacher education in our communities, we make choices about the face of teaching and learning. Inevitably, the teacher education choices we make support the development of some teaching practices and make others less likely. But now—at a time when there is much talk about change—our choices, along with our questions about our choices, come into sharper focus. With respect to the professional development of teachers, and therefore with respect to the shaping of teaching, we are at a time of change and choice. Unfortunately, we are also at a time of limited knowledge about the costs and benefits of our choices.

Yet even with the limits of our current knowledge, the broad outlines are being drawn for professional development that supports stronger teaching practices. From within each of the subject matter areas, there is a call for teacher preparation and in-service work that both helps teachers to deepen their own subject matter knowledge and takes place over considerably longer periods of time than has been commonplace (Ball, 1994, 1996; Calkins & Harwayne, 1987; Conference Board of Mathematical Sciences, 2001; Goldsmith, Mark, & Kantrov, 2000; Grossman, Wilson, & Shulman, 1989; Hammer, 1997; Rosebery & Puttick, 1997; Russell, 1998; Schifter, 1995, 2001; Schifter et al., 1999a, 1999b, 1999c, 1999d; Silver, 1996; Warren & Ogonowski, 1998; Wilson, 1991; Wineburg & Grossman, 2000).

In addition, increasingly there are calls for this professional development to be rooted in the study of student work and classroom practice. That is, increasingly there is a call to bring subject matter—as it looks in the context of elementary school teaching and learning—into the professional development setting for careful study by both teachers and teacher educators. Providers of professional development are responding by making this central to their own practices (Abdal-Haqq, 1995; Barnett, Goldenstein, & Jackson, 1994; Calkins & Harwayne, 1987; Carroll & Carini, 1991; Carpenter, Fennema, Franke, Empson, & Levi, 1999; Cohen & Hill, 2001; Conference Board of Mathematical Sciences, 2001; Duckworth, 2001; Franke, Carpenter, Fennema, Ansell, & Behrend, 1998; Graves, 1989–1992, 1994; Hammer, 1999; Heaton & Lewis, 2001; Lampert & Ball, 1998; Morse, 2000; Putnam & Borko, 1997; Rosebery & Puttick, 1997; Russell et al., 1995; Schifter, 1997, 2001; Shulman, 1986, 1987; Silver, 1996; Sowder, 2001; Stein, Smith, Henningsen, & Silver, 2000; Stein, Smith, & Silver, 1999; TERC, 1998; Wilson & Berne, 1999).

In this increasingly articulated view, the focus of professional development is on both issues of subject matter and issues of teaching and learning as they come together in classroom practice, and as real students work at building new understandings of specific content.

Beyond these matters of content for teachers' professional development are questions concerning the culture of teaching and learning established within the teacher seminar. It is a common goal of this new genre of professional development to build intellectual community among teachers—communities where disagreement and critique are welcome as teachers redefine teaching practice and engage in the often difficult and messy work of learning (Featherstone, Pfeiffer, & Smith, 1993; Grossman, Wineburg, & Woolworth, 1998; Lord, 1994; Wilson & Berne, 1999).

Further, this genre of professional development, unlike the one it replaces, tends to be relatively nonprescriptive. Instead it aims to help teachers build knowledge on which they can draw as they face difficult choices about how to best help their students build stronger understandings of subject matter (Ball, 1993; Sassi & Goldsmith, 1996; Stein, Smith, Henningsen, & Silver, 2000; Stein, Smith, & Silver, 1999). This aim raises the complex issues of what knowledge might best support these new teaching practices and of what learning opportunities for teachers are most likely to succeed in helping teachers to build this knowledge. These complex issues are far from resolved.

Although at this level of generality there is considerable agreement about some of the characteristics important to teachers' professional education, there is also a good deal of variation if we look more closely. The *means* of grounding professional development in subject matter, student work and classroom practice, the *balance* among these, the *settings* for the work, the explicit *intentions* for these choices, and the *subject matters* focused on are varied.

A few examples might highlight both the common threads and the variations among exemplars of this kind of professional development. These examples are by no means a complete review. Instead they are offered to illustrate two points. First, this is a broad trend in professional development for teachers—one that crosses subject matter lines. Second, with all of the similarities, there is still considerable variation in method, setting, and the particular intentions of the work.

In addressing the first point—the general similarity of professional development trends across subject matters—we look to one example from science and one from language arts. Then to better appreciate the variation that exists, we sample from professional development offerings all within elementary mathematics.

With respect to the professional development of teachers of reading and writing, the National Writing Project, its affiliates (e.g., Root & Steinberg, 1996), and individuals such as Donald Graves (1989–1992, 1994) and Lucy Calkins (1987) have long supported teacher study of both subject matter—emphasizing the importance of teachers engaging in their own writing and reading—and the development of subject matter knowledge in students. The latter has long been essential to a process writing pedagogy in which teachers, based on their analysis of student strengths and weaknesses, devise mini-lessons to help move student work forward. The Web site for The Reading and Writing Project, headed by Lucy Calkins at Teachers College, succinctly captures the important role their program accords to teacher study of student work as a piece not only of classroom practice, but of the professional development that supports these developing practices:

> The teachers and staff developers become co-researchers, observing what children do in writing and in reading, theorizing about what their behaviors mean, and planning teaching moves to help them learn. (www.rwprject. tc.columbia.edu/about_us.htm)

This same attention to student work, and to teaching moves in response to student work, is evident in David Hammer's work with secondary school science teachers. Hammer (1999) met over the course of a few years with a small group of teachers, offering them opportunities to share and consider snippets of one another's practice. He notes the intellectual challenges involved when teachers work both *with* student conceptions and *toward* stronger understandings of the collected knowledge of a field. For teachers facing these challenges, Hammer underlines the importance of professional development opportunities in which teachers jointly analyze the classroom work of students and teachers.

> We do not pretend that our conversations capture more than a fraction of teacher thinking. But by capturing that fraction, these conversations allowed the teachers to exchange and compare not only methods and materials, but perceptions of students in particular moments of instruction. Our conversa-

tions, grounded in specific instances from the teachers' classes, provided not only ideas for instructional strategies but also new diagnostic possibilities, an exchange of resources to support the intellectual work of teaching. (p. 6)

In elementary mathematics, this same approach to teachers' professional development is evident. Yet as we hold up a few different initiatives next to one another, we can begin to see differences as well as commonalities. We might think of these professional development projects as bearing a family resemblance to one another. Each draws from a common pool of features—those described in general terms a few pages ago. But the exact set of features and their relation to one another is unique in each project.

Let's begin with Lampert and Ball's (1998) creation and use of a multimedia representation of 1 year's worth of elementary mathematics teaching in two classrooms. They have linked daily classroom videotapes with teachers' journals, student work, interviews, and more for each of the two classrooms. This multimedia database provides a way for the investigator teachers and others to bring teaching practice and its study into the university so that intending teachers, teacher educators, and researchers can engage in careful, reflective study of practice. Although the multimedia representation itself is still far from being a professional development curriculum, it quite dramatically makes student and teacher classroom work available as a professional development resource.

The Lampert and Ball multimedia project is unique in many ways, but it shares with the Cognitively Guided Instruction (CGI) project the practice of shaping teacher professional development, at least in part, around the study of mathematical understandings as they develop in children. Today and since its inception in the mid-1980s (e.g., Carpenter, Fennema, Peterson, Chiang, & Loef, 1989), CGI has focused on K–3 teachers, sharing with them university researchers' knowledge of the development of children's mathematical thinking and working with them at building teaching practices that are based in, and that enrich, this knowledge (Franke et al., 1998; Franke & Kazemi, 2001; Carpenter et al., 1999, 2001). Although Lampert and Ball (1998) and CGI share the goal of helping teachers acquire more knowledge of their students' mathematical thinking, they also differ with respect to the source of that knowledge and with respect to the role in professional development of images of practice. These images of practice are central for the Lampert and Ball work and much less so for CGI.

In a very different venue, the *Investigations* (TERC, 1998) curricular materials offer another forum for engaging teachers in the study of children's mathematical thinking and the teaching of mathematics. *Investigations* is a set of mathematics curriculum materials for use in Grades K–5. In the sections of these materials addressed to teachers, the *Investigations* authors use classroom dialogue boxes to present teachers with transcriptions (or near transcriptions) of classroom conversations around central mathematical issues. These samples of practice and student thinking, and their further discussion in the accompanying teacher notes, provide opportunities for professional development that are embedded in the curricular materials. It is professional development that focuses on student work, the development of mathematical ideas, and classroom practice, all situated in the mathematical problems that make up the curricular materials.

Lesson study is a different approach to professional development that is, like the *Investigations* teacher notes and dialogue boxes, situated in the consideration of classroom lessons. Although *Investigations* lessons are not designed by the teachers studying them, teachers involved in lesson study are engaged in a collaborative, reflective process of designing lessons. Further, whereas the *Investigations* materials might be used in any number of contexts—by individual teachers, by informal grade-level groups, or in ongoing, facilitated teacher seminars—it is essential to lesson study that it takes place in a committed, professionally collaborative group of educators. Lesson study is a fundamental piece of professional development for teachers in Japan and is beginning to be used by some communities in the United States (e.g., Fernandez, Ertle, Chokshi, Tam, Allison, Appel, & Schafer, 2002; Lewis, 2002; Stigler & Hiebert, 1999). It is based on the assumption that, in a context of stability and continuity, teachers can evolve as professionals by focusing carefully on content, lesson goals, and student understandings. Teachers engage in collaborative work around the planning, teaching, and revising of particular lessons. They work jointly to set goals for and plan a lesson that one member of the study group will teach while the others and invited guests observe. These observations are focused opportunities for joint research into the pedagogical and subject matter issues that arise in the teaching of these jointly planned lessons, and they are used in a cyclic process of lesson revision.

These are just a few examples of this new genre of professional development, its family resemblances, and its differences. Many others exist. The work cited here is based on the many years of experience and the best professional judgment of thoughtful and talented educators. As the literature stands, we know little about the relative value of the different design choices or about the different contexts in which the different designs might be most effective. Yet we can add to the voices of the professional development initiatives described here a large-scale, quantitative study that supports the efficacy of this genre of professional development.

Cohen and Hill (2001) studied California's efforts to improve mathematics instruction. They found that teachers who spent at least 1 to 2 weeks of the prior year working at understanding student work, new assessments, and new curricula—subject matter issues like the kind teachers would encounter in any of the professional development opportunities just described—showed more instructional improvement than did teachers who either had less professional development or who engaged in professional development that focused on nonsubject matter issues such as diversity or use of small-group instruction.

Cohen and Hill summarize the characteristics of effective professional development as follows:

> instructional improvement works best when it focuses on learning and teaching specific academic content, when there is a curriculum for improving teaching that overlaps with curriculum and assessment for students, and when teachers have substantial opportunities to learn about the content, how students are likely to make sense of it, and how it can be taught. (p. 151)

Thus, Cohen and Hill's study supports the earlier characterization of the features of effective professional development. They also provide us with a general picture of the effects.

Cohen and Hill's evidence indicates that this kind of professional development supported two kinds of teacher change. Teachers added new practices as well as reorganizing their core approach to teaching. It is interesting to note that when teachers engaged in *less* of this subject matter-intensive professional development, they commonly added some new beliefs or practices, but they did so without letting go of or reassessing their core approach to teaching. These results are further supported by the finding that the more time teachers devoted to this kind of professional development, the greater the effects.

Further, Cohen and Hill found that the students of the teachers who had spent 1 to 2 weeks in subject matter-based professional development, and had most shifted their teaching practices and beliefs, scored higher on mathematics tests than did the students whose teachers engaged in less subject matter-relevant professional development and who continued to teach in more traditional ways.

This finding—that improved student performance and new teaching practices result when professional development provides teachers with opportunities to explore the content they teach and to explore children's thinking about this same content—is consistent with the findings of other studies of this issue (Brown, Stein, & Forman, 1996; Gearhart et al., 1999). Similarly, Sconiers, Isaacs, Higgins, McBride, and Kelso (2003) found that student performance improved when teachers used any of three mathematically ambitious curricular materials, all designed to work toward the goals of the national standards.

Combined, this research and the trend toward a new genre of professional development signal an emerging and coherent point of view about the general nature of professional development that supports teaching practices that are better aligned with the national standards and improve children's opportunities to learn. More and more, teacher educators and researchers call for subject matter-intensive, long-term professional development rooted in the careful study of student understandings and classroom practice. There is reason to be hopeful about this approach.

Developing Mathematical Ideas, the seminar that provides the setting for the stories of this book, is an example of this kind of professional development. Whereas Cohen and Hill (2001) and others have begun to spell out the characteristics of professional development that improves elementary classroom practice, this book offers a detailed look at what happens in professional development of this kind and at how it happens. The detail that the stories provide allows us to look at the "big ideas" that this kind of professional development raises for teachers, at which ideas take more time and which take less time, as well as at the aspects of the seminar design that emerge as particularly powerful. In other words, we will look both at the kinds of change processes set in motion and at the aspects of the seminar that make these changes possible.

What this book is *not* is an in-depth analysis of all of the mathematical knowledge that supports effective teaching of elementary mathematics. Others—notably Ma (1999), the Conference Board of Mathematical Sciences (2001), and even the DMI materials—have provided a good beginning in that analysis. Further, Ma (1999) establishes clearly for us the mathematical starting point of elementary teachers in the United States. In this book, we see similar mathematical starting points. But here we concentrate on what happens when these teachers begin to tackle the mathematics of the elementary grades through DMI seminars. The changes we see are in part mathematical and in part psychological and social. I argue that these are importantly intertwined, each serving the development of the other.

PART 2: THE DEVELOPING MATHEMATICAL IDEAS SEMINAR

It is not enough to know simply that DMI belongs to this new genre of professional development for teachers. To consider how the teacher learning depicted in the stories of this book might have come about—and, for that matter, how it could be built on—it is important to understand the DMI seminar in more detail. We begin with a general description of the DMI seminar, and then we consider three core aspects of the seminar design. We give attention to these core aspects of the seminar to situate DMI within the family of professional development to which it belongs and to provide a structure for our consideration of some of the features of this genre of professional development.

A General Description

DMI is a set of curriculum materials for the professional development of teachers working in Grades K through 6. It differs from the teaching and learning experiences that are most commonly available to teachers both in its content and its approach to that content. DMI seminars are intended to support teachers' own study of the mathematics of the elementary school curriculum, as well as their study of the development of children's mathematical ideas. The seminars are also intended to provide teachers with ongoing experience as students in a teaching and learning environment that is consistent with the teaching practices envisioned by the Standards. This kind of teaching and learning, and the relationships it encourages students to have with the subject matter, with other students, and with the teacher, are likely to be unfamiliar to most.

The materials are for use, over time, in seminar or inquiry group settings guided by a group facilitator who is knowledgeable about the aims and content of the materials. Most commonly, these materials are used in seminars for practicing teachers, meeting once every 2 weeks for 3 hours, although other formats are used. The materials also serve in many locations as mathematics methods courses in teacher preparation programs.

The DMI series consists of several volumes, each focusing on a different mathematical topic. Two volumes or modules address number and operations: *Building a System of Tens* (Schifter et al., 1999a, 1999b) and *Making Meaning for Operations* (Schifter et al., 1999c, 1999d). Two modules address geometry, examining both shape and measurement: *Examining Features of Shape* (Bastable et al., 2001a, 2001b) and *Measuring Space in One, Two, and Three Dimensions* (Schifter et al., 2001a, 2001b). Finally, one module, *Working with Data* (Russell et al., 2002a, 2002b), explores data collection and analysis. (Project directors also hope to develop materials on early algebra.) For each module, the course materials include a casebook, videos, and an extensive facilitator's guide. Each casebook consists of cases written by K–6 teachers to present some aspect of the mathematical thinking of one or more of their students. Although the cases certainly include the teacher-writers' thoughts and questions about the student work, the focus of the cases is primarily on the mathematical ideas. Within each module, the cases are organized by mathematical subtopic. The facilitator's guides contain introductory materials orienting facilitators to the seminar, detailed agendas for each session, a rather lengthy journal of a fictitious facilitator, Maxine, and two portraits of teacher change through the seminar.

During seminar meetings, teachers analyze the mathematical thinking of the children depicted in the cases (both video and print), listening to the students for the logic of their thinking, the parts of their reasoning and understanding that are strong, and the mathematical issues on which the children are still working. The teachers not only work on the mathematics as it appears in the cases, but spend a portion of each seminar meeting working on these and/or similar mathematical topics for themselves. In addition, there are times for discussion of the pedagogical issues that arise in the teachers' daily teaching practices.

Teachers prepare for each seminar meeting with both reading and writing assignments. The reading assignments are mostly the case materials, although for the last session of each module teachers read an essay that connects the case materials to research. The writing assignments include a variety of tasks designed to help participants examine the work of students in their own classrooms, including student interviews and cases, and several pieces in which the teachers write about their own thinking concerning the mathematical and pedagogical issues raised for them by the seminar. The writing serves several functions, including providing opportunities for participants to focus their thoughts and make them explicit, documenting participants' thinking over the course of the year, and serving as a vehicle for participant–facilitator communication. Seminar facilitators are strongly encouraged to respond in writing to the written materials submitted by participants.

The DMI seminars studied and reported on in this book are the pair of modules on number and operations. The mathematical theme in the first module is the base-10 structure of our number system. In the second module, the mathematical theme is the meaning of the operations. These two modules together formed a year-long course for elementary school teachers who met once every 2 weeks for 16 three-hour meetings. Appendix A provides an overview of the 16 DMI seminar sessions that comprised the course. The table in Appendix A portrays DMI as it was at the time of the research for this book[1] and enumerates—for each session—the mathematical topic, agenda, and portfolio assignment.

Articulating Three Core Aspects of DMI Seminars

There are three core aspects of DMI that deserve more attention in these introductory pages. These are (a) the solidity and complexity of the math-

---

[1] Some of the sessions and the portfolio assignments in the published material are different from those shown in Appendix A. One of the most notable changes is the addition in the published versions of several opportunities to analyze innovative curricular materials, with an eye on the mathematical ideas the lesson targets and how a lesson might be adjusted for use with children for whom it is either too difficult or too simple.

ematics under study, (b) the concurrent examination of teachers' and students' mathematics, and (c) the parallel between the seminar's pedagogy and elementary classroom pedagogy as envisioned by both national Standards and DMI designers. Together these aspects of the seminar help describe DMI's particular place within the new genre of professional development. Each characteristic was deliberately integrated into the seminar, and each is articulated to some extent in the DMI materials (Schifter et al., 1999b, 1999d). The following articulations are, in places, more explicit and detailed than they are in the DMI materials, and so may reflect my particular view of these aspects of DMI design.

The Solidity and Complexity of the Mathematics

DMI seminars provide a structured set of opportunities for teachers to engage in the study of the meanings and complexities of the mathematics of the elementary curriculum. Each module is designed to engage teachers in the rigorous study of a related set of mathematical ideas—ideas that are central to the elementary study of, for instance, number, operations, geometry, and so on. Appendix A lists the topics for the two number and operations modules. The topics for each seminar session are not a serendipitous collection of interesting classroom stories that happen to be about number, for example. Rather, the cases and mathematical activities for each session are selected so as to highlight fundamental ideas in the domain—ideas that in designing DMI we believed to be important subject matter knowledge for teachers.

The topics that each module focuses on are not only mathematically fundamental, but are also topics that we know to be relatively difficult for people to understand. That is, the mathematics is complex for both children and adults who have had little opportunity to explore it. Some examples of these are keeping track of 10s while operating, especially with large numbers, and operating with fractions (e.g., Ball, 1990; Borko, Eisenhart, Brown, Underhill, Jones, & Agard, 1992; Cohen, 1999; Ma, 1999; Yaffee, 1999).

As we read the stories of the following chapters, we might consider the impact of this aspect of the seminar. What do the stories reveal about the mathematics teachers are learning and the ways in which they are using their mathematical knowledge? We return to these questions in chapter 5.

The Concurrent Examination of Teachers' and Students' Mathematics

A second core aspect of DMI seminar design is that the key mathematical ideas of these topics are approached with a dual focus: (a) on the ways in which they are constructed by elementary school-age children, and (b) on the teachers' own understandings of these ideas. DMI is designed to offer teachers many opportunities to study each aspect of this dual focus and to do so concurrently, putting the two in juxtaposition to one another (Schifter et al., 1999b, 1999d). Let's consider each focus for a moment as well as their juxtaposition.

Teacher Study of Children's Mathematical Ideas. Participants study children's mathematical thinking both in and out of seminar sessions. Teachers engage in the careful analysis of children's mathematical thinking as they read and discuss the written cases or view and discuss the video cases. In addition, the teacher participants' own portfolio writing—their own and their seminar colleagues' written cases, student interviews, and analyses of student work—provides still more opportunity for learning about the development in children of mathematical ideas and cultivating the skills necessary to hear them.

Finally, at the end of each module, a different kind of opportunity for teacher study of children's mathematical thinking is offered. Teachers read and discuss an essay connecting the mathematical topics from that module to existing research on the development of these understandings in children. For example, at the end of the *Building a System of Tens* module, participants read an essay that presents an overview of the research on the following topics: the relationship between children's knowledge of written number and spoken number, seeing a 10 as a 1, inventing 10s-based procedures for adding and subtracting, inventing 10s-based procedures for multiplying and dividing, and understanding decimal fractions. In addition to presenting a brief summary of the research on these topics, the essays also refer back to the examples of similar findings from the classroom cases of the seminar. The purpose of the research essays is to invite teachers to take a step back from the detail of each individual case in order to build a larger picture of what might be generalizable from each case and of the relationships among the ideas they have been studying. Further, the essays are intended to help teachers situate their own inquiries about the development of mathematical thinking in children in the bigger picture provided by the broader research community.

Teacher Study of Mathematical Ideas for Themselves. Although the mathematical topics addressed by DMI are familiar to teachers, we know from the work of researchers such as Ball (1990) and Ma (1999) that their knowledge of these topics tends to be mostly procedural. For instance, American teachers know how to calculate, but they are less able to discuss the meanings or validity of these procedures or to investigate mathematical terrain that is new to them. This is likely to be equally true of most American adults who, like the teachers in Ma's and Ball's research, studied elementary mathematics in U.S. elementary schools. The DMI seminar was designed to offer teachers opportunities to engage in a deeper study of the mathematical topics of the elementary curriculum. During the seminar meetings, participants often work on mathematical tasks in both small groups and as one large group. The multiplication and division by fractions problem, which is the basis for the first story in chapter 3, is an example of this kind of work.

In addition to the mathematics activities, seminar activities such as case writing, interview preparation, and analysis of student work samples offer opportunities for teachers to engage in mathematical analysis. Similarly, in some instances, reading, viewing, and discussing cases are occasions for teachers to do their own mathematical work, especially when children in the cases present ideas or solutions that are new to or unexpected by the teacher. Schifter (1997, 1999) provides evidence of the mathematical challenges involved for teachers in analyzing, responding to, and working with student expressions of mathematical ideas.

The Two in Juxtaposition.   Within the seminar, this work on *teachers' own* mathematical understandings happens minutes before or minutes after teachers work at understanding *children's* mathematical thinking on these same topics. Thus, the structure of each session offers a juxtaposition of these experiences.

The juxtaposition happens *between* seminar sessions as well. Because the seminar was offered every other week during the school year, teachers went back and forth between their role as students in the seminar and their role as teacher in their own classrooms. Often they did so with an assignment to write about the mathematical thinking of children in their classrooms or to write about their own learning within the seminar.

In designing DMI, we intended for this juxtaposition both within and between seminar sessions to invite teachers to consider the ways in which their mathematical inquiry is different from or similar to the experiences they see children in their classrooms having or read about children in the cases having. Thus, the materials were designed to create opportunities for the experiences to inform one another. Of course hoping for such a dialectic is one thing, whereas ensuring that it occurs is another. The stories that follow offer the opportunity to assess whether, how, or in what kinds of situations teachers draw on their own experiences as mathematics learners while teaching children, or on their experiences of children's mathematical thinking to enrich their own work in mathematics.

*The Parallel Between the Seminar's Pedagogy
and Elementary Classroom Pedagogy
as Envisioned by National Standards*

A third core aspect of DMI seminar design is the commitment to a pedagogy for teachers that parallels the classroom practices we would like to see the teachers developing. Thus, the vision of teaching and learning in the DMI seminar parallels the visions for teaching and learning in elementary classrooms evidenced in the National Council of Teachers of Mathematics Standards (2000). A succinct statement of the pedagogy for both might go as follows: *In these learning communities, students jointly consider ideas, in a supportive environment under the guidance of a teacher who focuses both on student understanding and on her own sense of the ideas toward which students are working.* Next we will look more closely at the elements of this pedagogy and the rationale behind the teacher seminar pedagogy paralleling that of the elementary classroom.

Why This Pedagogy?   Both in the DMI seminar and in elementary classrooms aligned with national visions for improved practice, the aim is to create classroom communities where students' thoughts and ideas are welcome, where they are expressed, and where they are jointly considered and explored. This aim grows out of social and emotional concerns about students and the classroom communities to which they belong (and to which they become acculturated), as well as from concerns about how learning occurs. The social and emotional value of encouraging students to articulate their ideas, and then respectfully considering the ideas that they express, is likely to feel familiar to many. Truly hearing another person's thoughts and joining with them in considering these is generally accepted as an important component of building both trust and self-esteem. The value of such practices for *learning*, however, may need more comment.

There is a good deal of empirical research and scholarship from psychology that suggests that people learn by (a) confronting the limitations of their existing understandings (e.g., Duckworth, 1987; Piaget, 1975; Piaget & Inhelder, 1969); (b) further examining, reorganizing, and making more efficient procedures that already work, and that thus embody some truth about the world (e.g., Karmiloff-Smith, 1979, 1986, 1992a, 1992b); and (c) making explicit connections between and among ideas not previously connected (Karmiloff-Smith, 1992b). The first in this list—confronting the limitations of existing understandings, or *disequilibration*, to use Piaget's term—is probably the kind of learning opportunity most familiar to us. It builds on error detection. But the others, which build on successes, are equally important opportunities and are likely to be essential for the construction of some knowledge.

Making Ideas Explicit. To maximize classroom opportunities for all of these kinds of learning, representing student ideas, making them explicit, is essential. It is essential because, in making ideas explicit, in representing them verbally, graphically, in some notational form, or even in gesture or action, they become more available for reflection, analysis, and critique.

Clearly, this external representation of thought is essential to opening up ideas for *group* discussion because if ideas are not expressed, they are available only to the person thinking them. The more an idea is articulated, the more group members will know about an individual's thinking, and the better able they will be to join with that individual in considering those ideas.

Explicitly representing ideas also plays a crucial role in an individual's consideration of his or her *own* understandings. Some everyday experiences hint at this. For instance, imagine that you have a personal or professional problem and you go to a trusted friend or colleague to talk. In these situations, many of us find that even if the friend or colleague says nothing, we often come to see the problem differently. Perhaps we now see a solution we didn't see before, perhaps we become aware of a flaw in our original reasoning, or perhaps we become more certain of something that before had seemed too complicated to fully grasp. Similarly, anyone who composes—whether with words, music, or dance—has no doubt had the experience of beginning a piece only to realize that there is some aspect of the idea they had not yet thought through, and that they only discover *exists* in having begun their composition. In these experiences, we encounter our thoughts not only as we initially think them, but also as we think *about* them in whatever form we are able to give them at the time. The representations reflect the thought back to us; in that reflection, we are sometimes able to see new sides of it.

A good deal of work in psychology supports these everyday kinds of observations about learning from our represented ideas. Annette Karmiloff-Smith (1981) summarizes a long program of research in a number of domains, including children's developing language and notational skill, by noting that "what was functioning for the child as a *tool* progressively becomes part of the problem space itself" (p. 154). This applies to mathematical tools as well. Hence, this taking of a working procedure or representation to consider the information it embodies is a key piece of the pedagogy that both DMI and national visions for improved instruction strive toward. Providing students with opportunities to represent their understandings, whether this be in the form of a solution to a math problem, an observation, a question, or a piece of writing, creates opportunities to reflect on what that representation embodies and thus opportunities to learn.

Lehrer, Schauble, Carpenter, and Penner (2000) illustrate the utility of external representations such as these for group learning in a classroom setting. In a piece of classroom-based research that involved Grade 3 children's observations and explanations of patterns of plant growth, they found evidence that the children built on one another's representations, and that with children's increasing efforts at *representing* their observations came increasing *theorizing and conceptual change*. In their words:

> a cascade of inscriptions was accompanied by a cascade of conceptual change. As children inscribed growth, their ideas about growth became both more varied and more differentiated, and also became more tightly coupled to potential explanations, such as resource allocation in plants. [. . .] Like working scientists, children increasingly worked in a world of inscription, so that, over time, the natural and inscribed worlds became mutually articulated, albeit not indistinguishable. (pp. 356–357)

Yet the process is not simple. Complex issues arise concerning timing, who generates the representations that a class considers, what kind of relationship the representations bear to students' existing ideas, and what kind of forum for exploration and discussion of the representations is provided (Lehrer et al., 2000). These are issues that we see teachers grapple with in the stories of teachers' changing practice in chapter 4 of this book. Further, these are issues that teacher educators must also consider in designing and offering professional development that supports teacher learning. The first story of chapter 3 offers a glimpse of one DMI facilitator as she navigates this terrain.

Although this view of learning—a view that puts such emphasis on the importance to learning of expressing thoughts—may be common among psychologists and some educators, in our culture at large many of us have trouble taking our own ideas seriously. Eleanor Duckworth (2001) writes:

> We have found that most people, and adults in particular, are nervous about expressing their own ideas, especially in a realm where they are quite sure that there is some appointed wisdom to which they are not privy. They think, then, that their own ideas are not worth attending to; they should drop them, and catch on to the real, authenticated knowledge. We believe, on the contrary, that one's own knowledge—tentative and incomplete though it may be—is all one ever has; and that the only way to develop it further is to pay attention to it; figure out what needs to be further thought about, modify it, and keep striving to make it more adequate to one's experiences. (p. 184)

Between the relative difficulty of taking our own ideas seriously and the important role that making ideas explicit plays in learning, the value of classrooms in which ideas are neither ridiculed nor dismissed, but respectfully considered, becomes clear. This does not mean that all ideas are seen as equal in power, but that all ideas expressed by a student are seen as that learner's starting point. The work of teaching involves providing opportunities for students both to represent what they know and to build from that base.

Although considering student thought is essential to teaching, it is not—on its own—sufficient. Helping students move forward in their thinking requires the guidance of a teacher who maintains a dual focus on *students'* ideas and on *his or her own* conceptions of the subject matter. It is from this pedagogical stance that teachers are best positioned to consider which next opportunities to provide so as to best encourage students to move beyond their current understandings. All of this pertains whether the students are children in classrooms or teachers in professional development seminars.

Dual Focus as a Teaching Stance.   In a preceding section, we talked about a dual focus in the DMI seminar on both teachers' and children's mathematical understandings. We treated children's developing mathematical ideas and teachers' mathematical knowledge as two topics—two kinds of knowledge—that teachers need to support their teaching. Further, we looked at the ways in which DMI provides opportunities for teachers to gain both kinds of knowledge.

However, there is another sense in which the DMI seminar maintains a dual focus on both teacher and student thought. The dual focus, in this sense, is intended as a pedagogical stance. Whereas in the last section we looked at this dual focus as a focus on two types of knowledge for teachers to build, here we look at the dual focus as a way of teaching. Teachers' attentiveness to their own ideas and their students' ideas is a piece of the *pedagogy* of the seminar and, similarly it is hoped, will be a piece of the pedagogy that seminar participants are building in their own classrooms. In this way, the DMI seminar was intended to provide teachers with learning opportunities that are unusual not only in their mathematical content, but in their opportunities for learning about learning.

The seminar facilitator plays an important role in creating the chances for participants to learn about learning. Throughout the seminar, the facilitator aims at making student thinking visible. *Student thinking* here refers to the thoughts of the teachers participating in the DMI seminar: the facilitator's students. It also refers to the thoughts of children who are students in the teachers' own classrooms and those who people the cases. It is the facilitator's goal for the participants that they deepen their attention to both their own understandings and those of others, especially the children whom they teach. The facilitator's own stance as a teacher is one of the tools she can bring to bear in addressing this goal.

Modeling is a critical component of the seminar's pedagogy. When the seminar facilitator works at teaching in this way herself, paying attention to the participants' ideas and to her own assessment of the topics they are working to understand, she acts as a model of the kind of teaching envisioned in the DMI materials and in the national Standards. Because, when facilitators *teach* in this way their modeling is paired with the participants' experience of *learning* in this kind of community, the modeling is likely to be of particular importance.

Yet there are other models of this dual focus in DMI as well. The teachers whose voices we hear in the seminar's video and print cases are models. They too model for the teacher participants a kind of thinking and teaching in which the teacher pays close attention to her own and her students' understandings and questions. Finally, a third potential source of modeling is each teacher's interactions with her seminar colleagues, any of whom might demonstrate this simultaneous attentiveness to her own thoughts and the thoughts expressed by others in the seminar. In these situations, participants are able to experience the effect this stance has on conversation and the building of ideas.

In all of these ways, the DMI seminar attempts to offer this kind of pedagogy to teachers who are themselves learning and provide models and experiences of the kind of pedagogy we hope they might enact in their own classrooms. In reading the stories of chapters 2, 3, and 4, we might look for clues about the extent to which teachers draw on this pedagogy in their changing beliefs and practices. If teachers are drawing on the pedagogy that is in play in the seminar and portrayed by seminar material, which aspects of the pedagogy are most salient to participants? Which are less salient? These are questions to which we return in the concluding chapter.

How DMI Addresses Issues of Pedagogy With Facilitators and Participants. As may be clear, much of the work of the seminar depends on the facilitator's skill. The DMI materials explicitly lay out seminar pedagogy for the facilitators through the agendas and through Maxine's journal entries and other facilitators' guide material. Further, there is an explicit articulation for facilitators that the seminar pedagogy will hopefully parallel the kinds of practices that participating teachers will build in their classrooms.

Yet whatever information about pedagogy DMI makes explicit in facilitator materials, more is implicit. Whereas Maxine's journal entries in the facilitator guides sometimes offer direct statements about pedagogy, more frequently the entries offer pedagogical support in portraying a certain relationship between (or among) Maxine, the teachers in Maxine's seminar, and their respective ideas. The journal entries also portray a certain relationship between Maxine and the facilitators with whom she is sharing her journal. Similarly, the cases portray a variety of stances with respect to teaching and learning.

The information about pedagogy that is addressed to seminar participants is almost entirely implicit. It is embodied in the pedagogy of the seminar and in the seminar materials. The cases provide teachers with a window on pedagogy, offering samples of practice in narrative and video form. Although there is no explicit articulation to participating teachers of a classroom pedagogy that teachers are moving toward, there are some portfolio assignments in which *participants* articulate what they believe is changing and what is remaining the same in their own teaching practices. In the concluding chapter, we return to consider issues concerning the articulation of a pedagogical stance. In what ways does the seminar provide opportunities for these issues to be made explicit, when, and by whom? What is the impact of these choices on teachers' changing practices?

PART 3: THE RESEARCH PROJECT

So what happens when teachers participate in this kind of professional development? What happens when, over the course of 1 year, teachers' attention is focused on (a) an exploration of the fundamental mathematical ideas of the elementary curriculum, (b) the development of these ideas in children across the elementary years, and (c) this, all within the context of a teacher development experience where student ideas are expressed, explicitly represented, and built on both within the seminar where the teachers are students and within elementary classrooms as depicted in the seminar's print and video cases? What issues arise for teachers? What, if anything, changes in the teachers' thinking about mathematics? What, if anything, changes in the teachers' thinking about themselves, their students, and the processes of teaching and learning? What, if anything, changes in the teachers' actual teaching practices?

With these general questions in mind, I undertook the following study. I followed two DMI seminars. Each of the seminar groups met in western Massachusetts during the 1996–1997 school year. One group was from a rural community, and one was from an urban community. In the first group, there were 12 teacher participants; in the second group, there were 11 teacher participants. These teachers came from a variety of teaching situations. Some were first-year teachers, some had been teaching for 20 years or more. The participants taught in classrooms for children ranging in age from preschoolers through sixth graders. They taught in standard classrooms as well as special education settings and bilingual classrooms.

Two of the participants were not classroom teachers: one was a school psychologist, and the other was a librarian.

Each seminar was co-facilitated—in one case by two teachers and in the other by three teachers. Each of the five facilitators was a teacher leader in her school district, and each had participated in a minimum of 3 years of intensive mathematics professional development prior to teaching the DMI seminar. We should also note that each was teaching DMI for the first time. Thus, we see these facilitators—and the learning that they facilitate—while they are still new to this work.

I attended every other session of each seminar group videotaping and taking notes to record each of the eight sessions per seminar that I visited. I also collected the written teacher portfolios from these seminars. Each portfolio contained 16 entries, 1 prepared for each of the 16 seminar meetings (see Appendix A).

In addition to visiting the seminar meetings and collecting the portfolio writing from seminar participants, I also collected considerably more information about six of the teacher participants who volunteered to allow me to visit their classrooms. Four of the volunteering teachers were from one seminar and two from the other. All taught in public schools: two were preschool teachers with particular expertise in special education, one was a third-grade teacher, one was a fourth-grade teacher, one taught in a mixed-age special education class, and one taught in a fifth-grade bilingual classroom. I visited each of these six teachers' math classes three times during the seminar year—once in the fall or early winter, once in mid-winter, and once in the spring. I took notes detailing the conversation and activity during the math classes, and I videotaped each class visited. For four of the six teachers, I was also able to visit their math classes a fourth time during the fall of the following school year. After each classroom visit, I conducted an interview with the teacher. Interviews lasted approximately 45 minutes, and the questions centered around three topics: the issues on the teacher's mind in preparation for, during, and after the class we had just experienced; the issues on the teacher's mind in her seminar work at that time; and the connections, if any, that she saw between the ideas that she was most interested in from her seminar work and those she focused on in her teaching. All interviews were audiotaped.

PART 4: OVERVIEW OF THIS BOOK

The body of this book portrays three strands of work set in motion as teachers participated in these seminars. The strands are introduced to organize the rich and varied work that teachers undertook in the seminar. Their essence is well captured by the metaphor in the following quote:

"We all speak of having ideas but entertaining them is an art. You have to invite them in and make them feel at home—as you do company—while you get to know them" (Cox, 1975, p. 9).

Teachers worked to cultivate the art of entertaining ideas—in this case, mathematical ideas. We can think of the strands as three ongoing lines of work each in play to varying degrees as teachers in the seminar came more and more to invite their own, their colleagues', and their students' mathematical ideas in and truly entertain them. The strands are:

Strand 1: Teachers' increasing awareness of themselves and of children as "havers" of mathematical ideas and understandings, and their growing desire to give these ideas a central place in the classroom

Strand 2: Teachers deepening their own understanding of the mathematics they teach

Strand 3: Teachers building teaching practices that work with the children's understandings as together and individually the children construct new ideas

The first strand concerns teachers' growing sense that they and their students have ideas about the subject matter they study, and that these ideas belong, front and center, in the classroom. It has to do with teachers' proclivity to invite their own and students' ideas in so they can get to know them. Recall the two story lines introduced in the preface: the psychosocial and mathematical. In this strand, as in the others, both of these story lines are present, but in this first strand the psychosocial story line is in the foreground. We see teachers' visions of themselves, and of the children they teach, changing. We see teachers' visions of the possibilities for intellectual community expanding. Of course this is in the context of studying mathematics, but this strand focuses our attention less on the content of these ideas and more on coming to know people as "havers" of ideas and classroom communities as groups that productively entertain these ideas. Still as we hear from teachers, their own experiences doing mathematics in the seminar and their observations of children's rigorous mathematical work in the print and video cases provide the foundation that makes this strand possible.

The second strand foregrounds the mathematical story line. The second strand concerns teachers' growing subject matter knowledge. We see teachers' understandings of topics in elementary mathematics deepening both within the seminar setting and as teachers work within their own classrooms. In each of these settings, we see teachers learning to put forth mathematical conjectures, argue for or against them in substantive and mathematically valid ways, and reflect on the conjectures and arguments as they work to build stronger understandings. Although it is the mathematical story line that is highlighted in this strand, here too the other story line is present. To the extent that teachers have a vision of what (beyond the following of prescribed algorithms) mathematical thinking can be and believe in themselves and children as people capable of engaging in it, they are more likely to dedicate themselves to understanding the mathematics before them: both as problems are presented to them within the seminar and as mathematical issues arise in the course of teaching and uncovering the meaning of student work. Together Strands 1 and 2 make up the first half of the book.

The third strand concerns the work that teachers did as they came to change their teaching practices so that children and teacher could jointly entertain these mathematical ideas, making the classroom a place where ideas are not only at home, but well known. The second half of the book focuses on these changing teaching practices and the classroom opportunities that become available to children as their teachers' understanding of the subject matter grows and as teachers become more attentive to their students' and their own conceptions of the mathematics of their curriculum. In this third strand, we see teachers trying to keep the elements of both story lines in the foreground at once: focusing intently on the mathematical ideas and, simultaneously, balancing between the ideas as they are expressed by the students and as they compare to the teachers' own conceptions. This last sentence is so much easier to write than it is to enact.

It is worth considering for a moment the origins of these three strands. To some extent, each strand was targeted in the design of DMI (cf. Maxine's Journal, p. 109, of the Building a System of Tens Facilitator's Guide). Yet each also represents how the teachers—in the seminars, portfolio writing, after-class interviews—talk about learning. Each strand captures a recurring theme, and together they provide a useful structure for thinking about the work of teachers participating in these seminars, the work of transforming teaching practices.

One chapter of the book is devoted to each of the three strands. Each strand is introduced in broad-brush strokes to give the reader a general impression. This broad-brush stroke picture is then filled in with detailed stories. The stories of Strands 1 and 2 lay out some of the teacher learning and some of the changes in teacher thinking that make possible changes in teaching practices. These changes in teaching practice are portrayed in the Strand 3 stories. There are seven stories altogether: two for each of Strands 1 and 2, and three for Strand 3. One of the Strand 2 stories comes primarily from a seminar session. The other six stories come from the data collected from the six teacher participants for whom we have not only a record of seminar participation and portfolio writing, but also classroom visits and interviews.

The stories contain quotations from teachers' portfolio writing, as well as transcriptions of classroom conversations, seminar conversations, and after-class interviews with teachers. In these transcriptions, various symbols are used. In interview transcriptions, when either the teacher or interviewer says only "yeah," "uh-huh," or "mmm" in the midst of the other speaker's conversational turn, the "yeah," "uh-huh," or "mmm" is denoted by a double slash (//). Italics are used in all transcriptions to indicate that the speaker emphasized these words by their tone of voice. Square brackets ([ ]) surround words that are implied by, but not actually spoken by, the speaker. This might be the case, for example, where preceding text that would have made the referent clear is omitted. Square brackets surrounding an ellipsis ([. . .]) indicate a discontinuity in the text, which is a piece of transcript that has been omitted. An ellipsis without brackets (. . .) indicates a pause by the speaker. Finally, all of the names in the stories—teacher names and student names—are pseudonyms. Table 1.1 shows the correspondence in time of the stories of each strand with the ongoing seminar sessions.

For all three strands, it is in the stories of the book that we find (a) existence proofs that these kinds of learning take place among teachers engaged in a yearlong DMI seminar, and (b) form given to ideas of what some of the work is that teachers take on in these areas. Although the stories bring the strand to life, illustrating the kind of work we see at the heart of each strand, they are unable to provide an indication of how common that kind of work was in these seminar groups. For this information, we look to the portfolio writing available for all 23 participants in the two seminars. This larger data set helps situate the more detailed stories. To-

TABLE 1.1
Correspondence in Time Between Stories
of the Book and the DMI Seminar Sessions

Strand	Story	Corresponds in Time With DMI Sessions
1	Abby's story: Hearing students' ideas	Sessions 6 through 7
	Ella's story: Hearing one's own ideas	Sessions 3 through 14
2	Multiplication and division of fractions: A DMI seminar conversation	Session 14
	Tamar's story: Exploring the mathematics of counting	Session 1 through December of the year following the seminar
3	Ella's classroom story: Representing thoughts	Sessions 3 through 14
	Claire's classroom story: Using represented thoughts	Sessions 5 through 11
	Liz' classroom story: Working together to build new representations	Session 14

gether the two kinds of data give us a sense of the effectiveness of the seminar as an instrument of change.

For the purposes of this book the three strands are presented in an order. I have chosen to present them in this order because I believe it is the first strand that makes sense of, makes important, that the other two happen. It is in coming to see the power and complexity of mathematical ideas (their own and children's) that teachers see a need to understand more mathematics themselves and to develop ways to support classroom investigations into these ideas. Although these strands are laid out here in an order, I intend for them to be taken as ongoing, ever-evolving lines of work that continue to interact and influence one another as teachers engage in them.

In choosing an order for the strands, I also chose to present them separately. In reality, the teacher having these experiences is not doing so in such a neatly ordered and separable way. Although in the telling of the story of each strand I hold the three strands separate, this focus is somewhat artificial. It serves to illuminate some of the important ideas that the teachers are working on. Each story is told with a focus on its relevance to one strand, yet each clearly holds more, and the teachers themselves are no doubt working at all of these concurrently. We return to the interwoven nature of teachers' learning in chapter 5.

Finally, the concluding chapter of the book has two primary roles. The first section explores the benefits to children of having a teacher who is working on her teaching in these ways. To this end, we look at seminar participants' own characterizations of the changes in their classrooms and among their students. The next sections of this chapter summarize and articulate what we have learned about the work that teachers are doing in this genre of professional development, and how we can continue to support them as they do this work. We make two passes across the stories and portfolio data. One pass, focusing on the strands, considers the *what* and *when* of teacher learning in the seminar. The second pass, focusing on the three core aspects of the seminar, considers the *how* of teacher learning in the seminar. In both passes through the data, we consider the implications of the findings for how we think about teacher learning and for making wise professional development choices.

2

Seeing Teachers and Students as Sense-Makers

Strand 1: Teachers' increasing awareness of themselves and of children as "havers" of mathematical ideas and understandings, and their growing desire to give these ideas a central place in the classroom

Cox (1975) recommends to us the art of entertaining ideas. He advises us "to invite [ideas] in and make them feel at home—as you do company—while you get to know them . . ." (p. 9). Getting to know ideas in this way is at the heart of learning. Yet issuing these invitations, staying in touch with the ideas, and exploring new aspects of them is easier said than done. We differ with respect to our willingness to engage with new ideas. Indeed each of us, as individuals, may find some ideas easy to invite in and others hard. To the extent that we keep an idea at the threshold, however, we limit our understanding of it, its complexity, and its potential.

For most Americans, mathematical ideas are rarely invited in for a lengthy visit. Our everyday experiences show us little of the power and complexity of mathematical thinking—either our children's or our own. It is common, given our school experience with mathematics, for adults in our culture to experience mathematics as something to be remembered or told—procedures, rules, and facts that are given to us ready-made (Ma, 1999; Mokros, Russell, & Economopoulos, 1995; Morse & Wagner, 1998). It is much less common for adults in our culture to experience mathematics as something to be understood, created by our own work.

Over the course of the seminar year, however, the teachers in the DMI seminars became eloquent advocates for this second point of view. As the participants studied mathematics and the development of mathematical ideas in children, and as they experienced a teaching and learning environment built on making understandings explicit and public, they came to better know the existence, power, and complexity of children's and adults' mathematical ideas. They came to trust both children and teachers to productively participate in classroom explorations of mathematical ideas. They came to see children, for their part, as people who bring mathematical understandings to class, and who, when given support and opportunity, not only examine these ideas, but build new ones. Moreover, DMI participants came to see *themselves* in a similar light. They came to trust that they too bring to class an ability to understand mathematical ideas—their own and their students'. DMI participants spoke about developing these two kinds of trust—in the mathematical understandings of children and of teachers, as well as a commitment to developing their ability to work with children in the building of deeper, stronger mathematical conceptions.

These are the shifts in thinking that Strand 1 describes, and the two stories of this chapter focus in turn on each. With Abby, we hear from a teacher about her changing sense of children as mathematical thinkers; with Ella, we hear from a teacher about her changing sense of herself as a mathematical thinker. Both changes are important to reforming classroom practices. Each is essential to developing a teaching practice in which the teacher maintains a dual focus on the mathematics as she understands it and on her students' understandings.

TEACHERS' INCREASING AWARENESS
OF CHILDREN AS MATHEMATICAL THINKERS

From the start of the seminar, teachers worked both on their own mathematical ideas and on understanding the mathematical ideas of children. Yet teachers first wrote about noticing, acknowledging, and being surprised by the existence and variety of *children's* mathematical ideas. Without exception, all teachers in both DMI seminars talk and write about their changing sense of children as mathematical thinkers and their growing sense that it is important to bring the children's ideas into focus in the classroom. Yet this is neither a simple nor a fast occurring change in perspective. Abby's story, which follows, gives us a glimpse of one teacher's process of coming to acknowledge children's ideas and the impact of this discovery on her teaching.

The story begins with an experience that Abby has in one seminar session. She is trying to understand some of the mathematical work of a student she has read about in a case for the seminar. Seminar participants are frequently asked to find the sense in children's mathematical work. In this session, the participants have been asked to use a particular child's strategy to solve a problem similar to the one that a child has solved in the case. As Abby tries to use this child's strategy, she makes an error. She becomes confused and is helped when the seminar facilitator asks Abby, the seminar student, to articulate more of her own reasoning. This experience makes a strong impression on Abby. As the rest of the story unfolds, we hear Abby talk about the thoughts this experience set in motion for her, the roles of teacher and student, and the ways in which she would now like to change her own teaching to reflect her growing awareness of students' mathematical ideas. In the process of working to understand a student's mathematical thinking, and then working to understand her own thoughts about that same mathematics, Abby comes to see something new about the importance to learning of focusing on student ideas. Her story is one of a teacher who begins to think and feel differently about what student and teacher understandings are, and how she would like for them to interact in the classroom. In her story, we begin to get a feel for the important role in teacher learning of a seminar pedagogy that parallels envisioned elementary classroom pedagogy.

Abby's Story: Hearing Students' Ideas

It is the sixth seminar session. Abby, a teacher who works in a mixed-age special education classroom, is working with another teacher to understand the method for division that one child in a seminar case used. They are trying out April's strategy. April, in trying to divide 143 jelly beans among 8 children, began as follows: $10 \times 8 = 80$, $20 \times 8 = 160$, and so, April reasons, the answer to her problem, $143 \div 8$, would be between 10 and 20. April has noticed that the number 143 lies between 80 and 160, and she correctly reasons from this that the number of eights in 143 must fall between the 10 eights of 80 and the 20 eights of 160. It is this piece of reasoning that Abby and her partner characterize as doubling and try out on the problem $121 \div 3$. They begin as April did with 10 groups: $3 \times 10 = 30$. That being too small, they double it to $3 \times 20 = 60$. This is the move that parallels April's setting of boundaries: April reasons $10 \times 8 = 80$, $20 \times 8 = 160$, and 143 lies in between. Abby and her partner reason that $3 \times 10 = 30$, $3 \times 20 = 60$, and then Abby says that 60 would be too much.

The seminar facilitator, who is sitting with Abby and her partner, considers Abby's comment, notices that 20 threes, or 60, is actually less than the 121 of Abby's problem. The facilitator, paying attention to her own sense of the problem and trying to understand Abby's reasoning, asks an important question: "I'm confused, why would 60 be too much?" Although this question seems simple enough, it accomplishes a great deal. For the facilitator, it provides an opportunity to learn about Abby's thinking. For Abby, it establishes the facilitator's dual focus on her own and on Abby's mathematical reasoning, as well as providing Abby with an opportunity to make her thinking more explicit, and therefore more available to her for reflection. In response to the facilitator's question, Abby focuses her attention on the problem and on her thoughts about the problem in such a way that she now recognizes the error in her thinking and articulates it.[2] She explains that she had been thinking about "one block only"— that is, she had mentally divided the 121 by 3 and found that the number 60 exceeded the portion that would be allotted to each one of the three groups—she had, for the moment, lost sight of the whole, 121. With the whole 121 jelly beans once more in mind, Abby and her partner finish out the problem by doubling the number of groups again: $3 \times 40 = 120$. They now consider the 120, comment that this accounts for all but 1 of their 121 jellybeans, and that the last one must be cut into thirds to be shared evenly across the 3 groups; thus, they reason $121 \div 3 = 40\ 1/3$.

Several minutes later, during a whole-group discussion, Abby speaks about her experience of working through that problem and what she is now coming to realize. The facilitator's question "I'm confused, why would 60 be too much?" was a question that invited Abby to take a careful look at her thoughts and to express them. It invited Abby to focus on her own solution process; in doing so, Abby came to understand more about the mathematics of the problem and the particularly slippery issue of holding parts and wholes simultaneously in mind. For Abby, this interaction began to stand out as strikingly and disturbingly different from her own teaching practice.

> I realized tonight that . . . I thought I'd been doing relatively well with this, but . . . uh . . . when I'm trying to work with kids and I'm asking questions of kids, what I realized today is that I'm asking questions based on the answer that I already know to be true. Um . . . we were doing the 3 into 121 and I was just looking at one group 'cause I knew that, y'know, I wanted to get to [that number] and then I, and I ended up doubling it and I said, "Oh, 60", [I doubled] the 10 . . . "and the 60 is too much" and then [the facilitator] said "why is 60 too much?" You see—I knew, I knew what I wanted the answer to be. And I know . . . there was something else I did with a kid today, trying to like lead them down a path with my questions although I thought I was making inquiry. (Abby, Seminar 1.6, December 18, 1996)

Abby is struck by the parallel between her own reasoning as a student in the seminar and the kind of thinking she encourages in her students. In

---

[2]Although in this example the facilitator has asked her student to reflect on a piece of logic that is faulty, she might have made a similar request with respect to *correct* reasoning that she felt deserved closer inspection.

both cases, she notices that she can be blinded by an answer she holds in mind. She notices that in both seminar and classroom she accords a certain privileged position to an answer she has in mind, and she tends not to follow the mathematical reasoning—of students or herself—with the same attention. In the seminar, she becomes aware of the potential risks in her strategy. As the seminar student, she loses track of the meaning in working toward a target answer, and she now worries that her teaching methods might similarly derail the children in her class.

> And is anyone else having a problem with that? (pause) Using this stuff with kids? Because I don't know enough about the way that kids look at math and um . . . even feeling comfortable using different *methods* to get answers with math myself, what I am finding myself doing, and I only became aware of it tonight, is that I'm kind of framing questions with kids about what they're *doing* with math, with a hidden agenda in my mind. It's gotta be over here . . . instead of letting them go through the process and even if their answer was wrong, looking at the process. That's a *difficult* thing. I'm finding that that's *very* difficult. I'm just realizing it now. (Abby, Seminar 1.6, December 18, 1996)

In the seminar, the facilitator's question—"I'm confused, why would 60 be too much?"—provided Abby with an opportunity to consider a mathematical proposition and the reasoning behind it. Abby found that opportunity to better understand her own (in this case, faulty) reasoning valuable. Against the backdrop of Abby's seminar experiences, her relative lack of attention to student thinking in her own teaching practice now stands in bold relief.

> And I think what I've been doing is pulling kids through . . . for the last several weeks. Um . . . Instead of trying to find it out . . . um *really* finding out about *what, what they understand*, and then just stopping right there and building from *that* point. I think I'm *so* interested in getting them to understand how I can get them to get the right answer . . . (voice lower, with some emotion) And I thought I was doing a really fine job of this. (Sarcastically) Merry Christmas, Abby! . . . I think I'm *pulling* them down a path where *they* don't have all the skills to get it at a particular point in time. (Abby, Seminar 1.6, December 18, 1996)

In this excerpt, Abby shows us that she is beginning to see a different role for the teacher and, consequently, a different role for students. She characterizes her current practice as "pulling [children] down a path where they don't have the skills to get it" and as being directed by an interest in "getting them to understand how I can get them to get the right answer." This is contrasted with her newly emerging view that teaching can be "really finding out about . . . what they understand, and then just stopping right there and building from that point." Abby's image of the teaching practice she would like to build sounds very much like the pedagogical stance of the seminar.

Two weeks later during an after-class interview, Abby speaks about what had gone on in the seminar meeting. She talks about how surprised she was by the facilitator's question. Abby had been expecting the facilitator to ask a question that pointed out her error because that is the move that she—as the teacher—would have made. She had expected from the facilitator a move that emphasized the elucidation of one line of thinking—the teacher's—and paid less attention to getting a clear picture of the student's thought.

> I . . . , by the time that [the facilitator] intervened on the problem that we were working on, I realized where I had made my mistake and in my head I was saying, "oh, she's just going to say to me, look at the ten" or I don't even know exactly, // I knew what the mistake was. And I expected her question to be "look directly here // and tell me what you did."
>
> [. . .] Because I was expecting her to be me. If that was me in [the facilitator's] position and [she] was doing it wrong, what *I* would have done, and what I do in my teaching is, "Now, take a look right here in this area." . . . (Abby, interview, January 8, 1997)

When the facilitator instead asked, "I'm confused, why would 60 be too much?", she focused Abby's attention on their joint endeavor of understanding Abby's mathematical thinking. With this, Abby explains,

> I came to a better *understanding* of the process that I had taken, . . .
>
> [. . .] Because of her question. Yup. Now that's more meaningful to me in the *long* run. I was just always just looking for the bottom line, "here's the answer". And that's where I went wrong. (Abby, interview, January 8, 1997)

During this same interview, Abby speaks about how she sees this issue playing out in her own teaching practice. She speaks about it in general terms at first, characterizing what she now sees as a weakness in her teaching practice:

> Well, I think that . . . , I really believe that I identified a weakness in my teaching style. Um, and I don't know if it comes from the demand of having a curriculum and having to report progress so that I feel good about myself as a teacher and the kids feel good about themselves as learners and parents feel good about their kids on their report cards. Because there's this real sense of urgency with me, and the kid's got to get it, and you know, if I just give him, *if I give him* this piece here then they'll be over here. It always doesn't work out that way. // And instead of letting . . . , the difference there is letting the kid get the piece. And the way that I, what I was

doing, and what I still have a real weakness in doing is giving . . . , framing a question so that the answer in the question is inherent. Almost like giving the first three letters of the spelling word, because they're stuck. // And I'm a little bit stuck on it. // I'm more aware of it now that, you know, after, after that seminar. [. . .] But I feel really insecure about . . . , when I'm asking a question now, as to whether I'm leading, or whether I'm making a genuine serious inquiry. (Abby, interview, January 8, 1997)

Abby, having experienced in the seminar a teacher inquiring into her mathematical thinking—looking for a fuller explanation of her understanding of the mathematics of the problem—is convinced that she would like to provide those experiences of "genuine serious inquiry" to her own students. She is now dissatisfied with teacher questions that hand out answers, "almost like giving the first three letters of the spelling word." She has some sense of the direction in which she would like her teaching practice to move. She knows that she wants her teaching practices to allow "the kid to get the piece," but clearly this sense of direction is only a beginning. Abby still feels unsure about how she, as a teacher, can create the classroom conditions that support children as they "get the piece[s]" and can use her own knowledge as she enables the children's work on their understandings.

At this point, Abby is clearer about what she wants to change than she is about what her revised practice will entail. When asked in January for an example of something from her recent teaching that came closer to the kind of teaching she now was beginning to envision, nothing came to mind. However, when asked if she could think of an example from her recent teaching of the old way, Abby does not hesitate. She describes an episode from a class in which she introduced her students to the study of three-dimensional shapes; as part of this study, she asked the children to count the faces on one particular solid:

Abby: Oh, yeah. Yesterday I got right into it, but I kind of, . . .
       . . . Um, I know it was yesterday too. When . . . I have two kids who are pretty developmentally delayed in here so I make an assumption before I start to work with them, that they're just going to be incapable of doing this and I'm just going to have put their fingers all over the place with these hands-on manipulatives, instead of letting them *show* me exactly what they knew yesterday, I put the block in their hand, and hand over hand I went OK, we're going to go, on a solid cube, "one, two, three, four. Oh, look what's left. Five, six." // I'm sure that they could have rotated to do the full three or four, but I wasn't trusting enough in myself as a teacher or in their ability to explore materials that they were going to do that. I was . . . , I had to have them have six yesterday. I had to have *those* two walk away thinking six.

SC: And so how did you do that?

Abby: I physically put it in their hand and I rotated, it was hand over hand.

Although it is certainly sometimes appropriate for teachers to show children such things, Abby is saying more here than that this happened once. She is describing for us a teaching scenario that represents her primary stance in the classroom until now. She offers this as an example of how little room she feels her teaching leaves for students to try out their own ideas or express their own thoughts. Now, in the context of Abby's seminar experiences—where she had and valued such opportunities, and where she watched colleagues and children make use of similar opportunities—Abby wants to reshape her teaching.

SC: So your hand was on their hand. And you helped, . . . and with your hand on their hand you counted sides,

Abby: Yeah.

SC: So that you're literally taking their hands through the motions of counting sides.

Abby: And I'm sure that they could have done the "one, two, three, four," and they did, they counted without any prompting. "One," and I rotated, and went "two, three, four," which is great. So they can count, can say "one, two, three, four." But then I, even as directed as that was, I got caught in it again. Because there was this dead silence and they had neglected the . . . , and instead of saying something like "Is there anything more here, are there some other sides that we haven't counted yet?"

SC: So you have in mind now, after the fact, . . . you have in mind a different thing you could have tried, which is you might have said, "Is there anything more, did we leave anything out?"

Abby: Mm-hm. And then if they didn't get it, you know, in thinking about it today, thinking, y'know can you, . . . "Let me have [Jose] over here, Jose, when you counted this cube, can you show me when you counted the sides on this particular piece what you did?" [. . .] I did nothing for those two yesterday, basically is what I'm saying. They really learned very little from what I had to present.

SC: Why did they learn little from it when it's done that way?

Abby: Because they didn't do it. I did it. // It was just "Let me tell you what I want you to know, this is it."

SC: And why isn't that enough?

Abby: They don't retain it. It has no *meaning* to them, and there's no value in it. (Abby, interview, January 8, 1997)

This belief—that if "it has no *meaning* to them . . . there's no value in it"—stands in sharp contrast to Abby's characterization of her previous focus in teaching mathematics: "I was just always just looking for the bottom line 'here's the answer.' " It is also striking criticism of a teaching practice that this skilled teacher spent years developing. Abby is as certain now that this is not the kind of teaching she values as she had previously been that this would be helpful to children. In the interview, Abby explains what has convinced her that her "hand-over-hand" instruction had neither meaning nor value to those children.

> Each and every one of those children on the videos and in the cases that are given in the book is a testimonial to a particular child's thinking. And a lot of times, especially in [this city] where we make excuses for children, there's uh, cognitive delays, um, lack of experience with the materials and learning prior to their coming to the school, and on those tapes and in those writings I see the exact same kids, who are seven, who have the terminology to explain, . . . and they have the vocabulary development to explain what they're thinking. And they're coming up with some *absolutely*, . . . they're coming up, . . . those young children on those tapes are coming up with ways of solving problems that necessarily isn't the most expedient, but *that they understand*, and they're building a foundation. . . . In years previous, every . . . you go from addition, and then you go to subtraction. It was unrelated to my children. And then you went to renaming and re-grouping. And it was all unrelated. It was like going back and teaching the same skill from the start, and it was just a mechanics type of thing, it was like an instruction booklet type of way that they were doing it. (Abby, interview, January 8, 1997)

Through watching the video cases and reading the written cases, Abby has come to believe and trust that even very young children can have and express sophisticated mathematical understandings. Abby sees in the seminar materials what she takes as strong evidence of mathematical ideas that belong to children, children for whom mathematics makes sense. The video and print cases have also convinced her that this must be true for all children. She is seeing and reading about children who she recognizes as being just like the children in her school. Now in her own classroom, she believes these are also children who have mathematical ideas, and she is aware that she is not seeing or hearing their ideas. So Abby now sits with this question of what to do in her classroom so that student ideas become visible.

Although Abby's primary focus now is on critiquing her practice, embedded even in her description of the "hand-over-hand" episode are seeds for change. As she reflects on what happened in that class, Abby offers three ideas about what she might have done differently. Each of her ideas bears a good deal of family resemblance to Abby's own seminar experience with the facilitator question, "I'm confused, why would 60 be too much?" Each of her ideas involves asking students to show something about how they approach the question at hand, even such a simple question as counting the number of faces on a geometric solid. She is now inclined, in her after-class reflections at least, to ask the children who are counting the number of faces on a cube to count them in their own way, not holding and moving their hands for them. If these children stop after counting only four of the six faces, she is inclined to ask them if there are any more sides to count. If they see no others, she is inclined to take that as their opinion and look around her classroom to see if anyone—Jose, for example—believes differently. Abby, now convinced that her students have mathematical ideas, is beginning to see some of the possible openings in her classroom for mathematical discussions. Her hunch is that through those discussions students will begin to develop deeper understanding of the mathematics she wants them to learn.

Larger Data Set as Context for Abby's Story

Abby is not alone among her DMI colleagues in her new focus on students' understandings—in her expectation that children bring mathematical ideas to the classroom, which she as their teacher feels a growing commitment to acknowledge and explore. Indeed each of the 23 teacher participants in the two DMI seminars wrote in their portfolios about some aspect of this shift in focus. Fully 20 of the 23 participants wrote about this shift as early as their sixth portfolio assignment when asked: "Have your seminar explorations affected your teaching? Have you noticed any shift in what you are thinking as you work with your students?" Clearly, attention to student thinking was much on these teachers' minds.

Some of the teacher writing underscores the basic idea that understandings exist—that underneath the layer of computational procedures and answers is meaningful mathematics that children need to understand.

> Now I realize that just because a student may memorize an algorithm doesn't mean that they have true understanding. This alone is a valuable development in my thinking. (Substitute teacher, Grades 1–6, May 28, 1997)

> I am much more aware of how my students are thinking. I take little for granted anymore. I have the students explain themselves more to check for understanding. I find it amazing the way some of my students think. (Grade 4 teacher, January 6, 1997)

Clearly, these teachers are beginning to change their ideas of a teacher's role. They are now of the mind that it is the job of the teacher to be aware of and work with children's understandings. For these teachers, as for Abby, their focus is widening beyond answers and memorized algorithms to tapping into and building on children's reasoning and understanding.

Another teacher writes about the richness of children's understandings. During the spring of the seminar year, she reflects on a piece she had written just before the third seminar meeting.

> In Assignment 1.3, I wrote:
>
>> Numbers can be represented in several different ways: with manipulatives, tally marks and pictures, numerals, written word and spoken word. We, as adults, often assume that making the connections between these different forms is a simple matter when in fact it is very complicated. It is challenging for a young child to incorporate all these representations in his mind and to be able to move freely from one form to the next and do so accurately.
>
> This was really the beginning of my understanding of the depth of thinking and understanding necessary to do math. Prior to this I really didn't realize how much was involved in even very simple math. It was the beginning of my respect for the struggle in young minds to hold on to all this information at once and to use this information interchangeably. (Grade 3 teacher, May 28, 1997)

A fourth teacher, also writing about the mathematics she saw children in the seminar materials understanding and expressing, wrote:

> The point that really impressed me was the way children broke apart numbers. Watching the video was very helpful. It showed how the children worked in cooperative groups to solve number problems and then were able to explain how they arrived at their answers. I really felt the children understood what they were doing. They understood what groups of tens represented and grouping ones to make tens. I thought this was much more valuable than using the traditional method the way we were taught. Even in many classrooms today using base ten blocks for regrouping many children do not realize 14 is 1 ten and 4 ones. They just trade the 1 ten and call it one. (Grade 4 teacher, May 14, 1997)

Correct answers, the correct use of a taught algorithm or even the correct use of manipulatives do not necessarily indicate that a child understands the mathematical ideas that the curriculum targets. The seminar participants were beginning to make this distinction, and this drove their growing interest in understanding students' understandings.

This is especially clear in other pieces of teacher writing that focus on the existence of children's ideas *within* their own classrooms and that highlight the teachers' resolve to notice them, to make a place for them, to listen. Consider a few examples:

I think the video we watched about children learning addition in a first grade gave me the most info[rmation] about understanding. I had not considered much in the past the thinking of my students. [. . .]

After viewing the tape I returned to my classroom and put more emphasis on listening to what children said while working in the room and how they shared their knowledge with other students. Watching and listening has made an impression on me. I see many of the students differently now. (Kindergarten teacher, May 14, 1997)

I was "trying hard" at the beginning of the seminar to look at the understanding that children had about number and "try to guide their learning". Now at the end of this seminar I am thinking that this is not as hard as I thought. The children demonstrate understanding of number in many ways. It is there and I feel it is easier for me to see it. (Preschool teacher, May 28, 1997)

I would like to try having the students solve addition problems with regrouping on their own. Although I must admit this will be a little nerve wracking for me. It makes me both excited and anxious. What if this approach only confuses them? Or on the other hand with this approach will they show more understanding of place value and numbers than I think they have? It will be interesting to see. Normally, I've shown my students different ways to solve the same problems, now I want them to show me. (Grade 2 teacher, December 18, 1996)

One change that I am aware of is that I allow children more time to struggle with ideas and develop their own strategies more on their own. Also, as kids explain their problem solving strategies, I am less apt to assess it as right or wrong as I did before. Instead I think more about how they are trying to solve the problem—why are they using the strategies they chose, what are they thinking, and how to help them move on to the next level. I also listen more closely to their explanations seeing them as possibilities albeit not my first choice. In one situation a student was trying to explain her method to me but was stuck and could not take it further. I did not understand where she was heading and proceeded to suggest to her another method which she used successfully. Later I realized what she was trying to do and her way would have worked. Perhaps if I had spent more time "thinking her way" we could have worked it out "her way" allowing her to feel more successful and maybe to understand better. (Grade 3 teacher, December 4, 1996)

Each teacher's comments echo those of Abby: Children have mathematical ideas; I, as a teacher, want those ideas expressed in the classroom, and I will be listening.

TEACHERS' INCREASING AWARENESS
OF THEMSELVES AS MATHEMATICAL THINKERS

Although the excitement around student ideas was often first expressed early on in the seminar, it was typically somewhat later in the seminar, most often as teachers worked to better understand multiplication and division of fractions, that teachers expressed delight and awe at the power of their own mathematical thinking. Teachers came to know more about the distinction between mathematical procedures that we memorize (such as to divide by a fraction, "invert and multiply") and procedures that we understand (such as why that might be a valid computational procedure). They could feel the difference. Their written and spoken comments make clear that, although the mathematical topics they explored were not new to them, their understandings of those topics were. Not only were the mathematical understandings new, but the idea that there was something to understand and they—as mathematical thinkers—could gain access to it was also new.

The process was not an easy one. The participants came to the seminar with little experience of mathematics as something for them to understand. The seminar needed to help them beyond this disconnection from mathematical ideas, often learned through their own experiences with mathematics poorly taught in K–12 schools and higher education. Although participants eventually began to feel more empowered—more able to understand mathematics—the first stages involved feelings of frustration, fear, self-doubt, and general discomfort. Having the time and group support provided by DMI allowed teachers to see what happened if they continued to work at understanding mathematics that at first seemed impenetrable. Ella's story, which follows, illustrates these points.

Early in Ella's story, we learn with her about the difficulties of truly knowing one's own thoughts—of holding onto a thought, articulating it, and examining it. She begins the seminar year with these struggles to know her own mathematical thoughts. As the seminar year progresses and Ella does more and more mathematical work in the seminar, she finds that she does not always know how to solve the problems posed or understand the mathematics they present. Ella also finds that this not knowing can be quite unsettling and even scary. Determined to get beyond her uncertainties, and the frustration and anxiety that often accompanies them, Ella's first reaction is to ask others to tell her how *they* solve the mathematical problem in question. However, by the end of the seminar year, Ella has a newfound conviction that *she* is able to reason through difficult and unknown mathematical territory. She comes to see the work of understanding as something that each learner, including herself as teacher, both must and can take an active role in accomplishing.

Ella's Story: Hearing One's Own Ideas

Ella teaches third grade. From early on in the seminar, she makes a distinction between correct computation and understanding. She is clear that she wishes for her students understanding as well as correct computation. During our first interview in late October, she speaks about the importance to her of her students having alternatives to the standard algorithms for computation—of their being able to approach a problem in more than one way.

> I think that it makes numbers more accessible to them. If they are always having to line something up vertically and carry or borrow or however that they're working, that it limits, it limits their thinking about numbers. And that's what I'm fearful of. That they're not always understanding that they're carrying over. You know. How much are they really carrying over? How much are they really borrowing from? // And then they lose track of what the numbers actually mean. (Ella, interview, October 28, 1996)

Later in the same interview, Ella speaks about an earlier teaching experience prior to the seminar. In this piece, it is clear that Ella's focus on student understanding not only is evident early in the seminar, but predates her involvement with DMI.

> The year prior to that I had taught in a parochial school where I had to use the book, I didn't have a choice. I was required to hand in my lesson plans, the principal needed to approve them, and they needed to, I had to follow this book. I did interject things, like, you know, I did a lot of estimation, I am very fond of this book, "Estimation Destinations". [. . .] but when I started falling behind, you know, I would get the finger (she wags her index finger), you know, that we need to, you need to be at this place. And the teacher who I was teaching with or under, depending on how you want to look at it, would also say to me that, you need to move them along. And I would say, "But they don't *understand* this." "Well, it doesn't matter. They'll get it next year or the year after. You need to move them along." And I realized I could not continue to teach there because I, it just, it was very difficult for me. (Ella, interview, October 28, 1996)

Although Ella's focus on student understanding is there from the start, across the seminar year her sense of what understanding is and the world of ideas that it refers to seems to deepen. Her own experiences doing mathematics in the seminar are instrumental in this shift. In the first interview, after three seminar sessions, Ella talks about what has been most on her mind in the seminar. She speaks about her experience of mentally adding and subtracting multidigit numbers and trying to put her computational procedures into words. Several issues stand out for her, most prominently that the steps of her own procedures are sometimes so automatic that it is difficult for her to think about them, analyze them, and put them into words. In response to these difficulties, Ella feels frustrated when, in the seminar, she is asked to speak about a thought she is still working to uncover.

> Well, one of the things that comes to mind is, um, it's very, it's very different to be in a, in a classroom setting where you are now the student. And you are having to think about your own strategy. And, I mean, I did that back in college. Not quite as focused as this is. // Um, but it had me really thinking about strategies and the one strategy that I tend to rely on, and why do I do that? And so I was trying to explore other ways that I was learning. And I think that that has really helped me in the classroom with realizing that sometimes these kids really are stuck. // They can't always think of some new way to come to things. And maybe that's really very difficult for them. // It was very difficult for me sitting down when I add very quickly in my head and really can't figure out how I do it, to have to think about, well, how do I do it? And when I ask the students, particularly when we do the calendar math and we do it on the overhead, "well, how did you know that?" "Well, I just knew that." Not to press them so much because that can be very frustrating. // That's the one thing that I have taken away. . . . (Ella, interview, October 28, 1996)

Ella, having been asked in the seminar to focus on her own thinking, finds that it can be surprisingly difficult. She finds that she is sometimes frustrated, especially when asked to explain what she is thinking, and ends up saying "I don't know." She also notices that she, and perhaps children as well, "can't always think of some new way to come to things." New ideas take time. As Ella sees it now, this time for thought is still a private process. She continues:

> Or if you don't give the children time enough to think about it. You can't expect, that if they don't know right away, that they're going to come up with it. They need some time to mull it over, and then you can go back and ask them. I know that I need to step back and say, "Well, I need some time to think this over, before I can answer this intelligently." And kids want to answer things intelligently, too. (Ella, interview, October 28, 1996)

At this time, Ella's image of thinking something over is of something that takes place alone and internally "before I can answer this intelligently."

As the mathematics explored during the seminar becomes more challenging and as Ella takes on these challenges, digging more deeply into the aspects of the problem she does and does not understand, her worry about the gaps in her mathematical understanding becomes stronger. In the ninth seminar meeting, the group has the following mathematical problem: "On your own, figure out your age today counted in years, months, and days. Then exchange your age with your partners and figure out one another's birth dates (year, month, and day)." For this problem, we have no standardly taught algorithm. Ella and each of her colleagues have to devise a computational procedure out of their own understandings of the problem situation.

Ella: [. . .] I was approaching it completely wrong. I mean, I thought it was very easy. I just looked at it and. . . . And I realize I was tired, it was—you know—report card week and I labor over these report cards, I don't like the reporting system, so . . . I mean, I think there was a lot of that involved. But I left there, because we never had a chance to get to that, . . . and I left feeling, "But don't leave me like this. Because I don't know how to figure this out." // Um, . . . and that was enlightening for me because I thought "I wonder if I do that to any of my students." We don't get to it. so. . . . I mean, we worked at something, but we don't get to it . . . , and we don't, we don't even get back to it, at least I hope, but you never know. In their minds, I could think I've covered it all and everyone's clear, but there could be one student that I didn't get to, that wasn't vocal, and do they ever leave math thinking, "But, wait a minute, but wait a minute. I *didn't* get it." You know?

Ella's description makes clear her worry about being left alone to work through mathematics that at first she does not understand. She worries about putting her students in that position. At this point, Ella does not trust that she or her students will be able to productively work through a problem that is initially difficult for them. Ella's description also makes clear that her seminar experiences as a mathematics learner are feeding her reconsideration of her own teaching.

SC: And what, what happens I mean what happened to *you*, or what would happen to them if they did leave feeling "I don't get it"? Or when you left feeling "I don't get it"? What happens?

Ella: Well, it leaves you with a feeling that "what's wrong with me? It seems like everybody else is OK with it. Everybody else seems to have gotten it. What did I do wrong or what am I doing wrong?" and "can I really go on if I didn't understand this?" And so, putting, . . . being put back as a student . . . always you know, cues us in on what it's like to be a student, no matter how old we are. And I think that it's important for us, in learning about these mathematical approaches, to be put in the position that we may be feeling a little frustrated. It may be a little beyond what we're understanding. Because if it isn't challenging *us*, then we're not going to get that true sense of what it's like for them.

SC: So what did you *do*? You left class and you weren't getting it. // Did you just feel frustrated and put it away? Or what did you do?

Ella: No. I didn't. I took it out when I got home and had . . . uh . . . great intentions of asking my husband about it, and um, and then I didn't. But I have it out. And it was a very busy week last week, // so I didn't have any chance to think about anything, and I was away this weekend. But I'm going to put it out to my family. I have older children, and my husband, and have them figure it out. And I'm going to look at the way that they figured it out, // and see if I can learn something from it. My husband will have no problem with it. I, . . . I, I know that. Um . . . but it will give me a different perspective on it. And I can't just leave it hanging because I want to be able to figure out where I went wrong on this. And, um . . .

SC: And, . . . but it feels to you like you don't want to continue on your *own* with it? [. . .]

Ella: Well, no, because I tried. I was sneaking trying to do it when they were continuing on lecturing (laughs).

SC: So the feeling of not understanding it, then, was something that made you want to keep working on the problem. // The feeling of "I don't get this" was connected also to a feeling of "I want to get it and I'm going to keep trying."

Ella: Right. But that comes from an adult's perspective. I don't think we can always say that an *eight* year old may do that. (Ella, interview, February 10, 1997)

At this point in time, Ella, facing a mathematical problem for which she does not yet see a solution, feels uncomfortable. She comes up against feelings of self-doubt: "What's wrong with me?" Although she does tackle the problem on her own for a little while during the seminar, her inclination is now to "put it out to my family" and "to look at the way that they figured it out, and see if I can learn something from it." This is heartening because she does not abandon the problem in the face of not understanding it, yet it is also telling: Ella is asking someone else to solve the problem, and she will learn from what they do. She is not proposing to tackle the problem herself. Ella goes on to express some doubt about whether this work of persevering as one works to understand a mathematical problem is really something that she could expect her third graders to do—not surprisingly because Ella is still questioning the utility of her own perseverance.

By May, the time of our third interview, Ella's discomfort at coming up against mathematics that she does not yet understand is still present. Yet her sense of her own ability to understand, and the importance of this in her teaching practice, shifts. She speaks about a time in the seminar work when she was feeling particularly uncomfortable with her mathematical understandings.

It is during the 14th seminar session, after the group has been working hard at understanding what happens to fractional quantities as they are multiplied and divided by other fractional quantities, that Ella talks about her experience of studying fractions in this new way.

It's kind of like *thinking* that you know so much and *realizing* you know so little. That's what it was for me. I was an eye-opener. (With strong emotion) The last . . . the last class I sat there and wondered "Geez, should I even be teaching?" . . . but that's the way I was feeling. Having thought that I knew it. But I wrote, . . . what I wrote was "while it is true I have a good grasp, it's certainly not strong enough to give me a good hold". And that's very true. (Ella, 14th seminar meeting, April 30, 1997)

She elaborates on these feelings during the interview:

Ella: *But* the reason that I came to that, that *feeling* of "I shouldn't even be teaching" is because I felt *stupid*. // I *really did*. I felt stupid.

SC: Because, because you weren't being able to figure out the math?

Ella: I wasn't connecting it right away, no, no I wasn't. And even, I even wrote that in my paper this past, this past week, that I wasn't even thinking of division such as, you know, two divided by five is [two over five] as a fraction. // Now I *know* that. I did that for years. But I wasn't even making that connection. I mean, that's how *far* away it was. // And I think that, um . . . I think that I have this, you know, this drive that I have to just *know* all. You know? Don't let myself get, you know, caught and to have, to just kind of *share* that, it makes yourself very vulnerable // because you're thinking "Well, what do your colleagues think about you?" // So, . . .

SC: So what happened with those feelings during the last seminar then?

Ella: It was nice when someone else shared. [Pam] shared that she was feeling somewhat the same, // that, uh, and also the um, [. . .] One of [the facilitators] said it was like going into a *deep*, dark forest or something, when we, you know when we go into . . . // And that, and that, I guess set the tone, a little bit, that it was *OK*. . . . You know they're very good // about not making you feel about *this* (holds up slightly separated fingers, laughs), feeling about that big . . . But. . . .

SC: But you still sometimes feel that way.

Ella: You still feel that way, and, . . . and I don't even want to say that that's OK to feel that way. It's almost that I want to make sure that I don't feel that way too often, because I won't be effective in the classroom if I do. (Ella, interview, May 5, 1997)

Ella is clear that these mathematical ideas were difficult for her. She is clear that she felt stupid to find herself not understanding mathematics that she had assumed she knew. She is clear that this "deep, dark forest" of ideas is neither entirely comfortable nor familiar terrain. She is equally clear that feeling stupid, if it is an ongoing state, will interfere with her teaching practice.

Ella's evolving sense of what teaching is and who she would like to be as a teacher involves a teacher who has deep understandings of the mathematics she teaches, a teacher who is able to get through the "deep, dark forest" and who can take on the work of coming to new understandings when the classroom work demands it. This new view comes to light as Ella explains why her seminar work on multiplication and division of fractions made her wonder if she should be teaching. Again we see Ella using her mathematical and pedagogical experiences as a seminar student to reshape her ideas about teaching and learning in the elementary classroom.

> But the reason is is that I felt: if I can't understand [. . .], then am I not going to be able to tell, you know, tell my students, *have* an understanding, *be there* for them when something comes up, that maybe I'm not going to get, so how can I help them? // Because the teacher is supposed to guide, facilitate. How can I facilitate something that *I'm* not getting? // And that's where that was coming from. // And then feeling like I better stay down in the primary grades, . . .
>
> [. . .] Oh, you should have seen me that night. I went home in just sheer frustration, made myself a cup of tea, talked with my husband. He said, "Well, the worst, the worst that could happen here is that you'd have to go back and take a refresher course in math." I said . . . "No, you see, you don't *get* it. I can *do* it. I want to *understand* it. And no one's *going to tell me* how to understand it, I've got to figure it out myself."[3] And so what I've been doing, . . . and if I can admit, . . . but yeah . . . I can admit, my son in 7th grade brought home this summer math that he could do, // that was just these summer math activities. // And so I pulled it out, and I was looking through it, and looking at these, again, somewhat simplistic, and trying to look at it with an understanding of *how* would I understand this? . . . And that's a different way than I've *ever* thought of before. (Ella, interview, May 5, 1997)

Ella now aims squarely at her own understanding of the mathematics. She is not looking for someone else to show her how they do it; she is asking how she will understand it. Because this is such a shift in perspective, I asked Ella what, if any, impact this had had in her own classroom.

---

[3]Ella is both right and wrong here. Although college math classes that she is used to taking will not teach her these things, it is certainly possible to imagine mathematics courses that teach for understanding—courses that approach the content through problem solving (e.g., Schoenfeld, 1985) or that elaborate on the deep conceptual connections underlying school mathematics (e.g., Ma, 1999). DMI is an example of such a course.

Oh, it does. It definitely does. I think of where I was last year // teaching, and where I am this year teaching. And I just want it to grow though. // I'm worried that once I'm out of the class . . . , I don't think I'd ever, I don't think you'd ever fall back to . . . , I think it's kind of like once you, uh, *know* something, you you're exposed to it so you never let it go. // I mean, I'm hoping // that will always be, it will always be so exciting. But I also, I don't want to, uh, I don't want to leave this feeling right now of, // I want to, I want to *know* and *understand* what my students think. I really want to *hear* them and I want to listen to them. I want to give them opportunities . . . and so that has changed, and that's from the seminar. It's from working through it, being frustrated, realizing that, "Well, so OK, so I felt stupid, I felt dumb, um, what am I going to do to remedy it?" [. . .] And so what is important for us as teachers to leave our students with for that year . . . that's a great responsibility when you stop and think about it. (Laughs) You know, twenty children that you're responsible for, you know, teaching, more than skills, you know, but an understanding. Um, that's what I've come away with. The opportunity. Always having opportunities there. (Ella, interview, May 5, 1997)

Ella's own attempts to understand new mathematics, however difficult and frustrating, deepen her resolve "to know and understand what [her] students think" and provide them with opportunities to build their own understanding. Implicit in this is the belief that learning need not be such a private endeavor. Ella is no longer looking to provide her students only with "time to think" in order to "answer things intelligently" and "think of some new way to come to things," as she had said in the fall. Now she expects to engage with her students' ideas all along the way, and that this joint focus on the students' understandings is what generates the opportunities. Now in May she wonders, "How can I facilitate something that I'm not getting?" Ella has set a new agenda for herself and for her students.

Larger Data Set as Context for Ella's Story

Ella's growing confidence in her ability to understand mathematics, and her sense of the importance to her teaching of her doing so, is echoed in the portfolio writing of 21 of the 23 teacher participants in the two DMI seminars.[4] The following excerpts, all written near the end of the seminar, add three more voices to Ella's. Although all three voices are variations on the theme set up in Ella's story, each highlights a different point.

---

[4]The two teachers who do not write about this idea both had limited proficiency in written and spoken English. For them it is hard to know whether the absence from their writing of evidence for a sense of themselves as more powerful mathematicians was due to the absence of that experience, perhaps because of the language barrier, or to their difficulty in expressing it.

In the first excerpt, the teacher is clear about her changing sense of herself vis-à-vis mathematics. She is no longer someone for whom mathematics makes no sense; she is now someone who understands and can picture mathematical relationships, and she attributes this shift to her seminar work.

> In looking at my writing and my own thinking I see that the work on fractions is the most thought provoking of all the work. As I wrote in Assignment 2.7 I don't have the same reliance on rules as people who "know how to do math". I never could learn the rules and they made no sense to me until we started working through them in this very different way.
>
> In this example, I talk about being one of the slow thinkers, one of the confused ones and I find that even now as soon as someone starts talking about numbers I begin to panic. I feel much more able to say "wait a minute, I need to draw a picture" or "that may make sense to you but I think about it this way. . . ." I hope that I can bring this same perspective to my students in the questions I ask. I go back to the interview we saw of Jill trying to figure out what her student knew about numbers. I hope that I am now more able to approach a student with "what are you thinking we need to do" or "Show me how you can make this" or "Is there another way we can do this."
>
> In 2.7 I write about the moments of true understanding that came to me. These occurred as we were fighting our way through some tough questions. I had taken the time to allow myself to try and "see" what we were talking about and it actually worked. For me the crux of understanding has been being able to "picture" what we were talking about. This is very exciting. (Preschool–Grade 6 Special Education Resource teacher, May 1997)

This teacher, like Ella, traces this change in her thinking to her own mathematical work in the seminar, her own experiences with focusing on her mathematical thoughts, and making them explicit. By virtue of her own attempts and successes at making sense of mathematical problems in the seminar, this teacher has come to know and strive for being able to "picture" rather than only "learning the rules." She is also clear that she wishes to support the same kinds of sense-making among her students.

The second teacher speaks of a similar shift and connects it to the mathematical thinking that she now does as she considers her students' ideas:

> I value student thinking because it creates the desire in me to become a stronger teacher. Looking at pieces of work, like what zero means (1.4), or what to do with the extras (1.8), I realize that I construct deeper understanding of math because of what my students think and do. I ask questions about the content, skills, strategies, and investigations that I explore with my students that I didn't do when I became a teacher. Actually, I'd never thought to think this way or ever been required to reflect on my own understanding. As my thinking develops, I feel shakier, rather than "qualified." This might

turn others away from learning to think differently but it is the richness of this kind of experience that keeps me needing to do more. I believe now that the fundamentals of math are not that one can compute quickly but that one can reason, using numbers and patterns to make the computation meaningful and therefore more accurate. (Grade 4 teacher, May 1997)

Committed to "construct[ing] deeper understanding," this teacher, like Ella, speaks about the shakiness she experiences along the way. Both she and Ella meet these feelings with resolve to understand more for themselves, but also, and importantly, in the classroom context facing children's work.

Finally, a third teacher, speaking of her changing relationship to mathematics, like the others, highlights this resolve to understand. She adds to this that she is noticing a concurrent and similar change among her students.

I have also begun to develop a real appreciation for the richness of math, and I am liking it a great deal. I used to feel uncomfortable with math, probably because I never truly understood some of it. Now, I feel a different sort of discomfort, . . . a frustration, as I struggle to make true sense of something mathematical. It's really a puzzle sometimes, but I'm challenged by it, and instead of preferring to accept what I am told because I don't understand, I now work to figure out what I am confused about, because I have a greater sense of being able to do it. The same seems to be true for a number of my students who previously were totally frustrated with math. Many of them are now exhibiting good problem solving strategies, along with less frustration. (Grade 6 teacher, May 1997)

As this teacher develops more of a "sense of being able to do it," to "figure out what I am confused about," she notices that her students' engagement with mathematics is also changing. As she begins to think of mathematical understandings as accessible to her, she becomes more able to support the same in her students.

Teachers like these, coming to class poised to embrace, wrestle with, and understand mathematical ideas as they encounter them, are poised to do so with the mathematical problems in their textbooks and with the mathematical issues raised by children investigating mathematics. Should these teachers be likewise poised to assess children's developing mathematical ideas, vigilant for expressions of these, then the stage is set for a kind of teaching that is different from that which has been predominant in most of our communities.

Abby and Ella show us both sides of this shift that is Strand 1. Their stories are flip sides of the same coin. Each shows us an individual who comes to know people as "havers" of mathematical ideas. Each shows us an individual who gains a new respect for the strength and elegance of people as sense-makers. As Abby speaks about these issues, the piece of this strand that has to do with the power of children's mathematical ideas is at the forefront. As Ella speaks about these issues, the piece of this strand having to do with her own mathematical power comes to the fore. Yet for each—for Abby and Ella—both aspects are present. Indeed we know that Abby is feeling more able to explore mathematics herself because it was this kind of experience in the seminar that was a catalyst for some of her thinking about student ideas; and Ella, who speaks so powerfully about her changing sense of herself as a mathematician, brings it back to the classroom and her students. She wants "to know and understand what my students think. I really want to hear them and I want to listen to them."

Increasingly, DMI participants came to believe that teaching and learning mathematics is about students' and teachers' mathematical understanding. The more deeply held this conviction became, the more teachers came to call on themselves for a different pedagogy—one that depends more on sense-making than on memory and, in so doing, changes both the intellectual and social climates of the classroom. Thus, the relatively simple proposition that human beings are mathematical thinkers has revolutionary ramifications in the classroom.

Yet finding ways to support the expression of ideas and productively work with them in the classroom is a considerable undertaking. It not only requires from a teacher what she brings from Strand 1—a respect for and an attentiveness to her own and her students' mathematical ideas—it also requires a good deal more. It requires (a) considerably more mathematical expertise than does the exchange of unexamined algorithms offered for memorization; and (b) teaching practices that work with the children's knowledge as together and individually the children construct new ideas. As Abby's and Ella's stories illustrate, the desire to pay attention to student ideas is only a beginning, and by itself is not enough. The next two chapters take a careful look at teachers building deeper mathematical understandings (Strand 2) and new teaching practices (Strand 3).

3

Deepening One's Understanding
of the Subject Matter

Strand 2: Teachers deepening their own understanding of the mathematics that they teach

Abby and Ella show us a good deal about recognizing ourselves and others as builders of mathematical understandings. Yet in those stories, we do not see substantial demonstrations of mathematical understanding itself. In this chapter, we look at teachers building stronger, richer, more nuanced understandings of topics in elementary mathematics.

Let's consider for a moment the meaning of *elementary mathematics*. Elementary mathematics is *elementary* in the sense of being about the elements or fundamentals of mathematics, but it is not *elementary* in the sense of being simple. Elementary mathematics is complex. There is an enormous amount to understand in each of the mathematical topics of the elementary school curriculum. Given the kind of education that most of us have had, it is often, as Ella says, that we only know how to do some piece of computation without understanding why that computational procedure works (Ball, 1990; Ma, 1999), much less having some familiarity with the paths that children might take in building their understandings of these topics.

Thus, teachers of elementary mathematics have before them two substantial pieces of mathematical work: to understand the mathematics of the elementary curriculum in deep and connected ways, and to become knowledgeable about the development of mathematical ideas in children. Participants in the DMI seminars were doing both kinds of work. They worked at building this knowledge in the seminar meetings and, at times, quite independently in their own classrooms. The following stories provide examples, illustrating what it might look like when an individual or group of adults investigates elementary mathematics and its development in children, and providing evidence that teachers involved in these seminars engaged in this work of deepening their subject matter knowledge.

The two stories of this chapter portray teachers working on different mathematical topics under different learning conditions. The first story offers a detailed account of teachers working together during a seminar session to better understand mathematics that is typically an upper elementary (or middle school) topic—the multiplication and division of fractions. In this story, the teachers' mathematical work takes place in a facilitated group context where the mathematical problem has been assigned. The focus of the story is primarily on the mathematics that teachers are learning and on the nature of their learning experiences—experiences in which the representing and re-representing of ideas play crucial roles. At the end of this first story, another theme emerges. As teachers write about their experiences of building their own mathematical knowledge, they slip easily into observations about learning and conjectures about pedagogy. It is clear that in learning mathematics these teachers are also learning about learning.

In the second story, we see one teacher, a preschool teacher, who is coming to understand in more detail the mathematics involved in counting. With the benefit of her seminar experiences, now in the context of her own classroom, she works by herself to unpack the mathematical ideas involved in counting. Here it is the *teacher* who poses the mathematical questions, and it is *she* who pursues them. She uses her observations of the children's work to better understand both the mathematics of counting and the development in children of these mathematical ideas. Together these stories and the surrounding context offered for each give a sense of the power and range of mathematical work that teachers took on in the seminar.

TEACHERS LEARNING MATHEMATICS IN SEMINAR MEETINGS

Multiplication and Division of Fractions: Representing and Re-representing Ideas in a DMI Seminar Conversation

Math activities made me have ♥ palpitations all over again! I had to work hard! I felt like quitting! I loved working with partners because I trusted that I wouldn't leave without learning something I couldn't see before. (Liz,

It is the 14th seminar session. It is now the end of April, and the group has been working together about once every 2 weeks since September. Today the teachers are continuing their work on multiplication and division of fractions. They have been working in groups of three or four on the following problem:

a. Solve the following problem with a diagram:
   Wanda really likes cake. She decides that a serving should be 3/5 of a cake. If she has 4 cakes, how many servings does she have?
b. Solve the problem by writing an arithmetic sentence.
c. How does your arithmetic sentence match the diagram?
d. After 6 portions are eaten, how much is left?
e. Why is the answer to the division problem 6 and 2/3 rather than 6 and 2/5?

(Math Activity, p. 69, *Making Meaning for Operations: Facilitators' Guide*, 1999)

(Before continuing to read, readers might want to spend some time working on this problem and thinking about the mathematical issues it raises. Those issues turn out to be surprisingly complex.)

Pulling the small working groups together for a whole-group discussion of this problem, the seminar facilitator begins by pointing to the numbers 6 2/3 and 6 2/5, which she has written on a piece of chart paper, and asks "how can 6 and 2 thirds and 6 and 2 fifths both be correct answers?" Julie, a seminar participant, appropriately points out that both are not correct.

Julie:	They're *not* both correct. They each answer a separate problem. They don't answer the same question, they answer separate questions.
Facilitator:	So . . . which, which of these answers . . . what would be the question that um 6 and 2 thirds would answer?
Julie:	How many servings? She has 4 cakes, and each serving is 3 fifths of a cake, how many servings does she have? She has 6 and 2 thirds servings.
Facilitator:	So this would have to be 6 and 2 thirds servings. Anybody else? Any reactions?
Kate:	When you draw a picture though, she has 6 servings and then 2 fifths of a *cake* left over.
Facilitator:	Should we draw the cakes?
Kate:	Yeah.

(Laughter, a few side comments about people choosing to draw rectangular cakes rather than circular ones.)

In inviting the group to draw the cakes, the facilitator follows up on Kate's comment "when you draw a picture though, she has 6 servings and then 2 fifths of a cake left over." Kate has a picture in mind in quantifying the leftover cake after six whole portions have been served. The facilitator encourages the participants to jointly create this drawing—a more detailed and lasting representation—as a support to understanding the meaning of 2/3 and 2/5 in the context of this problem.

(The facilitator draws 6 rectangles [Fig. 3.1], rather than 4, each representing a cake. Perhaps she does this to check on the participants' understanding, or perhaps she is momentarily confusing cakes, of which there are 4, with servings, of which there are 6.)

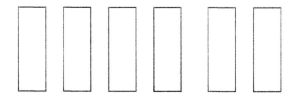

FIG. 3.1.   Facilitator's first drawing: six rectangles.

Julie: She only has 4 cakes though.
Facilitator: Thank you Julie.

(The facilitator crosses out two of the rectangles she has just drawn and divides each of the remaining cakes into fifths [Fig. 3.2].)

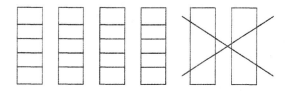

FIG. 3.2.   Facilitator's second drawing: four cakes each divided into five pieces.

And so where would the 6 and 2 thirds be?
Kate: Take 3 sections out of the first cake for one serving. And then the next 2 and 1 from the next cake for the 2nd serving.

(The facilitator points to the first 3 fifths of the first cake.)
Kate: That's 1. (Then telling the facilitator how to label the fifths of the cake) One, one, one. Two, two, two. Three, three, three.

(The facilitator completes the drawing of 4 rectangles [Fig. 3.3] divided into fifths with 3/5 of a cake designated as a portion.)

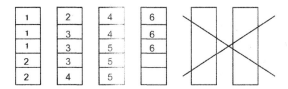

FIG. 3.3.   Facilitator's final drawing: four cakes divided into fifths with 3/5 of a cake designated as a portion.

Kate: So there are 6 servings and then 2 fifths of *one* cake left over.

Facilitator: So . . . you're saying that . . . it can be . . . it *can* be 6 and 2 fifths if . . . ?

Kate: Yeah. Mm-hmm. Depending on whether you're . . . the 2 fifths you're talking about . . . There are 2 fifths of a whole cake, or 2 thirds is of a *serving.* But if you're talking about the whole cake, it's 2 fifths of a cake that's left over, but there's 2 thirds of a *serving* left over.

Facilitator: And the thirds come from *here* (pointing at 1,1,1, the first three fifths of the first cake). And if you compare those 2 pieces (the 2 unlabelled fifths of a cake in cake 4) to these (the segments labeled 1,1,1), it's 2 thirds. Is that pretty much how everybody was thinking about that?

(Lots of nods)

As this discussion begins, one participant, Julie, reframes the facilitator's question, taking issue with the proposition that both 6 and 2/3 and 6 and 2/5 are correct answers to the cake problem. Julie clarifies that each of these numbers is a correct answer to "separate questions," and that 6 2/3 is the answer to the question "how many servings does she have?" The facilitator reiterates Julie's claim that 6 2/3 refers to servings, and then asks if there are any reactions to this. Kate lays out for the group what relation 6 remainder 2/5 has to the problem, establishing that the remaining chunk of cake is 2/5 of a cake in size. Kate continues to speak about the meanings of these numbers: "2 thirds is of a serving. But if you're talking about the whole cake, it's 2 fifths of a cake that's left over, but there's 2 thirds of a serving left over."

The group has, at this point, diagrammed the problem, and in the context of the drawing, the participants have established that there is enough cake for 6 whole servings with some left over. They have also begun to consider with one another the equivalency between 1 third of a serving and 1 fifth of a cake. Both the problem and this equivalency have now been represented in a variety of ways. The idea is a complicated one, however, and the facilitator's next question proves to be challenging. As the participants consider the facilitator's question and a participant's answer to this question, the group continues to work at understanding what is going on in this problem.

Facilitator: And what was the number sentence that people came up with for it?

(Laughter from the participants presumably because the mathematical relationships here are still difficult for many in the group, and expressing them in an equation feels out of reach.)

Julie: 4 divided by 3/5 (some "mm-hmms," in agreement. Pause as the facilitator writes this equation on the chart paper) equals 6 and 2/3.

Other participant: She's just gonna jump right to it.

Facilitator: You gonna just jump right to it?

Julie: Yup.

Other participant: Just jump right to the answer. . . .

Facilitator: So how do you figure that out when you do it, when you do it that way?

Julie: I know how to do the inversion now.

(Some uncomfortable laughter from other participants)

Facilitator: Tell us more Julie.

Julie: Well . . . I can see that the cakes are divided into 3 *fifth* portions. When it comes to solving it, . . . the 4 cakes, like you do the inversion, so it's 4 times, (the facilitator begins to write these numbers on the chart paper) 4 over 1 times 5 over 3. And each cake is divided into 5 thirds. Like in the first cake, there's the first porsh, the first portion is in thirds and there's 2 thirds of the next portion, so there are 5 thirds in each cake.

Others: Ooooohhh. . . .

Julie's equation for this problem is $4 \div 3/5 = 6\,2/3$, and she can solve the problem by diagramming it, dividing each of 4 cakes into fifths, creating servings by making groups 3/5 of a cake large, and counting the number of groups; but she hasn't stopped there. Julie is beginning to articulate her dawning sense of why $4 \div 3/5 = 4 \times 5/3$. Julie is working at understanding why she can numerically solve this problem by taking 4 groups of 5/3. Her explanation focuses on the meaning of 5/3—5/3 of what?—and Julie makes use of her diagrammed representation of the problem as she explores these questions. Some in the group are following her logic, some are on the verge, whereas for others this reasoning is not yet making sense. As each seminar participant asks questions, puts the ideas into her own words, or challenges the reasoning, each individual in the group has the opportunity to reconsider the mathematics. It is as if with each comment, question, equation, and drawing each participant gets the chance to look at this mathematical object from a slightly new angle.

Other participant: Wait a minute, say that one again.
Julie: Each cake has one whole portion, which each, each has thirds.
Other participant: And so 3 thirds.
Julie: And 2 thirds of the next portion.
Other participant: Yeah!
Julie: So there's 5 thirds altogether. Like the first portion, the 1, 1, 1 . . .
Other participant: Right.
Julie: You see those each as thirds of a portion. Right?
Other participant: Right.
Julie: OK. So the 2.2 is 2 thirds of the next portion. So if you're looking at the portions in each one, there are five thirds.
Other: Mm-hmm.

Julie has now twice put into words the relationship she sees represented in the diagram—that one cake is equivalent to 5/3 of a serving. Although some of the others are in agreement with her, Sarah assesses the argument as she hears it and finds that it does not make sense to her. She offers this to the group, creating an opportunity for another participant to put her thoughts into words.

Sarah: It sounds good, but *I* don't see it.
Liz: (apologetically) Oh, Sarah . . . I do.
(All join in long laughter—a release)
Sarah: You sound so apologetic about it.
Facilitator: So Liz, would you like to try to say it ? Say it out loud. I mean if you feel like you see. . . .
Liz: OK. But I have to *touch* it (she goes to the chart paper). I'm tactile. (More laughter. The facilitator offers her a marker.) No, I don't need the pen. (At the chart paper with the drawing of cakes and portions on it) When she's saying about the 5 thirds, now this is the one portion, so there's 3 pieces to that. And there's only 2 thirds of the next portion so that's why you have to go up here (the 2nd cake). So every portion makes up 3 parts, so you have 3 thirds, 3 thirds, 3 thirds (indicating portions 1, 2, and 3 in turn). And every time you count those 3 thirds, 3 thirds is equal to 1.

Other participant: Mm-hmm.

Liz: Is that helping Sarah? (pause) A little bit?

(Sarah shakes her head, looking confused.)

Rose: Each serving is . . .

Liz: So in here you have one serving and 2 thirds of another serving. In every cake. One and 2 thirds servings. (pause) Because each serving part, out of the 5, you have to take 3 pieces away each time because somebody's having 3 fifths of a serving [cake].

Liz adds her voice to Julie's. Although Liz seems to have seen Julie's argument and to agree with her that $4 \div 3/5 = 4 \times 5/3$, we see in Liz's use of the word *serving* in place of the word *cake* in this last comment a clue to how slippery the units of measure are, and how difficult an idea it is that the same amount of cake can simultaneously be 1 serving and 3/5 of a cake—or similarly that 1 cake is equivalent to 5/3 of a serving. At this point in the discussion, Liz's slip of the tongue is not discussed, but as the conversation progresses the issue is made explicit.

Julie: Do you see the 1 and 2 thirds part? One serving and 2 thirds of the next serving?

(Sarah makes a struggling face . . .)

Julie: Because if you, if you invert that fra . . . if you um . . . what's it called? If you make that an improper fraction, it'll be 5 thirds.

(Sarah nods her head yes.)

Julie: One whole serving and 2 thirds of the next serving, one and 2 thirds.

Liz: (pointing to 1 serving in 3 parts) Here's 1 serving.

Sarah: (nods) Yes, I see that.

Liz: And you can divide that into 3—into thirds.

Rose: Right, 3 thirds? So that's 3 thirds and then those lower 2 are 2 thirds.

Sarah: Yeah.

Rose: So that's 5 thirds. That's where you can get that.

Sarah: Mm-hmm.

Julie: So each cake has to be multiplied by 5 thirds.

Liz: So then every time you would count them, Sarah, here's 1 whole serving (points to 1, 1, 1) or 3 thirds, so you would go 1 (points to 1, 1, 1), 2 (points to 2, 2, 2). So that's actually like you have 5 thirds here (first cake) plus your next one (points to the top section of 2nd cake), 6 thirds. So there's your 2 cakes . . . 2 pieces . . . 2 servings that you've done already. And then here's your next one (points to 3, 3, 3).

In this segment of the group's discussion, it is Julie, Liz, and Rose who together express their understandings of why $4 \div 3/5 = 4 \times 5/3$. They are expressing the idea that each cake can be thought of as 5/3 of a serving. It is quantifying this equivalency between portions and cakes that is so difficult to understand.

Again in Liz's attempts to put her new understandings into words, we see the difficulty that she and presumably others are having. In Liz's last comment in this section of conversation, she says that the 6 thirds she has just pointed out are "2 cakes . . . 2 pieces . . . 2 servings." Holding onto the units being counted is not a simple matter. In this case, 2 servings is what she settles on and what is correct. Yet she has labeled for us and for seminar participants what some of the alternative units are that she must be keeping in mind as she is working on this problem. In addition to servings, there are cakes and there are pieces. By *pieces*, I take Liz to be referring to the 1/5 of a cake size slice that is represented on the chart paper drawing in which each cake is divided into fifths. Although she could be using *piece* as a synonym for *portion* or *serving*, if she is, she seems to recognize some ambiguity in the term and finally settles on *serving*.

At this point the seminar group is ready to make explicit some of these confusions about what is being counted; in doing so, the group creates a stronger representation of the mathematics this problem involves. The conversation continues as follows:

Ella: But you know, if you were to ever look at that and say that that was 5 thirds, people would think you were off your rocker!

[Other participants intersperse comments: "I know," "Right!", "Yeah," "Exactly!", "I agree."]

Other: The whole changes. From the whole *cake* to a serving.

Yet another: To the *serving* whole.

Ella: That's where I think it's confusing.

[Others: "Yeah it is," and "Mm-hmm."]

Ella: But Kate cleared it up for me because she said that 6 and 2 thirds *servings*, but the other one is 6 and 2 fifths left of the cake.

Others: Mm-hmm . . .

Three more teachers have now joined in the conversation. Key to this piece of the conversation is the idea expressed, in part, by each of three participants: "people would think you were off your rocker" to be calling one cake 5/3 of something, but that you can call it 5/3 because "The whole changes. From the whole *cake* to a serving"—"The *serving* whole." They are putting into words the ideas responsible for the confusion that most had felt at the beginning of this conversation when Julie offered the equation $4 \div 3/5 = 6\ 2/3$. Because even in this equation the issue of numbers referring to different units arises, and understanding both units and operations in this context is complicated. Yet now, having noted the difficulty surrounding the changing units (4 *cakes* and 3/5 of a *cake*, but 6 2/3 *servings* and 5/3 of a *serving*), Ella wonders about answering Wanda's cake problem with a whole number, thereby not having to choose between 6 and 2/3 and 6 and 2/5.

Ella: So what about the answer just being 6?

Julie: How many whole servings are there? Six.

Ella: Mmm . . .

Facilitator: So if that were the question, would the answer be six if you said how many whole servings, but getting, getting back to this—what are we paying attention to? Are we paying attention to the serving? Or the cake?

Julie: Right.

Facilitator: And what I think I heard somebody say—it depends on what the whole is.

Other: Mm-hmm . . .

Facilitator: What the whole thing is.

Although there is some response to Ella's suggestion, the facilitator quickly refocuses the group's attention on the issue of the unit: "Are we paying attention to the serving? Or the cake?" This leads to another seminar participant putting her thoughts on the matter into words.

Kate: So when you invert, when you're dividing, you're just flipping to think of the whole in a different way?

It was Kate who, at the start of the discussion, spoke about why the leftover cake, after making all of the whole portions possible, might be called 2/5. She spoke about the leftover cake as correctly being 2/5 of a cake in size. Soon after that, Kate also spoke about how the leftover portion might be called 2/3: "There are 2 fifths of a whole cake, or 2 thirds is of a serving." Now we hear Kate articulating something about the relationship of these units to one another in the "invert and multiply" procedure: "you're just flipping to think of the whole in a different way."

Facilitator: So . . .

Kate: You're changing the whole to get . . . or

Rose: Or finding how many servings—what is the whole?

Facilitator: Or paying attention to something else. (Pause) So we've changed the signs here. We've changed from talking about 4 divided . . .

Ella: I took it to 20 divided by 3.

Ella, having mentally cut all of the cakes into 1/5-of-a-cake-size pieces, now is thinking about the 1/5-of-a-cake pieces as the wholes to count. There are 20 of them, which she will divide into groups of 3, each group of 3 being 3 of the 1/5-of-a-cake-size pieces or 3/5 of a cake altogether. The 20 fifths of a cake divided into groups of 3 is another way to think about the number of servings Wanda can get from her 4 cakes. In Ella's method, she first divides the 4 cakes into 5 pieces each and then divides the resulting 20 fifth-of-cakes by 3. Represented mathematically, she has performed the following operations: $4 \div 1/5$ (or perhaps 4×5) yielding 20 and then $20 \div 3$ yielding 6 2/3. Although Ella's comment is not discussed directly by the group, as the conversation continues, another participant, Leah, brings up a similar idea. For now, the facilitator continues:

Facilitator: So 4 divided into groups of 3 fifths, or . . .

Other: Yup.

Facilitator: And then down here, and it goes back to what um, I think going back to the problem that the table in the back really spent a lot of time on earlier when they were trying to think about multiplication and why, why is that multiplying. (Pause, then very slowly) So . . . a serving is 3 fifths of a cake and a cake is 5 thirds of a serving. Does that sound . . . ?

Others: "Yeah." "Mm-hmm" "Yeah"

Leah: It makes some sense to me where it wasn't before. You have 4 cakes and they're each divided up into . . . all the cakes are divided up into servings that are 3 fifths of the cake. So that would be the division part of it, and then when you do the inversion part of it, there are 4 cakes and in each cake there are 5 thirds of a serving. And you want to know how many thirds you have altogether. And you multiply, you find out that there are *20* thirds.

Leah is focusing on the unit one-third-of-a-serving. She has shifted to thinking of the 4 cakes as 4 groups of 5 thirds-of-servings. She is now interested in how many thirds-of-servings there are in all 4 cakes. Her answer to this question, which she provides in the last sentence above, is that there are 20 thirds.

(Pause while the facilitator writes $4 \times 5/3 = 20/3$ on the chart paper.)

Sarah: (aside) That don't make *no* sense.

Although Sarah has a difficult time with this equation, the facilitator continues.

Facilitator: That's another true statement that you can say (pointing to the
               equation she has written on the chart paper) . . . that 4 times 5
               thirds equals 20 thirds. And then from there it is reasonable to
               think about this as . . . (Pause.)
Rose: How many servings?
Facilitator: Mm-hmm, mm-hmm—and that would be 6 and 2 thirds.

The 20 thirds-of-servings have now been composed into whole servings, yielding 6 2/3 whole servings.

The discussion has come to an end for now. This last segment of the conversation opened with the facilitator restating the idea with which she sees the seminar participants struggling: that a "serving is 3/5 of a cake and a cake is 5/3 of a serving." As she does this, Leah joins in with her articulation of the ideas that she and the group have been working on. Sarah still feels that the part of the conversation relating the equations to the drawings makes no sense. At this point in time, different members of the group have different understandings and different questions with respect to the mathematics underlying the problem before them. Yet all are involved in exploration of the topic together, and in the next session they will revisit the issues raised by dividing with fractions.

Wanda's cake problem is typical of the mathematics teachers do in DMI seminars in a few ways. It not only asks directly for a solution (in this case, the number of servings of cake that Wanda has), but also asks seminar participants to represent, in multiple ways, the mathematical relationships embedded in the problem. Teachers are asked to diagram the problem situation, write an equation that represents the problem, and consider the relationships between these. Further, the problem explicitly invites an exploration of a common and potentially enlightening flawed piece of reasoning—that 4 cakes divided into servings 3/5 of a cake in size might result in 6 2/5 servings. In exploring this idea, the seminar chooses to face, rather than avoid, a knotty but central aspect of the mathematics.

As the teachers' mathematical understandings and confusions are voiced over and over, the ideas become increasingly clear for increasing numbers of seminar participants. As we read their discussion of Wanda's cake problem, we hear the ideas turned over and over, expressed again and again. One expression or representation does not do it once and for all. Indeed the reader's own experience in reading the story of the teachers' seminar discussion may be a case in point. Perhaps as you read you found your own understanding of the mathematics involved in the cake problem developing bit by bit. Perhaps as you read the various voicings of the ideas the seminar participants grappled with you came to see and grasp new aspects of the problem that at first had been unclear, or to pose questions about issues that you had not noticed before.

As the teachers in the seminar group work together to understand the mathematics involved in Wanda's cake problem, they take their ideas farther by making use of both what group members understand and what they do not understand. Each provides its own kind of opportunity. In the small-group work prior to the whole-group discussion, Julie figured something out, and, as the discussion progressed, Liz, Rose, Kate, Ella, and Leah all joined her in some way. As they did, I would imagine Julie's own sense of the mathematics may have changed slightly.

Larger Data Set as Context for the Fractions Story

Although all of the teachers knew how to *solve* this problem from the start, they (like most U.S. adults) did not begin with a rich or complete *understanding* of the mathematics involved in the cake problem. These richer understandings were new to all of them as their portfolio writing makes clear.

> With the exploration of my own mathematics came an understanding that for many math operations I had never been taught why we did what we did. I (and many others in the seminar) was expected to memorize the process but not expected to understand the facts behind it.
> The math activities demonstrated this by challenging us to explore how and why we solve problems. It was especially evident when we got to fractions where many of us felt unsure to begin with. (Julie, DMI course evaluation)

It is worth noting that this comment comes from Julie, who, in the segment of the seminar transcribed in the previous pages, has such a strong grasp of the mathematics. Clearly, she had not begun with that same understanding or indeed even the knowledge that this layer of understanding—beyond successful computation—exists and might be something to aim for.

Rose, another seminar participant, writes about her learning this way:

> The most exciting new insight I gained during the entire seminar was the development of my own personal knowledge during the sections devoted to fractions. I especially enjoyed learning how and why multiplying a fraction by its reciprocal works. The mathematics activities and discussions for these sections were fun as well as useful.

It was interesting to focus on the parts and wholes in the various cases and to see how the changing of the "whole" in problems involving fractions[5] can change your answer. Seeing adults struggle with these issues, helped me gain insight into the mistakes children make. (Rose, DMI course evaluation, May 1997)

In Rose's writing, we hear testimony to the mathematics she learned, as well as to the new sense she is developing of struggle as a part of learning. We return in a bit to this struggle that Rose mentions. For now, we can note that both Julie and Rose spoke in the DMI seminar segment presented in this chapter. Yet even for teachers who did not speak during this piece of seminar discussion, the mathematical experiences were powerful.

In reflecting on the development of my own thinking as I reviewed my portfolio the area that has had the greatest impact on me is the work we did with fractions. I found the work challenging and enlightening, and yet it was hard and confusing. I am amazed at how much I have learned over the past several weeks, for myself as an adult learner.

The math activities forced me to look at what was happening to the numbers when different operations were employed. Although I thought I knew what was happening I came to realize that I was just going through the process of following the traditional algorithm and producing a response. Now I feel I am able to make sense of the math because I can picture what is happening to the whole when it is divided into equal parts and then divided again and so forth. (Grade 1 teacher, Portfolio Assignment 2.8, May 26, 1997)

This teacher, like Julie, comments both on her own mathematical learning and its effect on her sense of what mathematical knowledge can be. In coming to *understand* something that she had only had procedural knowledge of before, this teacher now recognizes this understanding as something of value.

Another participant who did not speak during the portion of the seminar transcribed in this chapter writes:

---

[5]Rose attributes issues of unit to the fact that the problem deals in fractions. However, the same issues of unit arise in many multiplication and division situations. For instance, we can imagine the following whole number version of the cake problem: Philip has 4 cakes; 2 cakes is one serving. How many servings does Philip have? Here we can represent this situation with the equation $4 \div 2 = 2$, where 4 is the number of cakes Philip has, 2 is the number of cakes per serving, and the 2 on the other side of the equality is the number of servings Philip has. This is precisely the same set and variety of units that the original Wanda's cake problem holds. The existence of fractional quantities in Wanda's cake problem highlights these issues of unit, but is not the source of the issue.

The seminar had been focusing on fractions. We had been exploring fractions in a way I don't recall ever doing before. We were creating story problems for numerical multiplication and division fraction problems. This task proved to be quite challenging. I believe I had always done problems like the examples when I was younger, however I had never applied the algorithms with content problems. This activity was of particular interest as it clarified how important problems presented in context are when determining how to solve a problem. Another interesting fraction discovery, [. . .], was the understanding of the reciprocal that occurs when dividing fractions. This discovery was enlightening and also made complete sense (for the first time ever, I believe!). (Grade 4 teacher, Portfolio Assignment 2.8, June 4, 1997)

Here again we hear that a teacher has, from her seminar work, understood mathematics that she had not previously understood. She also remarks on the value of meaningful context in making meaning of new mathematical topics.

For some of the teachers these newly understood mathematical ideas felt like solid acquisitions, whereas for others the terrain felt less solid. The experience of feeling that one has hold of an idea only to feel it slip away at a later time and have to regain that hold is a common one. This kind of experience not only opens up for teachers new areas of mathematics, but also opens up for inspection some of what can be involved in learning.

During the math class, I found that I was sometimes moved to feeling totally confused as we approached the math activities. I was especially confused when we discussed division of fractions. I knew that you could invert and multiply, and that would work, but, I never knew how or why. I guess I just accepted it as the proper way to complete such a problem, because I was told to do it that way. I now find that I was living in the dark as far as my understanding of math. Through working on those activities, I now feel that I am coming out of the dark. There are times when I really I have a strong understanding of what that all means. But, then I slip back into a confusion, and have to revisit it all over again. But, I feel much better about my math confidence. (Leah, Grade 6 teacher, DMI course evaluation)

My most recent growth in mathematics has happened over our past three classes as we worked through the issues surrounding multiplication and division of fractions. The math involved confounded me: there were many pieces that I could hang onto, but the "whole" eluded me. I knew that the math, the algorithms, worked during our discussions about brownies and pizzas. I could even make lots of fancy number connections that all fit together. But the issue of "what part of what whole" was right, wrong, the same . . . AAAAARGH!

I kept going because I had enough to hang onto. And as we struggled as a class to make sense of this, the energy we all gave working to make sense was sustaining. I would not have pursued my questions on my own. And when the light dawned for me at the end of our sixth class, I felt successful. I now knew why we can "invert and multiply." At least I thought I did, until our 5/14 class.

When I was asked to apply my new knowledge during the first May class, I froze. I couldn't figure out how to draw 4/3 of a serving of ice cream. I drew diagram after diagram and it eluded me. I had to be shown again. Then the concepts about inverting fractions seemed to be reinforced, but I wonder if they will remain almost there, become more solid, or fade once more. Certainly, I will need to use the idea, to practice the concept, or it will slowly disappear. But I may now be able to call upon it more readily.

I was interested in the development of my thinking during these weeks for a number of reasons. The sequence of events reinforced the idea for me that self-discovery, accompanied by a guiding hand, is the most satisfying type of learning for me. Although the struggle was difficult, I felt that I was really learning, and that I have a deeper understanding of fractions *and* of all number patterns. I believe that I have achieved something. As a result of this learning on my part, I feel more assured that my students need to struggle with and discover number patterns and concepts in the same way, in order to experience genuine learning, not just learn how to regurgitate facts. The interplay of ideas in our class helped all of us. We used and reshaped other people's ideas to come to better understandings. (Kate, Grade 1 teacher, Portfolio Assignment 2.8, May 28, 1997)

Thus, participants commented not only on having learned mathematics, but also on the nature of that knowledge and the nature of their learning. They had new respect for the knowledge, the process of struggling to gain it, and the ongoing work of maintaining it. Further, they were beginning to consider the implications of all of this for their own teaching practices.

All 12 of the teacher participants in the seminar group whose fractions discussion we have just considered wrote about their fractions learning in their portfolio assignments or in their written course evaluation. In the other seminar group, 7 of the 11 participants wrote about the importance of their fractions learning, while an 8th teacher spoke about her learning about fractions in our interview, although she had not written about it for her portfolio. Thus, altogether 20 of the 23 participants highlight their learning about the mathematics involved in the multiplication and division of fractions as among the most powerful of their seminar experiences.[6]

The fractions story is offered as a particularly powerful example of teachers learning mathematics in the DMI seminar. It is an example of

---

[6]Although there was a portfolio assignment asking teachers to write about their own mathematics learning as they worked on fractions, only 2 of these 20 teachers who wrote about the importance of their fractions work did so only in that assigned piece. The fractions work had such an impact that it was a common topic for portfolio writing during the last few seminar sessions.

teachers working on mathematics for their own understanding, where the mathematical topic is one that some of the teachers also tackle with their own students. Although the fractions experience was powerful and nearly universal, teachers also learned other mathematics in the seminar context. Teachers did important mathematical work in each of the seminar meetings, and parallel stories could be told of these explorations on topics such as multidigit multiplication and division and the variety of situations modeled by subtraction, to name just two. The teachers learned important mathematics from these explorations.

In addition, as the quotes we have just read suggest, these kinds of seminar experiences also create a vision for teachers of engagement with mathematical ideas: what it might look like, what it feels like, and what it accomplishes. Further, teachers wrote about the importance to mathematical learning of having group support. They wrote about the importance of working through a difficult conceptual issue and struggling with it, rather than avoiding it. They wrote about the experience in learning of sometimes losing one's grasp and having to reconstruct the notion. They wrote about the importance to them, as teachers, of having the experience of learning in a teaching and learning environment that mirrors the one envisioned by NCTM Standards (2000). The mathematical learning these teachers engaged in enriched their mathematical knowledge. It also enriched their pedagogical knowledge.

By the end of the seminar, the sense that comes from the teachers' portfolio writing is that teachers universally felt they had learned an enormous amount of mathematics in the seminar. However, they did not feel they now had covered it all. As Abby put it in June of the seminar year:

> You know, I think the most significant thing, and it just doesn't have to do with the last part [of the seminar], um . . . but it emerged again during the multiplication and division, and the multiplication and division of fractions // it's humbling . . . is that I had no mathematical idea myself as a teacher about what I was doing, or how it was done. I mean . . . I had a formula, I had an algorithm and I did it, and I did the math appropriately, I calculated appropriately, it worked. And then when I was . . . we were given word problems to figure out, which we often do to children, um, I had a very difficult time fighting my way through it. Or when they said develop a word problem for this particular algorithm, it was like . . . "OK, well, would this be applied?" . . . It was very *humbling* for me to know that here I'm a teacher and I'm standing in front of a classroom of children whether they're special needs or not, teaching mathematics, when I realized that as a student and as a learner, my own foundation, in understanding math . . . , mathematical procedures and how they related to each other, and what they actually *mean*

to us in real life, is not . . . is less than I'd like it to be as an adult. (Abby, Interview, June 9, 1997)

Even in June, Abby speaks in present tense: ". . . my own foundation . . . is less than I'd like it to be as an adult." Rather than feeling she had learned it all, by seminar's end, Abby, like others, felt ready to learn mathematics.[7] Indeed some were ready to do this on their own in the context of teaching mathematics in their own classrooms.

TEACHERS LEARNING MATHEMATICS IN THE CONTEXT OF CLASSROOM TEACHING

Tamar is such a teacher, and we turn now to her story. Tamar's story gives us a particularly good opportunity to look at a teacher learning mathematics from her own classroom teaching. Not only is Tamar working on mathematics that is *not* covered in the seminar, making it possible for us to see the mathematical work she takes on on her own, but she also revisits the same mathematical topic several times in the course of the year, making it possible to see the changes in her thinking.

Tamar discusses her sense of the mathematics her students understand and are working on as she observes their classroom counting. In Tamar's story, we hear her discuss counting on three separate occasions: one prior to and in preparation for the seminar, one early in her DMI seminar year, and the other 1 year later. Over the course of this year, Tamar builds on her ability to observe her children and reflect on their work, and she comes to do much more work to understand for herself the mathematics on which her children are working. To some readers, the idea that mathematics as basic as counting is something to be understood (not just remembered) and, further, that adults might have work to do to understand counting may sound quite odd. Yet as we follow Tamar's story, we see by her example what more mathematical sense one might make of counting.

As Tamar comes to focus more intently on her students' mathematical understandings, she also comes to focus more intently on her own exploration of the mathematics. She learns more about *counting* as she learns more about the *development in children of counting understandings.*

---

[7]Dr. Stephanie Smith led a DMI Seminar at Brigham Young University in 1996–1997. She also noted (personal communication, July 1, 1999) that at the end of the seminar, the teachers in her seminar felt as if they had just begun to explore and understand the mathematics they teach. Many reported to the course evaluator that, for this reason, they did not want the seminar to end.

Tamar's Story: Exploring the Mathematics of Counting

In preparation for the first seminar meeting, Tamar and each of the seminar participants has the following assignment: "Collect work samples from three children. Choose one whose work you think is strong and two whose work is not so strong. Explain why the first sample satisfies you. What is your analysis of the other two? What are your learning goals for the three children?" (Portfolio Assignment 1.1 from Appendix A, also p. 25, *Building a system of tens: Facilitator's Guide*, 1999).

Tamar, who teaches in a prekindergarten classroom in which half of the students have special needs, selects three examples of student work and finds all to be "strong examples of preschool math" (Tamar, Portfolio Assignment, September 1996). They are: "matching beads to a project card to create a pattern; sorting pegs by color and counting each color," and a third brief observation of one student's use of counting. Tamar writes about this third child, noting that she observed a student: ". . . counting pieces of a game to six adding a few more and then saying 'Now I have thirty.' . . . [This example] is very interesting because there were only 10 pieces and I do know this child can count to 10. He took a look at the pile and estimated (or wished for) 30 pieces." Tamar's goal for this child is that he "practice his estimating skills" (Tamar, Portfolio Assignment, September 1996).

Tamar comes to the first seminar meeting already making careful observations of a child's use of number. Although she does not actually pose a mathematical question about her observations here, she seems to be on the verge of posing one or more in her comment that this "is very interesting because there were only 10 pieces and I do know this child can count to 10." At this point in time, although Tamar notices that the child, able to count to 10, is not using counting to arrive at the quantity or cardinal value of the set, she does not seem to go further in trying to understand what this reveals about the child's understanding of number. Here, before the seminar has begun, counting and estimating remain unanalyzed. At least there is no evidence of any analysis either in Tamar's stated goal for this child—that he "practice his estimating skills"—or in the collection of student work that she selects for this portfolio assignment. The three pieces of student work are relatively unrelated mathematically and are presented as such by Tamar.

It is not long, however, before Tamar begins to focus more on the mathematics of counting. Armed with her seminar experiences of mathematics and pedagogy, Tamar begins to take a new stance in her teaching. Tamar shifts to a view of mathematics teaching that includes understanding the child's mathematics, and this brings her to a practice that involves her own exploration of the mathematical topics that she teaches.

Tamar begins to write about this shift in early November as she describes a math interview she conducted with a student as homework for the seminar. She is feeling frustrated at the difficulty she experiences trying to understand how the child she interviews is making decisions about which of two piles of objects has more in it. Tamar makes two piles of objects and asks the child which pile has more, but she has difficulty keeping the conversation going once the child offers an answer. Their conversation does not go much beyond the simple choosing of this pile or that pile. Tamar writes: "I think that I am just used to getting at ways to see if children can *do* these tasks rather than listening to *how they understand* or *what they are thinking*" (Tamar, Portfolio Assignment 1.4, November 5, 1996, italics added).

A few weeks later, in mid-November, Tamar is still considering what her children understand about number, and she decides she would like to introduce a number line to her preschool students. She writes about coming to this decision in this way:

> One thing I have been learning in the seminar and trying to focus on in my class is to "step back" and really look at the understanding children already have about numbers and to try to guide their learning and try to provide opportunity for self discovery. Rather than saying look this is how I do it, saying tell me how you do it. I think the readings and the class discussion have focused on the idea that children need to make their own sense of numbers. . . . (Tamar, Portfolio Assignment 1.5, mid-November 1996)

Thus, Tamar introduces the number line to her children as a representation that she hopes will *provide children with opportunities to make their own sense*. She does so based on her seminar experiences. Perhaps introducing the number line is at least a partial answer to the question on Tamar's mind a couple of weeks earlier—How could she keep the conversation about comparing quantities alive?

For Tamar, providing children with the opportunities to "make their own sense of numbers" coincides with her own efforts to make sense of her students' numbers. Each is central to her changing classroom stance. If she is to assess where students stand vis-à-vis the important mathematical ideas of her curriculum and then design and provide opportunities for them to learn more of what is there to know, she must not only have access to student thinking, but, of equal importance, her own knowledge of the mathematics must be strong and explicit. For example, she needs not only to know *how* to count, but also to understand the layers of meaning that the counting numbers hold and the relationships they express. That is, she must unpack the mathematical meanings implicit in her own knowledge of counting.

We get a glimpse of Tamar as she begins this work in an interview in early December. Tamar shows us that she has separated out order and value as two important aspects of number. Although in September Tamar spoke simply of counting, now she is looking at *aspects* of counting and is noticing that her 3- to 5-year-old children are sorting out issues relating to number order and number value. Tamar uses these observations as the mathematical rationale for introducing a number line to her students.

Tamar: Well, I think um, a couple things for me, for planning the number line activity um, we were, or *I* was listening to kids counting in the classroom, counting objects and stuff, and they were having a hard time with number order. Or I would ask them, sort of, out of con-text, "Well, um, you know, what number comes after five?" Or, you know, they would, they would say, you know, "what number would . . . how old will I be next year?" They were asking a lot of questions about number order and seeming kind of confused about number order. // And also um number value. // Because um, you know, we were asking um which is a bigger number, eight or, you know, three, or whatever, and kids were not real solid with that kind of thing. They were confused.

SC: That's with or without objects around, for that question?

Tamar: Um, both. // In both cases. Because we would be, you know, counting blocks or whatever, and "how many," "who has more," or "who has less," and "let's see if we can make, make 'em, or pass out bean bags so that everybody has the same amount," // you know, those kinds of things. Kids were still, you know, "She has more," when she would, you know, have four and the other person has seven. You know, things like that. // And they seemed really confused about those kinds of skills, so I thought of introducing the number line and just kind of talking about how, you know, the numbers go in order from . . . , and you know, just kind of a visual thing. We can hang it up in the room when we're done and it will help, you know, kids kind of have a reference.

SC: As a way of representing number, and . . .

Tamar: Right. Because what I was thinking was we have a lot of um words around and we write up our songs and we do a lot with um liter-acy, but we don't have any number symbols in the room. // So I was trying to incorporate that in the room, but before I did that I thought it would be neat to, you know, introduce it to the kids and show them different ways to use it. (Tamar, Interview, December 2, 1996)

Tamar notices that her 3- to 5-year-olds often have trouble with the or-der of numbers. Her evidence for this is that the children cannot answer questions like "what number comes after 5?", and they ask questions such as "how old will I be next year?" Tamar also notices that her students have difficulty with number value. They do not reliably answer correctly questions such as "what's bigger, 8 or 3?" So Tamar introduces the number line as a representation of number or at least the order of numbers.

Although Tamar seems quite clear and definite about the use of the number line as a support for investigations concerning the order of numbers, she raises and considers important questions about how to use it to address her interest in the children's understanding of quantity.

> I decided to introduce a number line but I was troubled as to how to explain it. We could use some counters but should we visualize value on a number line? Have one cube for each number (my preference) or should we count out the correct numbers of cubes for each number. Well I decided to trust the children. First we talked about numbers, which numbers could they recognize etc. Then I showed them some unifix cubes. They decided to count out cubes and place them on each number: one cube on the number one, two cubes on the number two etc. Now they can place the stacks of cubes together and see which is the biggest stack. So does this accomplish my goal? (Tamar, Portfolio Assignment 1.5, mid-November 1996)

Now that Tamar is paying attention to answering for herself questions about what the children understand, what they are working on, and what experiences in class might support that work, she is in the midst of a mathematical exploration. Does representing order necessarily represent quantity? How might *she* represent quantity? One counter on each number? Tamar's own idea about representing quantity here is that each number is a one. The children chose to represent each quantity as a separate quantity, not including the one cube of "1" in the one, two cubes of "2." Although Tamar prefers her method, she has not yet analyzed why. She asks herself whether the child's representation accomplishes the goal she has for them of understanding the value of the numbers. Tamar wonders whether the child who builds the quantity one and who separately rebuilds the quantity one in the building of two understands the quantitative relationship between one and two. If a child builds stacks of different size in this way, how can he or she use these representations to better understand something about the quantities and the relationships among the quantities?

Although Tamar's questions about the use of a number line are part of her own mathematical investigation, her interest in using this representational tool with children to support the children's mathematical investigations bears a strong resemblance to the seminar pedagogy, the kinds of mathematical experience DMI participants engage in in the seminar, and the kind of explorations portrayed in the print and video cases of the seminar. Both the mathematical inquiry and the pedagogical world of the seminar are echoed in Tamar's work on counting.

One year later, in December of the year following the DMI seminar, Tamar speaks of her recent thoughts and observations concerning counting. At this time, Tamar proposes a set of stages in the development of understandings about counting and number. She is using her observations of the children, as well as her own mathematical analysis of number, counting, and the children's use of each, to propose these stages. In doing so, she has laid out more explicitly what the mathematical ideas are that she wants her children to work on and has taken some steps toward answering her own questions from 1 year earlier. She talks about some of her ideas in an interview.

> ... I've been thinking a lot about counting and numbers and how children learn about numbers. And sort of looking at the different developmental stages that we have in the classroom. // So, um, I tried to, um, pull out three examples of children working on the same issue, 'cause we don't really do a lot of math activities where they're all doing the same activity that I could compare. (Tamar, interview, December 8, 1997)

Tamar's focus on actively exploring the mathematics that her students are engaged in is much stronger here than in the first portfolio assignment—the one she prepared prior to the first seminar meeting. Even in these few sentences we see Tamar's interest in collecting mathematically related samples of student work so she can compare them with one another to illuminate "the different developmental stages that we have in the classroom."

> Tamar: The first one was, um, someone counting. And he can count to about ten but he doesn't have, he's not always accurate in his counting. // It seems to be more, um, counting by rote. But there is some understanding of, you know, you put one bean in and you say a number, and the next one. But it's still clearly not, um, really proficient at it. // And the next example was, um, number cards. They're numbered one to ten and the student was able to put them in order . . . , // from zero to ten. Um, so that, you know, I was trying to figure out where, where she was on this developmental scale. Is that, you know, seemingly more than, um, counting by rote, 'cause she, she had some idea of what order to place them in. Um, she would use counting to help her, if she would come across a number that she didn't know quite where it would go in, she would start counting again, you know, "one, two, three, four, five, six, seven, *eight*." Um, on the cards there, // are pictures of um, different animals and so forth, and, you know, two animals on the number two card. And she used those as clues too, um, she was really, um, she would notice that there were *less* animals on the, you know, number one card than there were on the ten, // and, and

things like that. And then the third student, who actually knows a lot about number, does a lot of counting, um, talks about number in a lot of different ways. He had these, um, unifix cube, you know, the value trays, // and he would, he put them in *order* but what he was really surprised was that, um, you know, the number three you put three cubes in, and the number four you put four cubes in, // like that was a *new* experience for him. And he was asking questions about why, why did that, why did it happen that way? And why did it, why did all the numbers go up? Um,

SC: You mean, why was four more than three?

Tamar: Right.

SC: And six was more than five.

Tamar: Right.

SC: And five was more than four.

Tamar: So I think he's just beginning to, um, understand, maybe, place value, um, val, um, maybe not place value, but value of numbers, um, and that numbers increase as you count. // Um, and, you know, I think he was actually making a lot of discoveries there that were pretty neat. What I was trying to figure out was, you know, if he didn't *have* that understanding, that basic understanding that four is more than three, and five is more than four, you know, what would he be missing? Um, // so, you know, and, and there's a lot of children in, in the room that don't really have, I mean, they could, if you gave them two numbers, like we did on the chart today, um, "which number is bigger?", // um, "three is bigger," um, a lot of children have that sort of basic understanding, especially if they can see it. But, um, that little discovery that he made, you know, that each number was one more than the next, and it sort of made little stairs and, you know, I just thought that was kind of interesting. . . . (Tamar, interview, December 8, 1997)

Tamar, along with her student, sees clearly that "each number was one more than the next." In counting, each number has nested inside it the previous counting number plus one more. That is, four is four, a quantity in its own right, but it is also three, the previously counted quantity plus one more. Similarly for three, which is three, as well as being two plus one more, and so it goes all the way back down to one. The act of counting adds one, and so the numbers we create by counting can be understood as a set of numbers bearing particular numerical relationships to one another. This is far more than the rote string they begin as. Tamar's student makes this discovery while building and comparing unifix representations of the quantities associated with consecutive counting numbers. This contrasts with Tamar, who at least implicitly understood this relationship 1 year earlier when she preferred to represent quantity on the number line by placing one cube on each of the counting numbers. Perhaps this representation highlighted for Tamar an idea that she was working on making more explicit: that each counting number is nested within the following numbers, each of which in turn contributes its own one. Tamar had not yet figured out why she preferred to represent each counting number as a one. Now in December, 1 year later, Tamar has worked out more of the mathematics involved in counting and along with it a developmental sequence that will help her to make sense of her students' work and of her work as a teacher.

SC: So did you tell them to me in the order of what, I mean, are they in the order of who you think's, . . . , are they in this developmental order that you're talking about? . . .

Tamar: I think so. // I think so. Because this first person is just, um, I mean obviously he can count really proficiently by rote. I mean, he knows his numbers from one to ten, but he can't really count objects // proficiently. I mean, he has some understanding of it, he's getting there.

SC: So sometimes he points to the same objects, // twice, and this is one,

Tamar: Or he might miss a few or, um, he might, you know,

SC: So he has the number *names* down.

Tamar: Right. So, you know, it's just um, and then the next, the next person, she knows the number names, she knows, um, how to count the cards, how to count the objects on the card, and how to put them in *order*. // Um, and the third one, um, I think was making some nice discoveries about, you know, *amount* and the value of the number and, and, // and also number order, 'cause he put his trays in order from, from one to ten, um, as well. Um, but instead of . . . , I guess, I guess why I thought that,

SC: I don't know the trays very well. Is there a, . . . in the two tray, for instance, there's a one and a two?

Tamar: No, it's just, it has the number two at the top, // and then it will have a space here for two cubes, // and then the number three would be three at the top, // and it would have three,

SC: Three cubes. OK. OK, so each one is just, is a representation of that number.

Tamar: Of that number, right.

SC: So he put them together, meaning he put the one next to, he, he put the one next to the two next to the three next to the four.

Tamar: Right. But then he was trying to fill, you know, fill them all up with, um, cubes, // "OK, well, why, why does this one have more cubes than this?"

SC: Mm. And why is it three and a three?

Tamar: Right. Why are there three cubes in the number three?

SC: Now this girl who was doing the number cards, was she asking that same question about why there were three, or was she even noticing that it was three on the three, or just that there were more on the ten than the one? I mean, did she notice that it was ten on the ten? Not just more than one?

Tamar: No, she wasn't comparing the, the number [numeral] to the amount, // on the card. Um, she was just sort of, you know, putting them in order. One, two, three, four, five, six, seven, eight, nine, ten.

SC: It's interesting.

Tamar: Yeah. So, I guess I've been thinking a *lot* about, um, *number* this year and how . . . , I guess I could see, um, counting by rote, 'cause we do a lot of counting in the classroom when the kids go on the, um . . . , you know, when we cook, or when the kids go on the trampoline, or when I push kids on the swing . . . , so they *hear* the numbers a lot, but I guess that *step* between just knowing the numbers, and knowing that, you know, this is *three* things, and this is *five* things. // You know, I'm sort of wondering how they work that out. (Tamar, interview, December 8, 1997)

Tamar's observation of her students, now coupled with a keen interest in understanding the mathematical ideas that students either understand, are working on, or have yet to encounter, leads her to propose a developmental progression. Tamar now posits that children first learn number names, then understand these as an ordered set, and later come to understand something about the amount or value represented by each number. In doing the work of analyzing her students' mathematical thinking enough to notice this sequence, she has understood something about number that she had not made explicit before. She had always asked children to count, arrange in order, and make comparisons between two quantities, but previously she had not understood the ways that each builds on and is related to the others. Tamar has begun to explore the complexity involved in constructing meanings for these number names. Each represents a quantity, and the quantities are all related to one another in particular and predictable ways. Yet working this out is not simple. Tamar has not only understood this, but is now poised to consider in her own teaching what kinds of experience will be useful to children as they work on constructing *their* understandings of quantity.

As Tamar's own understanding of the mathematics deepens, she writes that it is "easier to evaluate children's mathematical thinking and observe critically what they are learning" (Portfolio Assignment 2.7, mid-May 1997). This stands in sharp contrast to Tamar's assessment of student work in the portfolio assignment she prepared before the first seminar meeting that "all are strong examples of preschool math." Although her prior attitude of acceptance provides a "welcome mat" for students to offer their thoughts, it leaves Tamar without any means to move forward with the students' offerings. Now with a stronger sense of the mathematics at issue, Tamar not only can welcome students' work, but she can also envision the terrain she will invite them to explore further.

Envisioning that terrain is crucial if Tamar is going to propose problems for her students to consider that, like Wanda's cake problem in the seminar, ask students to represent core mathematical relationships and to face head on the knottier issues. Although for Tamar's preschoolers these questions would not include a consideration of 6 2/5 as an answer to the cake problem, they might include something akin to Tamar's student's question about why there are 3 cubes on the number 3 in the course of working with a number line or with the value trays.

Larger Data Set as Context for Tamar's Story

To what extent are the other DMI seminar participants doing this kind of mathematical work in their own classrooms? There are several ways to look at teachers' portfolio writing to address this question. Yet no matter how we look at the data, it is clear that the kind of work that Tamar's story exemplifies is not universal among seminar participants after 1 year's time.

The portfolio pieces that offer the strongest, most direct evidence for teachers learning mathematics in the course of their teaching are pieces in which the teacher (a) asserts that she has learned mathematics in the context of examining student work, preparing to teach, and/or teaching itself; and (b) lays out the mathematics she feels she has learned in this way. This kind of evidence exists from 4 of the 12 participants in one seminar group and from 1 of the 11 participants in the other seminar group. Thus, from 5 of the 23 participants in the two seminar groups, there are portfolio entries of this kind. Two examples follow.

A first-grade teacher writes about her students' work and her own thoughts as she observes their work on the following problem: "I want to buy enough heart stickers so that each child in first grade has 3. If we have 13 children in our class, how many stickers do I need to buy?" After describing the ways that different children build models of this problem and find an answer, some children using materials in sets of one and others using materials in sets of three, the teacher comments on the mathematics in this way:

> I am also fascinated, especially in light of the cases that we are reading on
> the operations, how intertwined my students use of counting, addition, sub-
> traction and multiplication and division are—I am beginning to think that
> the distinctions that we have made among the operations are much more ar-

tificial than many people would like to believe, and that we need to acknowledge their interconnections more often, rather than emphasizing their differences. (Grade 1 teacher, Portfolio Assignment 2.2, February 26, 1997)

This teacher, like Tamar, uses the mathematical work of the children in her classroom, and her attempts to understand what they are working on, to push further her own mathematical understandings. In this case, she takes the opportunity to revisit her understanding of the relationships among the operations. This topic, as she acknowledges, is one she is also working on in the seminar.

A second, more detailed example comes from a fourth-grade teacher. She writes:

Two girls showed how to solve, 48 cows, farmer wants them in groups of 4. They again put tally marks into groups of 4, like Matt explained earlier. They counted them up for the group and seemed sure that they had divided the # 48 into groups of four.

Teacher: Do you think they have shown us that 48 was divided into groups of 4?

Simon: No! They are "building up," not breaking down!

T: Can you explain this, "building up?"

S: The whole field has 48 cows, so the 48 is what you take groups of 4 out of until you use up all the cows. That's when you see the 12 groups.

At this time, Simon got a discussion going among his classmates. Several felt that building *and* breaking were in the problem while others were convinced that it was building *or* breaking.

Simon was able to diagram his idea, as represented below:

48	44	40		4	count down ÷	count up ×
↓	↓	↓		↓	↓ breaking	↑ building
4	4	4		4		
↓	↓	↓		↓		
1	2	3 . . .		12		

It was interesting to have Simon explore his idea about the difference between division and multiplication in this way, especially when I was initially concerned with the ways students had explained $48 \div 4 = 12$, essentially relying on multiplication to represent the idea of division. He was able to move the class's thinking and "show" them breaking away from a large number by taking groups out of 48. (Grade 4 teacher, Portfolio Assignment 2.2, February 27, 1997)

This teacher's attention is focused directly on the mathematical ideas her students are working to construct. We hear her recount that most children's initial solutions involved beginning with 0 cows and repeatedly adding groups of 4 cows until 48 was reached. They then counted the number of groups they had made. Simon introduced a different way to think about this problem and was able to describe the connections between "building up" and his notion of "breaking down." We cannot tell from what this teacher wrote on this occasion whether Simon's diagram and the children's discussion deepened in any way her own understanding of division, multiplication, and their relationship to one another, but in the following portfolio assignment this teacher writes:

> In my last paper, I wrote about Simon's idea called, "Building or Breaking," where he was able to present repeated subtraction as the division, and the breaking down of a large number into smaller, equal groups to the class. Even for me, the way he explained his strategy was a BIG STEP! (Grade 4 teacher, Portfolio Assignment 2.3, March 12, 1997)

Although this kind of writing is relatively clear evidence that a teacher is in fact learning mathematics in the course of her teaching, it is interesting that only 5 of 23 participants write portfolio entries of this kind. It raises questions. Is this number lower than that found for the other kinds of learning already considered because fewer teachers actually come to engage in this kind of independent mathematical investigation after 1 year of DMI? Or might the choice of indicator—that teachers write explicitly in their portfolios both *that* they learned mathematics while teaching and *what* mathematics they learned—be too narrowly defined, hiding from view other teachers who perhaps were also engaged with their students' mathematical work in this way?

To address this question, I looked at the portfolio data for two other kinds of evidence. My aim this time was to make the criteria as generous as I could so that if the numbers remained low it was likely to truly indicate that this independent investigation of mathematics in the classroom context was a less common or perhaps a later occurring change than was, for instance, coming to see children as havers of mathematical ideas.

To this end, on a second pass through the data, I looked at the portfolios for simple assertions by teachers that they did learn mathematics from their teaching interactions with students, without also articulating the mathematics that was learned. On a third pass through the data, I looked for writing that showed a teacher's careful analysis of the mathematics of her students' work, such that if the content *were* new to the teacher, she would have the opportunity to discover some new ideas. By combining all three types of data, we get an upper (or, in any case, larger) estimate of the number of teacher participants whose writing shows evidence of learning mathematics in the course of teaching. Interestingly, as we add in the various kinds of data, this number ranges between about 1/5 and 1/2 of the participants—far shy of the nearly universal occurrence of teachers' learning mathematics in the seminar sessions or coming to consider children and teachers as mathematical thinkers.

The second pass through the data—counting teachers' simple assertions that they did learn mathematics from their teaching interactions with students without articulation of the mathematics learned—adds another five participants to the original, more stringent count, for a total of 10 of the 23 seminar participants.

Two examples of the simple assertions are included next:

I have come to truly appreciate the powerful benefit of talking about math, in discussing how various students chose to solve a certain problem. For myself, this has been educational, as I have come to SEE how people think differently, and I now am better able to know where and what thinking is occurring. This has helped me, both as a teacher and as a student of math. I have learned some new ways of thinking about math from my students, and sometimes, their thinking causes me to think about something very different, which I really don't think I would have thought of on my own. (Grade 6 teacher, Portfolio Assignment 2.8, May 26, 1997)

One of the things that I noticed in my writings from the beginning of the class [seminar] to now was that as I progressed through this class, my papers grew longer and more reflective. I have learned along with the children. Sometimes they teach me new things. Sometimes they come up with ideas that really blow my mind. (Grade 2 teacher, Portfolio Assignment 2.8, May 28, 1997)

Further, with the third pass we can count the portfolio pieces that show a teacher's close and careful analysis of the mathematics of her students' work without also asserting that the teacher learned. From this kind of evidence alone, we learn that a teacher creates opportunities for her own learning in her teaching: that she does the kind of analyses that bring her into contact with mathematical ideas, some of which might be new to her and that she shows a willingness and ability to examine the mathematics outside of the seminar context. Including this kind of teacher writing with both of the kinds of evidence already counted, the total number of teachers rises from the previous 10 of 23 to 13 of 23.

For an example of this type, we return to Tamar for her thoughts on whether or in what way her preschool students have an understanding of division. Although this particular piece comes from a teacher whose writing we have already examined at some length, I have chosen to include it because it allows for interesting comparisons with the fourth-grade teacher's writing about *breaking down* and *building up*—the relationship between multiplication and division. Tamar also analyzes her students' understanding of division and its connection to other operations, although of course her very young students have quite a different understanding of both number and operation than do the fourth graders in the example we have already seen. However, in both cases, the children's ideas can be fertile ground for a teacher's own mathematical work. From this pair of examples, we can see that a teacher whose aim is to engage mathematically with her students can use the work of children at any grade as a springboard for her own explorations. In doing so, the mathematics that she learns will be particularly well suited to the teaching of students at that level.

Tamar writes:

I have been thinking a lot lately about how to relate the readings and class discussions to preschool, especially now when we are getting into division. How can I relate these discussions about division to preschool learning?

What is really important to preschoolers is that everybody has the same amount. Fairness is very important. One morning two girls were playing a beanbag toss game. There was a conflict because one of the girls had grabbed up all of the beanbags leaving only two for the other. We decided that to be fair they should each have the same amount. What they ended up doing was each took a handful and counted them and then compared. "Eight," "Six." With just a few words to help they each got to seven beanbags. However the girls started the game and each time they tossed the beanbags they needed to complete this entire process again.

What I was thinking about afterwards is that there were several ways they could have divided the beanbags. "Dealing" was what I thought would happen. But they found this way and I think that since it worked the first time they continued with it. I was really confused as to why they didn't hang on to the number seven each time as if they were afraid that the numbers would change. There were some things they were doing that I was glad to see. This continual counting and recounting was good practice I was really glad about that. They did a lot of comparing numbers; "which had more?" The addition and subtraction to each get to the number seven was also good and it got me to thinking about how much we use addition and subtraction in division problems. So is there any division going on in preschool? I'm still not sure. (Tamar, Portfolio Assignment 1.8, early January 1997)

Tamar knows what function and meaning the number 7 would have had for *her* in this bean bag problem, and she notices its relative instability for her students. She also knows that from her point of view the children's work accomplishes division, but she is thinking carefully about the nature of division and to what extent the preschoolers' counting-based solutions constitute evidence of children carrying out division. This is an example of a teacher who is working to understand (a) the mathematics as she works to understand (b) the students' own conceptions of this mathematical terrain.

Although each reader may have his or her own point of view about which of these kinds of evidence is most compelling, we can take the data to show that somewhere between 5 and 13 of the 23 seminar participants—or roughly between 1/5 and 1/2 of the teachers—wrote about engaging in this kind of mathematical work while teaching. That up to 1/2 of the DMI participants had begun to work in this way is an important accomplishment. However, it is interesting to note that even at 13 of 23, the numbers are still considerably smaller than they were for learning mathematics in the more supported context of the seminar group explorations, where virtually all of the seminar participants comment on learning mathematics.

Indeed the teachers' portfolio writing on all of the topics considered until now—that *children* have mathematical ideas (illustrated by Abby's story), that *teachers* have mathematical ideas (illustrated by Ella's story), and that teachers learn mathematics from the seminar work (illustrated by the fractions story)—has been resounding and nearly universal. With respect to this topic, however, the teacher's learning of mathematics for herself while also focusing on understanding the students' mathematics, we hear less from the teachers in their portfolio writing. Perhaps this is not surprising because it involves putting together two complicated agendas and carrying them out on one's own.

This kind of independent exploration of the subject matter might be expected to come somewhat later in a teacher's development. Both the seminar work on mathematical topics for the teachers, such as that illustrated in the fractions story, and the seminar work on understanding children's mathematical ideas in the cases are likely to serve as bridges for teachers to the more independent work of exploring mathematics in one's own classroom.

As the stories in this chapter illustrate, there is an enormous amount to understand in elementary mathematics, even for intelligent, well-educated adults. The teachers who participated in the DMI seminars were seriously engaged in building these understandings. For a teacher to develop a strong knowledge base of the mathematical topics in and beyond her own grade level takes time, support, and, as the latter half of this chapter suggests, probably group effort at least in the beginning years. The portfolio evidence concerning teachers' independent mathematical learning in the course of teaching raises a number of questions. Among these, it is perhaps most important that we consider what kinds of experiences, over what kinds of time, are likely to offer the continuing support that this learning appears to require. This is a topic to which we return in the concluding chapter.

4

Creating Teaching Practices
That Focus on Understandings

Strand 3: Teachers building teaching practices that work with the children's understandings as together and individually the children construct new ideas

In the last chapter, we saw teachers working with one another and with their students to learn mathematics. Inasmuch as the stories were about fractions and counting, they were also stories about people laying out their thoughts for themselves and for one another, making their reasoning and their ideas explicit, reflecting on those newly explicit ideas, and, as a result, learning. In the case of the fractions story, the mathematical work and the representations and interactions that supported it took place in the teachers' seminar with the help of the seminar facilitator. In the case of Tamar's story, the teacher's reflection on her students' in-class representations took place on her own outside of both seminar and classroom.

It is one thing to engage with the intellectual content of represented ideas in the seminar or even before or after conducting a class, and quite another to do so in the act of teaching. In this chapter, we look to the elementary classrooms of DMI participants and focus carefully on the nature and outcomes of the mathematical interactions that take place there. Over the course of the seminar year, what, if anything, was changing in teachers' practices?

As the stories of this chapter illustrate, the DMI participants began to build their own classroom practices in ways that—like the teaching of the seminar facilitator from the fractions story—involved careful attention to students' and teacher's mathematical thoughts. More and more, their practices seemed to aim at the creation, representation, and exploration of what I call a *jointly holdable mathematical idea*. Key to this process is supporting and eliciting from students representations of their thoughts so that the thought is "on the table" for group consideration. A second, equally key aspect of this pedagogy is taking these ideas, once expressed, as objects of mathematical reflection—a reflection that is shaped by the details of both student and teacher mathematical understanding.

The following stories of DMI participants' changing classroom practices illuminate the teachers' growing ability to support both student expression of mathematical ideas and the mathematical investigation of those ideas. As we see, these two aspects of teachers' practices are intimately intertwined. The more deeply a teacher understands the topic under study and the more deeply she grasps the strengths and weaknesses of the students' ideas, the better able she is to elicit clear representations of student thought. This same depth in a teacher's mathematical understanding supports her attempts to orchestrate classroom conversations that begin with what her students believe and challenge them to take next steps. The relationship works in the other direction as well. The more able a teacher is to invite, encourage, and support learners as they represent their ideas, the richer the mathematical terrain that is opened to the group for study. It is this complicated interaction—between the proclivity and ability to elicit and hear others' ideas, and a teacher's own connection to and understanding of the mathematical topic—that is central to the following stories of changing practice.

Characterized in this way, it is clear that both Strands 1 and 2 are essential elements in these stories of change, but they alone are not sufficient. Clearly working in a classroom on jointly held ideas requires of a teacher an attentiveness to children's and teachers' understandings of the ideas of the curriculum (Strand 1). Equally important is a teacher's familiarity with the mathematical ideas themselves, their development in children, and a readiness to engage in an investigation of these ideas (Strand 2). All of the progress a teacher has made in Strands 1 and 2 helps equip that teacher to understand the thinking children represent in the classroom and to make choices about guiding its development. However important Strands 1 and 2 are to this kind of practice though, learning to facilitate the processes of representing thoughts and productively reflecting on these representations—that is, developing new teaching practices—is itself a large piece of work.

The three stories of this chapter show teachers who are taking on this work. Each story describes a different facet of what is involved in developing this kind of teaching practice. The first two stories are stories of teacher change, and the third is an illustration of some of the power and complexity of this kind of teaching. In the first story, we revisit Ella (the third-grade teacher from Strand 1), this time in her classroom. Over the course of the year, we see Ella's teaching shift so that she more often encourages students to hold ideas still long enough to describe and make them explicit. We also see Ella's—and the class'—mathematical focus strengthen. Classroom conversation in May involves both more detailed representation of student thinking and a clearer mathematical purpose than it did the previous October. Thus, in Ella's classroom story, we are able to look carefully at a teaching practice that comes more and more to support *children representing their mathematical thoughts*, for themselves, for their classmates, and for their teacher.

The second story, Claire's story, shows the work of a teacher who grapples with *the function of children's representations* and, related to this, the function of her own knowledge in teaching and learning. In Claire's story, we see a teacher who comes up against the limits of trying to *tell* students what *she* knows. Instead she comes more and more to look for opportunities for children to use their own representations of a problem as tools for investigating and illuminating the underlying mathematics toward which Claire, as a teacher, aims. In Claire's teaching practice, over time there is a shift in the functions served by both teacher's and students' mathematical knowledge.

In the third story, Liz's story, we see a teacher *working to orchestrate the classroom interactions as different children represent their differing ideas* about a mathematical topic and, in reflecting on these, try to resolve some difficult mathematical questions. It is in this third story that we see more clearly the potential that lies in a classroom full of students, in interaction with their teacher, jointly holding an idea, turning it over and over as they get to know it better. It is in this story too that we can see more of the mathematical and interpersonal complexities that make this teaching such a challenge. Yet without the kinds of changes in teaching practice that Ella and Claire show us, teaching such as we see in Liz's story would not develop.

Throughout we might remember that no one gave the teachers in the DMI seminars assignments about what to work on in their teaching practices—or even requested that they change anything about their teaching. The stories that follow show us the work that each teacher took on in her classroom because, presumably, something in the seminar experience stimulated her to pay attention to certain aspects of the classroom interchange and to respond differently to them than she had before. We turn now to Ella.

REPRESENTING THOUGHTS

Across the seminar year, Ella changes her classroom practice such that children come to hold their thoughts still and in focus long enough to represent them to themselves and one another. The thoughts become more visible to Ella and the children and, once visible, become the subject of their mathematical scrutiny. At the heart of the story are excerpts from Ella's math class in October and the following May. At the beginning of the year, while children take many turns to speak in class, they do so only to report the *results* of their thinking—their answers. The classroom conversation probes no deeper. Neither Ella nor the children inquire into the reasoning that leads to an answer, the relationship between one answer and another, or the mathematical validity of any of the offerings. By the end of the year, we hear a different kind of conversation in Ella's classroom: one in which children represent their reasoning in spoken words, and the teacher probes for more detail and student comment about this reasoning. Representing thoughts becomes an important aspect of classroom conversation and provides the forum in which mathematics becomes better known and understood.

In reading Ella's classroom story, it is useful to recall Ella's story from Strand 1. In that story, we found Ella beginning the seminar (and the school year) feeling uncertain about her own ability to work through mathematical problems that she did not immediately understand. By the end of the school year, however, Ella has a new sense of herself as a mathematical thinker. She no longer shies away from making her own sense of difficult mathematics. In the spring of the seminar year, she is more likely to persevere when, in the seminar context, she is faced with a difficult problem. She talks about a conversation over tea with her husband where, to his suggestion that she could take a college course in mathematics, Ella replies that she does not need help knowing ways to *do* mathematical problems, but rather needs to work at *understanding* the mathematics. Ella adds: "And no one's going to tell me how to understand it, I've got to figure it out for myself."

In the vignettes from Ella's classroom that follow, we see how these two different stances with respect to mathematical engagement—the more tentative stance of October and the more empowered stance of May—play out in Ella's teaching. In May, Ella digs into the mathematics of her students' thoughts in a way that she does not in October. Ella's new relationship to mathematics enables her to invite her students' ideas in for lengthier, more intimate classroom visits. The parallels between Ella's Strand 1 story and her classroom story are telling. The impact of her involvement with both the mathematical content and her students is powerful.

Ella's Classroom Story: Representing Thoughts

It is October 28 of the seminar year, a few days after the third DMI session. Ella, a Grade 3 teacher, speaks with me about the math class she just taught and I just observed. Ella's sense of the class is that it was lacking what she called "the real meat and potatoes." When I ask her to tell me more about what the "meat and potatoes" is that was missing, she says:

Ella: Oh, well the meat and potatoes would have been a lot more talk. A lot more math talk. "Well, we could do this. Well, maybe we shouldn't do this." And to hear that is . . . , to me it's mind boggling.

SC: So you would want the room, . . . what you are aiming for as a teacher is to have the room abuzz with conversation among children about, "well we could do it this way," "this way," "here's what I did," "here's what. . . ."

Ella: Right. And talking about different strategies and showing different strategies and how we got them, and that they are able to work through how we got that, rather than just saying, "Well, I just knew it."

So at this point in time, at the end of October, Ella strives for a class in which children engage with the mathematics, devise solutions to problems, and talk about their reasoning. By Ella's own estimation, however, the actual classroom conversation in October falls short of this goal. We can better understand Ella's point by looking at an excerpt from this class early in the year.

The children are sitting at their desks, and Ella is at the chalkboard. She speaks to the whole class:

Ella: We're going to go ahead and do some calendar math this morning. This is the number that you're going to be working with this morning (writes "28" on the board). I would like you to see if in *some* of the ways that you're thinking about getting to twenty-eight, if maybe in one of those ways, or maybe two or three, however many that you think, you might have some doubles of numbers. (Pause) And what would I mean by that Angela? What would be a double of a number? (Pause) What number could I use a double of to get twenty-eight? (Pause) Can Dylan help you out?

Dylan: Fourteen plus fourteen.

Ella: (writing "14 + 14" on the board) Fourteen plus fourteen. That would give me a twenty-eight, right? OK. . . . Erica?

Erica: Ten plus ten plus four plus four.

Ella: (writing "10 + 10 + 4 + 4" on the board) How many doubles does she have there? . . . OK. Doesn't mean you have to use all doubles. Whatever it is that you like. We've been working with our addition, our subtraction, and we've been working some with multiplication. So see what you can do for ten minutes, OK?

(Students work individually, at their seats, writing in their journals.)

As we can see even in these opening instructions, Ella is a teacher who naturally and comfortably invites children to speak in the classroom. As the conversation progresses, Ella makes time for many children to speak. Yet as we watch the conversation unfold, it also becomes clear that, at this point in the year, once a child offers an answer, even when that answer seems more of a place holder for a conversational turn than the more substantive answers Ella is wishing for, the conversation seems to be over.

Ella: OK—I would like you to go ahead and stop and I am going to um, choose a few names to come up with um some of the ways you have gotten to twenty-eight. Let's see. I'm gonna pick 'em [names] from the basket like I always do. (Ella picks a piece of paper from a basket, and reads the name on the paper aloud.) Angela!

Angela: (walks to overhead projector, and writes "19 + 9 = 28")

Ella: Angela, what is it?

Angela: Nineteen plus nine equals twenty-eight.

Ella: And how did you know that?

Angela: (very quietly) I just knew.

Ella: You just knew it. OK, (Angela walks back to her seat) very good, thank you. (Then, calling on the next child) Noah.

Although Ella makes sure to offer Angela an opportunity to speak, and Angela has accepted a turn in the classroom conversation, neither the student nor the teacher goes beyond "I just knew" as a rationale for the answer. For now Angela's offering—19 + 9 = 28—is not explored.

The conversation continues as it has begun, and several more children take turns presenting their equations.

Noah: Does it *have* to be a double? (Walks to overhead projector with his journal.)

Ella: Nope. Choose whichever one is your favorite on there. How's that?

Noah: (Begins to write on the overhead.)

In this pause, as Noah takes time getting organized at the overhead, Ella provides an opportunity for another student to speak.

Ella: Noah, while you're writing that up, I'm going to ask Michael a question. Michael, what's the advantage of doing doubles? What did you find that you like about doing doubles? Was it easier for you? Was it harder?

Here, as in the exchange with Angela (Ella: "And how did you know that?"), Ella asks a question that provides an opening for talk about thoughts. However, as with Angela, Ella does not yet take the child's first response much deeper.

Michael: To me doubles was kinda harder, cause you can't like do eight plus eight equals twenty-eight.

Ella: So what do you hafta do?

Michael: Kinda get high numbers. Like twenty-nine take away one is twenty-eight. Doubles can be really hard sometimes.

This foray into the power of doubles ends here. Neither Ella nor the children move closer to the mathematical heart of the matter—in this case, the parts and wholes implied by doubles. Ella has posed the question and invited children to consider it. Yet the visit with these thoughts does not last long. The talk stays at the level of reading equations, and the class, including Michael, only gets the tip of the iceberg of his ideas. There is little exploration of Michael's initial offering or, as Ella puts it, little "meat and potatoes."

[Noah asks if the numbers need to be all together. Ella joins him at the overhead, where they confer privately. There appears to be some question about which of his equations to write on the overhead. Ella suggests a particular one. Noah writes: "10 + 10 + 4 + 4 = 28."]

Ella: (again to the whole class) All right, Noah, what do you have there?

Noah: Ten plus ten plus four plus four equals twenty-eight.

Ella: All right, so you have . . . how many doubles?

Noah: Two.

Ella: (calling on the next child) Suzanne.

Ella's conversation with Noah proceeds much like the conversations with Angela and Michael. Here Noah offers an answer—$10 + 10 + 4 + 4 = 28$. Ella responds with a question: ". . . so you have . . . how many doubles?" Noah answers her question.

Although Ella's question relates to Noah's answer, it does not probe Noah's reasoning, his understanding of the equation, or the underlying mathematics. For instance, they do not discuss how Noah came to find *these* particular doubles. Did he partition the 28 into 20 + 8, split the 20 to yield 10 + 10, and split the 8 to yield 4 + 4?

The question Ella chooses to ask keeps the conversation going, but stays at the surface mathematically—"How many doubles?" This was the case with Angela's offering as well. Although $19 + 9 = 28$ might have been considered in relation to 20 + 8 or in relation to doubling—perhaps leading to the discovery of, for example, $10 + 9 + 9 = 28$—this analysis of the parts and wholes involved in composing the number 28 stays just beyond today's classroom conversation. The children in this classroom are talking and their teacher is listening, but so far the talk is not about their ideas and the conversation does not seem to build from one child to the next.

Even when a child tries to connect his answer with another child's, as happens next in the conversation, Ella's response helps keep the conversation on the surface, rather than taking it deeper.

Peter: (with enthusiasm) I had the *same* one!
Ella: Did you have the same one?
Peter: Yeah, ten plus ten plus four plus four.
Ella: OK. Great.

With Suzanne, who presents her answer next, again Ella invites the child to speak and asks a question. Yet the content of the conversation is not the "meat and potatoes" for which Ella is hoping. Instead they speak about how Suzanne has written the numbers, and Ella asks Suzanne to read the equation.

(Ella asks one child to move his desk a bit so that whoever is at the overhead has more room to use the shelf at the side of the overhead cart.)
(Suzanne writes

$$\begin{array}{r} 8 \\ + \ 8 \\ \hline 16 \\ + \ 12 \\ \hline 28) \end{array}$$

Ella: Suzanne, you've written yours out differently. Why did you choose to do that?
Suzanne: (shrugs) I don't know, that's the way I usually do it. I usually do my math that way.
Ella: You usually like to do your math that way. OK, thank you. And tell us what your problem is.
Suzanne: Eight plus eight equals sixteen. Sixteen plus twelve equals twenty-eight.
Ella: Great. Thank you. . . . (Then, calling on the next child) Julia.

Classroom work on this problem continues for 10 more minutes, or a total of 28 minutes, and for six more children all in the same vein: children's offerings parallel to one another, not discussed, and little, if any, talk of mathematical thoughts. The more explicit conversation—about how answers are reached, about children's thoughts and strategies along the way, about the relationships among children's answers—the conversation that Ella wishes would fill the class is, in October, mostly missing.

Now in October, Ella's approach to encouraging children to speak about their thoughts relies primarily on providing many opportunities for children to speak and on showing her interest in what they say by asking a question or two. These are not negligible contributions. Still as we see, they are not enough to bring about the more thoughtful conversations that Ella envisions. Now if children do not speak about an idea, Ella is not challenging them to; if children do offer the beginning of a thought, she is not yet helping them to take it further. Ella's own role in encouraging talk about mathematical thoughts in her classroom is, in October, relatively passive.

From the October interview, we hear Ella comment on this:

SC: ... It sounds like you are also saying something about wanting that [... "meat and potatoes"] to come sort of from the efforts of the ..., that the *children* should know how to, that one of your goals for them is that *they* should know how to make those conversations, carry on those conversations without a lot of intervention and help from you.

Ella: Right. I would rather, thinking of myself as a facilitator rather than the in-struct-or. // But also I think that children have a lot of, a wealth of knowledge that we just need to tap into. And they don't even realize that it's there sometimes. And once they find it, wow, it just goes.

From Ella's teaching and from these interview comments, we get similar pictures—pictures of a teacher who asks a question and then looks to the children for the mathematical "meat and potatoes." Ella's October stance vis-à-vis mathematics in the seminar provides an interesting perspective on what we see in the classroom. During October, Ella looks readily to seminar colleagues or family members as mathematical questions arise. She is rather tentative about tackling the ideas on her own. However, things change over the seminar year. Ella comes to believe that she can do more mathematically. She also comes to believe that her students have more than answers to offer, and she has some ideas about how to gain access to their thoughts. By May, things look quite different in Ella's classroom than they did in October.

As early as December, Ella writes in her portfolio about a shift that she has noticed in her teaching practices. She puts it this way:

The shift that I see in my thinking, as I work with my students during math, is that I am more comfortable spending a considerable amount of time having the students explain to each other how they solved a problem. I am not quite certain if I would have been so at ease with this before this seminar. Mainly because of my worry that some students may become confused by this. ...

There have been many ideas that I have gotten from both the readings and the videos that I have implemented in my classroom. One that readily comes to mind is what I have explained in the above paragraph. In the very first video that we viewed, the teacher had the students explain their strategies for solving an addition problem. I was so moved by this video that the very next day I imitated a reproduction with my students. I was so impressed by the outcome that I have since used this same method many times and I will continue to do so. (Ella, Portfolio Assignment 1.6, December 1996)

A few months later, Ella writes:

My observations of my students this year have shaped me as a teacher and have directly impacted me as a facilitator of math instruction. In listening to them engaged in learning and talking about their different approaches with one another, I realize that these students have so much to offer one another. Being aware of how important this is to them as learners, I base my math curriculum around them problem solving with one another. (Ella, Portfolio Assignment 2.3, March 12, 1997)

Thus, in Ella's words, this is the shift in her teaching practice: She is "more comfortable spending a considerable amount of time having the students explain to each other how they solved a problem," and she has come to realize that "these students have so much to offer one another."

Another change for Ella by May is familiar to us from Ella's story in Strand 1. Recall from that story Ella's comment to her husband in May, after she worked in the seminar at understanding division by fractions: "No you see, you don't get it. I can *do* it. I want to *understand* it. And no one's going to tell me how to understand it. I've got to figure it out myself." By May, Ella is much more ready to engage with mathematical issues and ideas than she was in October, and we see this not only in the seminar, but in her classroom as well. A visit to Ella's classroom in May shows us what these changes in her practice look like.

It is May 5 of the seminar year. The children are sitting as one group, on the floor, facing an easel-style dry erase board. Ella sits by the board facing the children. She has just posed a multiplication problem for the children to solve mentally.

(Ella has written the following on the dry erase board: "35 × 5 =" and below this she has written " 35
                          × _5"
She waits for all hands to be up, signaling that everyone has an answer.)
Ella: Put your hands down. Michael, what do you know?
Michael: Mine . . . One hundred seventy-four.
Ella: One hundred seventy-four. Well, how did you come up with that?

Michael: Well, I added. . . . I took the five and added—actually I took the thirty-five and I, well in the air I wrote three, three, three, three, three.

Ella: OK.

Michael: And then I did five, five, five, five, five and, and I came up with one hundred seventy-four, and I know the right answer is something else, 'cause Tom told me.

Ella has asked Michael to tell about his thoughts: "Well, how did you come up with that?" Although this initial question is not so different from what we heard in Ella's class in October, now in May the conversation proceeds differently from here. Michael is able to put into words his reasoning, the sequence of thoughts by which he came to his answer of 174. He explains that he thought of the problem 35 × 5 as involving the repeated addition of 35s and then goes on to describe his method of adding the 5 "35"s. However, Michael also shows us that, for some reason, he has more faith in Tom's answer than his own. Here Ella continues in a way that seems quite different from her approach in October. Ella asks Michael to stick with his reasoning for a while longer, presumably assuming that he, the class, and/or Ella have something to learn by a closer examination of his thoughts.

(Ella writes on the dry erase board: "35
                                      35
                                      35
                                      35
                                      35")

Ella: (laughs in response to Michael's comment about Tom telling him the right answer) OK. All right. But this is what you were doing in your mind? (Pointing to the column of "35"s on the dry erase board)

Ella's question and her representation on the board of what Michael wrote in the air for himself help focus both Michael's and the group's attention on his reasoning, and to support its fuller consideration.

Michael: Yeah.

Ella: Which one did you add up first?

Michael: I added the threes.

Ella: You added up all the threes. And what did you get?

Michael: (long pause) Eighteen.

This 18 is neither a correct sum of the 5 threes nor consistent with Michael's answer of 174. It appears that either Michael's original calculation was incorrect, that his current recalculation is incorrect, or both. At this point, Ella does not challenge his computation. She continues to ask him to articulate his thinking.

Ella: OK. And then you added up the fives? And what did you get?
Michael: I don't remember.
Ella: You don't remember. OK. All right.
Michael: I came up with twenty-five.

Ella and Michael, together, have clearly represented Michael's method for solving this problem. We still have not heard from Michael how or if his method yields an answer of 174, but we know both the answer he arrived at originally and the solution method he employed. Michael's thinking about this problem is made explicit—explicit enough that its meaning and validity can be assessed. Indeed as the conversation continues, another student offers an opinion about the answer this method would yield. Ella does not choose to follow up on that offering now, but we do see that children are following the logic of one another's thoughts.

Nathan: One hundred . . . It is one hundred twenty-five, that right there is
         . . .
Ella: Right, right. (Erases what is on the dry erase board.) OK Carl, what did you come up with?
Carl: I, I just counted up (unintelligible).
Ella: You think it's one hundred ninety-five.
Carl: I just counted up all the thirties, all the thirties, all the thirties.
Ella: (to the whole class) Shhh . . . OK hold on just a minute. Carl, you counted up how many thirties?

Ella's question shows us how important the details of Carl's process are to her. At this point in the year, she does not just want to know vaguely what Carl has done to solve this problem. She wants to know in sufficient detail that she and the children can understand and follow his thinking. Of course, this also provides *Carl* with encouragement to pay attention to the details of his thoughts.

Carl: All of them. Five of them.
Ella: You counted up five thirties. OK so, this is what you were doing . . . (Ella writes on the board: "30
                                    30
                                    30
                                    30
                                    30")

OK. And what did you get?

Carl: (slowly) I have a hundred and fifty.

Ella: OK. (Ella writes "150" as the sum under the column of 30s.) And then what did you do?

Carl: And then I counted up all the fives so I took five plus five equaled twenty-five.

Ella takes Carl to mean that next he added 5 fives, and she represents his words this way.

Ella: OK. (Ella writes "   5
                                5
                                5
                                5
                               _5
                               25")

Carl: Oops—I already know what it is.

Carl, on seeing his thought written out and going by more slowly, now sees an error in his original work.

Carrie: I know, I know.

Ella: You know what it is now—what is it?

Carl: It's a hundred and seventy-five.

At this point, Ella decides to shift the class' focus from the content of student thoughts, where it has been as Michael and Carl have explained their reasoning about 35 × 5, to the process of having those thoughts.

Ella: Is it . . . , Carl, I have a question for you. And some of you, this is all for you too. And I'm wondering, . . . does it get confused in your head?

Carl: Yeah—all the time.

Ella: So you start and you know the numbers, . . .

Timothy: And then I lose track.

Ella: And then it's hard to keep track of them.

Jonathan: I had a thousand and five but then (unintelligible).

In reading this segment of conversation, it is interesting to think back once more to Ella's Strand 1 story and her description of her feelings about her own struggles with mathematical thoughts in the seminar. Ella's relationship with her mathematical thoughts, her vulnerability in the "deep, dark forest" of ideas she refers to in the Strand 1 story, come through in her practice now—now that she has come through that forest a first time, that is. She treats the children's thoughts as central to the work of the classroom and also addresses feelings she knows—firsthand from her DMI experience—that some may have.

Ella now seems to have a number of ways to ask children to pay attention to their thoughts, and, of equal importance, she more clearly demonstrates her own mathematical involvement with the children's thinking. The class continues by considering Richard's approach to the 35 × 5 problem.

> Ella: OK, OK. So Richard, what did you do with this?
> Richard: I basically did a hundred ... Thirty-five plus thirty-five is seventy.
> Ella: (writes "35 + 35 = 70" on the dry erase board) OK.
> Richard: And seventy plus, ... no seventy plus seventy is one hundred and forty ...
> Ella: Mm-hmm.
> Richard: And then I just had to add one more thirty-five and I got one seventy-five.
> (Ella writes "70 + 70 = 140
>   140 + 35 = 175")
> Ella: OK. How did you know to do another seventy?

Here Ella probes beneath the action. She not only wants to know what Richard *did*, but also *how he knew* to do that. With this question, Ella provides an opportunity and an invitation for the students to join with her in thinking about the mathematical validity of each step in a computational procedure.

> Richard: 'Cause we did before and thirty-five plus thirty-five was seventy and then you needed one more thirty-five.

Richard's answer is not yet very articulate. Perhaps in unpacked form the logic of his words is that he knows, from just having calculated it, that the sum of 35 + 35 is 70; he needs 5 thirty-fives altogether; the first 2 thirty-fives are in the first 70; 1 more seventy gives him 4 thirty-fives, and that leaves him with 1 more thirty-five to add on. Of course Richard is still a ways from having this so clearly in words, but these words that I have used do match the logic of his method. Ella leaves Richard's statement just as he offered it and moves on.

> Ella: That's right (smiles, nods, gives thumbs up sign), that works. That works out really well....

At this point, there is a behavior issue that Ella wants to address.

Ella: Noah, do you need to go to your seat for a little bit?
Noah: (unintelligible)
Ella: Do you need to go into the boys' room to take care of that?
Noah: No.
Ella: David, you need to stop that. . . . OK. Suzanne?

Yet Ella, maintaining her focus, returns to the math.

Suzanne: (unintelligible)
Ella: I'm sorry Suzanne, we need to hold on just a minute so I know
          your classmates are listening. . . . And can you speak up a little
          louder so they can hear?
Suzanne: I counted um . . . thirty-five fives.

Suzanne, rather than taking 5 thirty-fives as Michael, Carl, and Richard
did, has taken 35 fives.

Ella: (having trouble hearing) I'm sorry, can you say that again?
Suzanne: I counted thirty-five fives.
Ella: (writes "35 5s" on the dry erase board) You counted thirty-five
          fives—so you went five, ten, fifteen, twenty, twenty-five, thirty,
          thirty-five, forty, forty-five, fifty (touching a finger with each
          count)—that way?
Suzanne: Mm-hmm.
Ella: That works! Great! . . . (Pointing to a boy) OK.

Although Ella is willing to move on from Suzanne's method, another
student, in describing his own method, compares it to Suzanne's. Although the two children's methods differ in many ways, they share the interpretation of the problem as 35 groups of 5.

Simon: I did mostly like Suzanne, except for, I counted up—I knew five
          times ten was fifty and then I added fifty plus fifty plus fifty.
Ella: OK. So wait . . . (now writes "5 × 10 = 50") Five times ten was
          fifty, you knew?
Simon: Mm-hmm.
Ella: OK. So then what did you do?
Simon: Time, times three equaled a hundred and fifty.
Ella: (writes "50 × 3 = 150") OK so fifty times three equaled a hundred
          and fifty. And . . .

Simon: And then I added a twenty-five.

Ella: (writes "150 + 25") How did you know to add a twenty-five?

Again as with Richard, at this point in the year, Ella wants to hear the student's justification for his method. She is interested in his answer, as she was in October, and now in May she is also interested in a full description of computational method *and* the reasoning behind it.

Simon: Cause five times five is twenty-five.

The piece of Simon's logic that goes unarticulated here is that he multiplies 5×5 because he still needs to add in 5 more fives. He accounted for 30 of the fives, taking them 10 by 10 by 10. That left a group of 5 fives, which he now tells us he knows to equal 25. This is the end of this piece of conversation. The class now moves on to a new problem.

In this excerpt, as in all of the class' work on this day in May, we see Ella taking a much more active role in supporting the children's mathematical work than she did in October. She now probes, challenges, and digs deeper, helping children lay out some of the mathematical detail of their thoughts. This requires Ella to engage with the mathematical detail of the children's thoughts. Although at the end of October Ella was accepting of comments such as "I just knew" and "I always do my math that way" as rationales for answers, by May, both teacher and children create a new kind of conversation. Now in May, Ella works to get children to make their thoughts explicit. She does this whether they offer correct answers or incorrect ones—perhaps on the assumption that a careful look at the method will be instructive for all and allow the group to assess the validity of the answer. Ella now asks questions such as "But this is what you were doing in your mind?", while pointing to a list of 35s on the dry erase board, or "How did you know to do another seventy?" She even draws children's attention to the confusion they might feel as they try to mentally calculate. Both Ella and the children now expect, and participate in building, a conversation in which children's thought and reasoning are present and represented, and neither Ella nor her students shy away from the mathematics.

Larger Data Set as Context for Ella's Classroom Story

Indeed all 23 teacher participants write about this kind of change in their classrooms. Listening for and coming to understand children's mathematical ideas was a universal theme voiced by DMI participants. Although Ella's classroom story shows us what it might look like as teachers change their classroom practices so that children's thoughts become more visible and the mathematics comes into sharper focus, the portfolio writings give us a sense for the ways teachers express the shift taking place in their teaching. From several of the teachers, we hear simple and direct assertions of the growing importance to them as teachers of hearing students' thoughts. Among these, some also are explicit about the importance they see in exploring the mathematics of these student offerings. Teachers are clear that these are new stances for them—something that has changed since the start of the seminar. Some examples follow:

> In reflecting on the changes I see in my own thinking I find that I am more concerned with having students talk and explain their thinking. . . . (Grade 1 teacher, Portfolio Assignment 2.1, no date)

> I have changed in my thinking since the first assignment because I now look for more of an explanation of a child's thinking and for different strategies being used to solve problems. I also expect the students to give more detailed written explanations in their math journals. (Grade 4 teacher, Portfolio Assignment 2.1, February 5, 1997)

> Yes, I'm giving myself more time to explore students' strategies during class. The class participation has become more active. Students are willing to go to the board and explain their way of coming up with their answer. (Grade 6 bilingual teacher, Portfolio Assignment 1.6, December 1996)

> I feel like I am now looking at students' work in a very different way than before I took this course. I am seeing a lot more and wondering why they did things the way they did. I think I had a more cut and dried point of view before. Previously I would have looked for the correct answer first and only looked back at their work to see where they went wrong. Now I would tend to give more attention to their process of solving their explanations. It's a lot more interesting and I can learn a lot from their methods. (Substitute teacher, Portfolio Assignment 2.7, May 14, 1997)

Other teachers, also making simple assertions about a direction of change in their teaching practices, write in a way that reveals the value they place on *children* listening to each others' thoughts, considering each others' offerings.

> The seminar explorations have begun to affect my teaching in my classroom. I find myself encouraging the students more and more to explore other strategies and to try to understand other students' methods. (Grade 4 teacher, Portfolio Assignment 1.6, December 4, 1996)

> I am encouraging the children to become aware of respecting each others' thinking. We are working on some difficult ideas and practices for 6 and 7 year olds—really listening to peers and carefully articulating the ideas that

they are thinking, as well as attending to the mathematics involved. (Grade 1 teacher, Portfolio Assignment 1.6, December 4, 1996)

One of the effects of this seminar is a change in my thinking as I teach math lessons. I'm more cognitive [cognizant] of the different ways students may be thinking of numbers and ways to solve problems. I am trying to learn more about how they have found the solutions. I'm trying to have students share their strategies so they can see there are many different ways to solve problems and that even though their way of thinking is different it does not mean it is wrong. (Grade 2 teacher, Portfolio Assignment 1.6, December 1996)

In a somewhat more elaborated piece of writing, one teacher points to her increasingly strong focus on children's mathematical thinking and on what a child understands about a mathematical problem. She not only describes this change in her teaching, but articulates that representing thought can proceed verbally and nonverbally, and that both are useful in the work of teaching.

The seminar has also helped me to see that figuring out how a person solved a problem is an important step to understanding their thinking. Much of my work in both the Preschool and the upper grades is with children who have difficulty with either expressive and or receptive language. Explaining their thoughts is not an easy thing for many of these children. This step can be difficult to get at with young children who lack the language necessary to talk about their ideas or for older children who's language skills are weak. One of the lessons which I have been reminded about from the readings is to have children show what they did to solve a problem. This can serve as a catalyst for conversation about their work.

In my work in the upper grades, I am often entering a classroom in which a math activity has been presented. These activities vary greatly between classrooms due to different teaching styles. I am often called upon to help make sense of some child's thinking or asked to assist a child in understanding a particular concept or word problem. The work we have done in this seminar has been helpful to me in this situation because I am now spending much less time trying to figure out what the teacher wanted for an answer on a particular assignment. Instead, I am now more likely to focus on what a child was attempting to do and why they did it that way. (Preschool special needs and K–6 resource teacher, Portfolio Assignment 1.6, December 3, 1996)

This teacher speaks of her new focus on children's understandings and her use of children's nonverbal representations in the context of her work with special needs children. Yet all children, indeed all of us, often find it difficult to put new thoughts into words, and this teacher's point about the value of showing (i.e., representing) how a person solved a problem—

whether with symbols, blocks, diagrams, or gestures—has meaning in every classroom. From Ella's classroom story and from the collection of teacher writing we have just sampled, we see and hear about classrooms in which children's thinking has been invited in for children and teacher to get to know. The teacher has helped create a classroom in which she demonstrates an engagement with mathematical thoughts and ideas, and in which she encourages children to take a close enough look at their own thoughts that they can describe them. As they do so, they offer the raw material to the entire classroom community—teacher and children—for deepening student engagement with the mathematical topics before them.

DISCOVERING THE FUNCTIONS OF REPRESENTED THOUGHTS FOR LEARNERS

The next story, Claire's story, is about the function of representations for the child who is creating them. It is the story of a teacher's discoveries about the utility of explicitly representing student thought in the classroom. It is the story of a teacher who comes to rely more steadily on making use of children's thoughts as they work through difficult mathematics.

Claire's story begins in a math class during December of the seminar year. During this class, the students get off to a good start on a problem that Claire has posed. A few minutes later, Claire urges the class to record their work on a chart. However, the chart is not easy for them to connect to their initial and rich representation of the problem, and Claire senses that the students are struggling. She responds to the students' struggle by modeling a solution strategy—one that *does* correspond well to the chart she has asked them to use. The children take on Claire's method, but Claire soon sees that the method she has offered them does not hold the same meaning for the children that it does for her.

Given the children's difficulty making sense of Claire's method, they also have trouble assessing the validity of their work. Faced with errors that the children are neither noticing nor evaluating, Claire poses this question for herself. When I notice an error or a shortcoming in students' work, when I, as the teacher, see a mathematical issue that the children either are not seeing or are confused about, what can I do besides pointing out their error and telling them what is right? What can I do that is more likely to make a difference in *their* understanding?

In answering this question for herself, she purposefully comes to create a central place—in the work of the classroom—for children to represent their own ideas and encourages the children to make use of these representations to build on their mathematical understanding of the topic at hand. In Claire's story, we see a teacher who throughout the school year is engaged with classroom mathematics. Yet how she uses *her* mathematical thoughts and how she uses the *children's* thoughts shifts over the year. In December, she is more apt to respond to a child's struggle by telling or offering a solution, whereas in March, she is more likely to invite the struggling child to represent his own thinking, to himself and to her, as a way through the struggle.

Claire's Classroom Story: Using Represented Thoughts

It is December 16 of the seminar year. Claire, who teaches a bilingual Grade 5, asks her students to take out their math notebooks and write both the date and "Boxes of 200," the topic of today's math class, at the top of the page (TERC, 1998, *Landmarks in the Thousands*, p. 26). In introducing today's problem, Claire reminds the children of their work last week on "Rectangles of 100," and she draws everyone's attention to a large piece of chart paper on the board. On this paper are drawings of several rectangles, each having been drawn, colored, cut, and pasted onto the chart by a child during the previous week's work. Each rectangle on the chart is composed of 100 unit squares. For example, the rectangles drawn on the chart paper include these: 4 columns of 25 squares each, 2 rows of 50 squares each, 10 rows of 10 squares each, among others. Claire asks children to come up to the chart and label each rectangle with its factors. The children take turns labeling the drawings: 4 × 25, 2 × 50, 10 × 10, 1 × 100, and 5 × 20. Claire takes a clear interest in reviving last week's work and connecting this day's topic to the work on 100 that they have already done.

Claire continues to connect the work on 200 with the work on 100 as she asks the children to consider what materials they might use.

Claire: When you were working on these factors, you used certain materials to help you find the factors. Do you remember what helped you find the factors? We're going to use those same materials to help us find boxes of two hundred. What's one material you used?

Teresa: Calculator.

Claire: That was everybody's favorite.

Teresa: That was my favorite.

Other children name other materials that were used: snap cubes, paper, a 300 chart, their minds, and methods of counting. Claire writes all of these down on a chart she is making on the board.

In addition to connecting this day's work to previous days' work, Claire also connects the work on the number 200 to a concrete problem context. She provides this next.

Claire: This is the story behind it. We'll make a story up about two hundred to make it more interesting. There were two hundred pieces of candy . . .

(Several children chime in with other suggestions: gum, stickers.)

Claire: There are two hundred pieces of candy or gum that we need to fit into boxes.

Rafael: Two hundred pieces of marbles.

Claire: Marbles? Let me finish the story. Let me finish the story. Ready to listen?

Children: Yes.

Claire: There are two hundred pieces we need to stack in one layer so they don't get crushed and they don't get . . .

Children: Eaten.

Claire: They don't get eaten until they get to the person I need to. In *one layer*. Right? There are different ways you can package them. If I had one hundred pieces of candy (walks to the chart with the rectangles of 100 on it), and I wanted to find different kinds of boxes, how many different kinds of boxes could I find? (Claire points to the 10 × 10 rectangle on the chart.) Try to think of this as a box. This is one kind of box, it's a ten by ten box. Yes. This is another kind of box (pointing to the 2 × 50 rectangle), it's a really *long*, thin, narrow kind of box, but it works, doesn't it?

With these and the following comments, Claire maps today's concrete problem situation of packaging candies onto the rectangles of 100 chart.

(Miguel points to one of the rectangles on the chart.)

Claire: This one? It's a five by twenty, if you can imagine it, yes. A five by twenty is another kind of box. Here's a box (pointing to the 1 × 100 rectangle). I don't know if the post office would like you to send *this* through the mail, but that is a box, and that could be a box that you could send one hundred pieces of candy. I want you to see how many different kinds of boxes you can make with the number two hundred. With the number two hundred. You did it real well with the number one hundred. I'm imagining you could do it pretty well with the number two hundred.

Claire's connections have evoked an interesting thought for Samuel, who now tries to express his idea.

Samuel: You know what? It's like people could use those things (pointing to the chart of rectangles of 100).

Claire: What would you use to help you?

Samuel: Um . . . four times twenty-five, and two times fifty, and a hundred, one times one hundred.

Claire: And how would those numbers help you with the two hundred?

Samuel: Um . . . (gestures with his hands and says) You add them.

Claire: You add them?

Samuel: Yeah.

Claire: So what would you add? Let's say four times twenty-five and you wanted to use it for two hundred. What would you do?

Samuel: I'd add four times twenty-five . . . four . . . cuatro mas veinticinco . . . cuatro . . . four veces veinticinco and the answer mas veinticinco.

Samuel stumbles and struggles as he uses both Spanish and English, trying to express this complicated idea that involves both addition and multiplication: that to (4 × 25), he will add (4 × 25) again. Claire sticks with him and his idea. Her next question encourages him to continue and reflects back to him the nugget of his thinking that has made sense to her.

Claire: So far you've told me you'd multiply four times twenty-five, and it would give you one hundred. And then how would you get to two hundred with that knowledge?

Samuel: Veinticinco (unintelligible)

Claire: And then repeat the whole thing again. So you would do . . . four times twenty-five, two times, twice. That's a good idea. I bet that would help you. That sounds like your mind's already working. . . .

Claire not only follows and appreciates Samuel's reasoning, but she also, in listening and asking questions that require him to make his thoughts more explicit, helps him to bring his idea into sharper focus for himself, for the class, and for her. Claire continues.

Claire: Isabel, any thoughts about how what you did last week might help you with boxes of two hundred this week?

Isabel: Um . . . In two times fifty like, it's one hundred and you could add fifty mores, like . . . (makes hand gestures out in front of her describing the shape of a row of fifty squares) oh you add fifty squares like . . . um . . . straight and you add fifty more. That is one hundred (the two rows of 50 she describes adding to the cut and pasted 2 × 50 rectangle) . . . so that's *two* hundred.

Claire: So two more groups of . . .

Isabel: Fifty.

Claire: Fifty, are you saying? . . . Elena, do you have a thought?

Elena: I was going to do that

Claire: Same thing? OK. Anyone else have a thought? Pablo?

Pablo describes a method that is identical to the one Samuel and Claire expressed a few minutes before. Claire praises the thinking and points out that this is the method that Samuel had described.

At this point, several children in imagining the doubling of one or another of the rectangles of 100, have begun to work on this problem in a rich and meaningful way. They make good use of the representations of 100, both geometric and numerical, that they have already created. Some, perhaps all, of the children have begun to recognize that all of the arrays of 100 can be extended to build 200. This is an important mathematical connection. In addition, this is a representation that makes the more basic idea of multiplication as repeated addition very concrete. The array representations offer opportunities to consider multiplication as taking the number of items in a row (e.g., 25)—which is constant for a given array— as many times as there are rows (e.g., 4 × 25). We have seen the students in this class begin to use these arrays in this way. That the class has embarked on this work is likely due in large part to several of Claire's teaching moves: the connection she nurtures between today's work and the children's prior work on rectangles of 100; the concrete problem context she offers; and her interest in, and questioning of, the ideas the children begin to express.

We do not know exactly what guides Claire's next choices. Yet as the next 10 minutes or so unfold, the class, under Claire's guidance, moves to a different strategy for answering this day's question about Boxes of 200. As it turns out, the strategy Claire urges her students to adopt holds less meaning for the children than the one they began with, and as Claire becomes aware of this she faces an interesting dilemma. Her resolution of this dilemma is at the heart of Claire's story.

The shift in strategy, and Claire's entry into the dilemma, begins as Claire turns from the productive and thoughtful piece of conversation that we have just seen to revisit the list of materials that children might use in approaching the Boxes of 200 problem. From there, there is a brief conversation in which Claire solicits children's predictions about the number of different boxes they will find for 200. At this point, Claire asks for "educated guesses," but is not asking for the children's rationales for the guesses. Most children guess 5, the number of boxes they were able to make for the number 100. Two children predict that they will find 10 boxes for the number 200, perhaps on the logic that with double the number contained in the box, there might also be double the number of containers. However, this is not discussed today.

Claire next asks the children to copy the chart in Fig. 4.1 into their notebooks to record their work. She reminds them that this is the same format they used for working on 100. We do not know how fully Claire has, at this point, thought through the mathematical issues that might arise by introducing this chart on the heels of the opening discussion. Although there are certainly times when learning to use conventional representational tools is an important mathematical agenda, in this context the particular table introduced turns out not to be productive. The chart that Claire asks the children to create does not match up so easily with the most recent representations of the 200 problem introduced by Samuel and others: the doubling of rectangles of 100. In doubling the rectangles of 100, children build the factors of 200 out of representations of the factors of 100 and their knowledge that 200 is 100 two times. In this kind of solution, the children work with known pairs of factors. The chart, in contrast, is organized in such a way that children are asked to consider *a* potential factor and to discover how many times that number might go into 200. The chart does not lend itself so easily to representing the work that some of the children have already begun to do on this problem.

Just 3½ minutes after Claire has asked the children to copy the chart and begin their work, she addresses the whole class again.

Claire: When do you think we'll know when our predictions can be verified? When do you think I'll know the answer to this? (Points to question on the chart paper about the number of possible boxes of 200. Pause.) Elena, when do you think I'll know the answer to that question? That statement? (Pause) What would you have to do to verify, to know what the number is?
Elena: Count the numbers?
Claire: OK. Just count them? (Pause.)

Perhaps during these 3½ minutes—as Claire watches the children hesitate, struggling with how they will begin or rebegin—she is feeling some of the discomfort she describes in our after-class interview. In the inter-

Numbers we tried	Did we land exactly on 200?		How many skips to 200?
	Yes	No	

FIG. 4.1.   Recording chart for work on factors of 200.

view, Claire's first comment about what was on her mind as she was teaching this class was: "I like to sit back and watch them go towards something. I hate to see them stumble. That's my only problem." At this moment, when the children are trying to find a way into the problem or maybe trying to understand how they might use the chart that Claire has asked them to use, Claire responds by modeling a solution strategy. Her strategy is one among several options described for related tasks in the curricular materials she uses (TERC, 1998, *Landmarks in the Thousands*) and is one that corresponds well to the chart she asks the children to create.

Claire: Do you remember skip counting on the calculator? Does everybody remember skip counting? I want to just model it for you, . . . just in case you don't remember. If you wanted to skip count by ones . . . actually I won't do by one. Um . . . I turn on my calculator. Remember this Pablo? You were here for this, right? Marta, you remember? Just listen to me for a moment then. Elena, . . .

Elena: Mm-hmm.

Claire: Can you watch and listen to me for a moment? Let's say I'm going to pick the number three. I want to skip count to two hundred. I do three plus three equals . . .

Samuel: Six.

Claire: I should have six and I do on my calculator, and now I . . .

Children: Six, nine, twelve, fifteen, eighteen . . .

Claire: And I'm keeping track. So now I'm at twelve. How many times, how many threes have I skipped through?

Children call out: Two. Three.

Claire: I'm on twelve.

Children: Three.

Claire: (Unfolding one finger on an outstretched hand for each additional three counted) Three, six, nine, twelve. (Claire now has 4 fingers out.)

Children: Four.

Claire: (Counting as she adds in each new 3 to her running tally on the calculator) Five, six, seven, eight, nine, ten, eleven, twelve. I'm on thirty-six. . . . Thirteen, fourteen, fifteen, sixteen, seventeen, eighteen, nineteen, twenty, twenty-one, twenty-two. Twenty-two and I'm on sixty-six. Am I any closer to one hundred?

Children: Yes.

Claire: Twenty-three, twenty-four, twenty-five, twenty-six, twenty-seven, twenty-eight, twenty-nine, thirty. What number should I be on now?

Claire continues in this way until she reaches 33 threes equals 99. As she adds in the 34th three, a few comments are exchanged about what number

34 threes has landed them on and about whether 3 would go evenly into 300. Then Claire says:

Claire: So think back to how you used it last week. You did a good job of it last week. Record every number. Whether it works. Or it doesn't work. . . .

So I will give you calculators and I will give you the three hundred chart.[8] I would . . . Actually, you know what, I think that I will give you calculators first. (Now pointing at the chart paper on the board from which the children have copied the record-keeping chart into their notebooks) Please record the numbers you try. Give me an answer, either yes it goes to two hundred or no it doesn't, and then tell me how many skips it took you.

Claire has now chosen a solution strategy for the children and instructed them in it. It is unclear what connection, if any, the children see between their initial thoughts about the doubling of rectangles of 100 and this strategy of skip counting on the calculator. It is also unclear what the children understand about the relevance of this new strategy for this problem, and whether, for instance, any of them understand that each addition of a certain number on the calculator—5, for example—corresponds in the array model to the addition of a next row of 5 in the $5 \times \_$ rectangle they are testing out. The calculators may have addressed Claire's discomfort with the children's initial 3½ minutes of stumbling, but they soon put her face to face with a new discomfort as she pays attention to the mathematics and notices the kinds of errors the children are making.

In the half hour that follows, children work at this problem on calculators and frequently miscount the number of times they add in the particular number they are trying out. As Claire walks around the room looking in on the children's work, she notices these errors. She sees these as including too few or too many groups of the size being counted, but she also realizes from the children's reactions that the children are not seeing these entries in their charts in the same way she is. She tries out several approaches to bringing the mathematics to their attention and in the end is dissatisfied with all of her attempts.

Claire's first conversation with a child around a miscount takes place with Sarita, who first counts 39 "skips" of 4 and records them on her chart. At this point Claire asks:

---

[8] Three hundred charts are materials that are part of the *Investigations in Number, Data, and Space* curriculum. They are 10 × 30 grids with one counting number in each cell. Claire is offering the 300 charts as a representational tool presumably because there are no 200 charts offered by the program, not because of some special significance of the number 300 to this problem.

Claire: Did you land on it exactly in thirty-nine skip jumps?

Sarita calculates again on the calculator, keeping count, in Spanish, of the number of fours she enters. This time she counts 52 fours. So again Claire notices a miscount, notices also that Sarita is unaware of the miscount, and Claire continues to try to help Sarita make some sense of the numbers she is recording.

Claire: Did you count twice when you entered some numbers? Cause I'm going to ask you, when we had a factor of four and it was one hundred, how many times did we have to do it when we wanted to get to one hundred. This time I want to get to two hundred. Think of those cluster problems we were doing. I still have four as a factor. This time what changes is the total. (As Claire says these words, she writes the following equations on a paper that she and Sarita are both looking at: 4 × ____ = 100; 4 × __ = 200.)

Sarita tries the repeated addition of 4 one more time on her calculator.

Claire: This number has doubled right (pointing to the 100 and the 200 in the two equations she has just written), one hundred to two hundred has doubled. What could happen to this number (pointing to the spaces she has left in the equations)?
Sarita: (unintelligible) Fifty.
Claire: Fifty. So you were right around there. . . .

Claire's continuing concern that the children meaningfully connect the work on 200 with their earlier work on 100 is clear from her interactions with Sarita. Yet it is less clear, for Claire and for us, what sense Sarita makes of these equations or of her work on the calculator. Does Sarita understand, as Claire does, the connections between repeated clicks of the "+" button on the calculator, repeated addition, multiplication, and the array models implied by the candy box problem?

As Claire continues to circulate, it is not long before she notices another miscount that, like Sarita's, seems to go unevaluated by the student. Elena has recorded 42 × 5 as factors of 200. Claire is concerned both that Elena evaluate the validity of this claim and that she understand the relationship between 42 × 5 = 210 and 40 × 5 = 200.

Claire: OK, I like the way you are trying to prove it. You thought it took forty-two skip jumps to get to two hundred. Forty-two times five. But it was two hundred and ten. How much are you off by?
Elena: Oh, forty (now correcting her error).

Claire: It is forty, good. . . . When you had your forty-two skips, that really counted as ten extra. So change that.

A similar interaction takes place with Pablo, who has miscounted the number of times he added the number 8. He has written that he found 26 "skips to 200" for the number 8.

Claire: Explain to me eight and twenty-six.

Pablo redoes a count by calculator and this time arrives at an answer of 25. Claire now punches some numbers into Pablo's calculator. First she multiplies 25 × 8 and notes that this equals 200, next she tries his original factors, 26 × 8, and comments to him on the result:

Claire: I have too much. How much do I have too much?

In this case, as in her interaction with Elena, Claire asks the child to focus on the product of the two factors they find and compare that product with the number 200. Although Claire sees the difference between the 208 yielded by 26 × 8 and the 200 yielded by 25 × 8 as one group of 8, in fact the 26th group of 8, she does not get the sense that the children see it in this way.

When Miguel counts 41 groups of 5, Claire again shows her interest in helping her student to focus on the meaning and value of a group in a multiplication situation.

Claire: You're saying that five is a factor. If I wanted to check this, that means that five times forty-one should equal two hundred.
Miguel: (Recalculates on the calculator, and surprised) Two hundred and five?!
Claire: Talk to me about this number.
(Unintelligible because of announcement over intercom.)
Claire: Each one of those forty-one is worth how much?

Miguel looks like he does not understand what Claire means. At this, Claire reminds Miguel of a previous class in which there had been this same confusion over the value of one group. She describes the example they had worked through in which there were a certain number of children and each child held nine pencils. They worked at sorting out how much each child was worth or contributed to the total: how many groups and how many pencils.

All of these examples, and there were others as well, stand in marked contrast to the children's beginnings on this problem, in which they imagined the doubling of a rectangle of 100. In those first approaches, children *had* ideas about how to create a rectangle of 200 that was composed of 2 rectangles of 100, and Claire supported the children's consideration of these ideas. In that context, the children's sense of dealing in a number of groups of a certain size seemed much more stable. Their work and their solutions made sense to them, and they could evaluate each outcome. With the skip counting method that Claire asks the children to use, however, their work is disturbing to Claire in its superficiality. It is clear to her that although she has offered them a strategy that they are, more or less, able to carry out, the strategy does not hold much meaning for the children; not only are they unable to evaluate their answers, but they are unable to make use of Claire's answers.

Claire puts it this way:

Claire: ... I guess I like the question part where I can go up to them and ask them to explain to me, I like that. // That doesn't put me in a position of explaining, it puts *them* in a pòsition of explaining what they did. And hopefully when their, ... for instance, when he had forty-one instead of forty, ... [groups of 5], ... but they had forty-one. Um, "how come you have forty-one?" "Because I counted it. And that's how much it came out." "OK, well, OK, could you double check it by multiplying?" and they discover that it gave them one group more. ... But then they do *not* understand that that one group of [five] is that *one* from the forty-one. ... And *that's* frustrating for me. That part. And I ... no matter what I was saying to them, even though it was clear in *my* mind, definitely they had *no* use for that at all.

SC: ... And ... what *you* were seeing in that, what that calculator said to *you* was, "there's one extra group of five. That should be forty, not ...

Claire: Right.

SC: Not forty-one." But you, as the teacher, are standing there noticing that, "geez, it's not making ..., it's not *meaning* this to these children."

Claire: It doesn't mean anything to them.

SC: And so the question in your mind, I think, I think you were saying ... "huh, what now?"

Claire: Yes, how do I ..., *do* I explain it to them or do I ask them to do it over again? Easily, they could do it over again, I could tell them "you counted wrong." I could say that and I suggested to them that they counted, and when they do that sometimes they do count wrong, so it's good to double check. // And then they would get the right one. Or easily I could tell them, "well, four times whatever is going to give you ..., check it." But, *not* easily am I going to convince them that that two hundred and five was because they have one extra group of five down in their tally count.

Having noticed this, Claire now faces her dilemma. On the one hand, she can tell: She can tell the children how to solve the problem, she can tell the children what the meaning of their miscounts is. On the other hand, she can support the children's own exploration of the meanings *they* make of the mathematical problem before them. Although the telling—the offering of a solution or an interpretation—can alleviate Claire's own discomfort at watching her students struggle, she notices that *her* strategy and *her* interpretation hold little or no meaning for the children, and so the children's struggle is just postponed. Further, as Claire notices that telling the children about her understanding of their miscounts is not getting the results she wants, she asks herself an important question. As a teacher, what can she do, beyond telling, to engage her students in an exploration of the mathematical ideas she targets? "Easily . . . I could tell them 'you counted wrong.' . . . But, *not* easily am I going to convince them that that two hundred and five was because they have one extra group of five down in their tally count." Claire had tried to tell the children where they had gone wrong, hoping they would also see the mathematics she was seeing. It is now very clear to her that this did not work, and she has some ideas about what might work better.

Claire: . . . if I had just zipped my lips and said "OK, I'll take suggestions for numbers that worked for you," and we put them all out like we did. If you noticed, maybe I should have done it that way, but I did . . . , I took all correct answers, after we had already self-corrected. (Interruption) If I had taken all that *they* thought were correct, and said "OK, you take the forty-one, here's, uh, . . . *make* me forty-one groups, make me,"

SC: Out of?

Claire: Snap cubes. What happens? So,

SC: As opposed to using the calculator.

Claire: As opposed to using the calculator. Or . . . we could do the three hundred chart, but I think it's much more . . . manageable

SC: So you think the group, the notion of sets of five, or sets of twenty, or sets of something would be something that,

Claire: Might clear it up more than, not clear it up, but might cause them to say "oh, wait a minute, I have one group of five that I don't need here."
    . . .

Claire: I'll try it this afternoon. I mean, I can try it today or tomorrow with them, and say "OK, *somebody* got forty-one, but let's look at if we used forty-one groups, what would happen . . . ?"

Here Claire's idea is to ask the children to more explicitly represent the 41 skips of 5 they have taken on the calculator. She has begun to think that if they are unable to assess the mathematics in the numbers-only representation of the calculator, it would be a good idea to offer children materials with which they can represent what they *do* know about those numbers. She is now thinking that, for these children, building a physical representation of the groups—not so different from the children's initial work doubling the arrays of 100—would be a more effective way to make sense of this problem than was her own telling of the sense it made to her.

A few months later, in March, Claire describes a shift in her teaching practice that is consistent with her after-class thoughts on that December day.

> Claire: . . . I have to understand my word isn't gospel. Sometimes they come up with something that would be . . . , that . . . , it makes more sense for them. And I also have to think I'm this adult looking at it and they're a child looking at it. It makes . . . that's a huge difference. It really is. I can say "it doesn't make sense to me, because you're four off, you're four over, you went beyond," but I don't always think that they see that as going four over or four beyond.
>
> . . .
>
> So I guess I have to push them to find another way and, you know, and that's when you see . . . , and the way I'm *doing* it is "OK, prove it to me. Show it to me. Draw it for me. Show me how you got it."

In March, as we see in the classroom conversations that follow, Claire's students are proving, showing, drawing. By March, the children's representations of problems are more at the center of their work in class. Claire now works to support her students' representing to themselves, and to her, their own understanding of a problem. These representations become tools for solving the problem and illuminating the mathematics. Claire expects that children will represent to themselves the problem at hand, that they will do so in a way that is meaningful to them, that these representations will be the basis for children's solutions, and that, should any errors or questions arise, the children's own representations of the problem will be their starting place in working out whatever requires further attention. Claire's own work with her students now stays connected to these starting places.

In March, the children are still, or perhaps again, working on issues of multiplication and division. Claire asks the class to consider this problem: If she were to give 1 pencil to each of the 13 children in class today, and pencils come in packages of 12, how many packages would she need to buy? Soon Samuel says that Claire would have to buy 2 packages.

> Claire: I would need two packages. Why?
>
> Samuel: Because if we are thirteen . . . Because we'd just need one more pencil for everyone to have one.

Claire: So I would have to buy another . . .

Samuel: Package.

Claire: And when everybody had their thirteen pencils, their pencils, everybody had one pencil, how many pencils would I be left with?

Several children say "11," one voice offers "12." Claire calls on Pablo, whose answer was 11.

Claire: Why?

Pablo: 'Cause if . . . if in one package brings . . . um twelve and you're giving everybody one pencil . . . one person one . . . you need another package and you'll get . . . you will keep eleven pencils.

Claire praises Pablo's thinking and how he expresses it. She then walks through Pablo's model of the problem a little more explicitly than Pablo had. With packages of pencils in hand, she points around the circle of children, commenting that the first package will be all used up in handing out one pencil to each of the 13 children present, but that Carlos would have been left out, he wouldn't have gotten one. They would need to open a second package to give Carlos one also, and then she would be left with 11 pencils in that second box.

Claire puts up on the overhead, a copy of the questions that the class will be working on today. She asks the children to read the questions to themselves and then asks for them to be read aloud to the class. At the top of the paper, it says: "Pencils come in packages of 12." Question 1 reads: "How many packages of pencils do you have to open to give 2 pencils to everyone in our class?" (TERC, 1998). The second and third problems ask this same question about the number of packages that must be opened, this time to give each class member 4 pencils or 6 pencils. After the first question has been read, Claire clarifies that they will be using their full class size, 21, for these problems.

As with the class in December, Claire again asks for predictions and discusses materials. Unlike in December, however, this time Claire expects children to devise their own approaches to the problem.

Claire: My goal for you is that you get question number one answered in two different ways. So I would like to see question number one answered in two different ways. Here are the choices you told me you would use. (Claire writes these on the board as she speaks.) These are your choices: calculator, graph paper, snap cubes. I need question number one answered in two different ways. Either using the calculator and the graph paper, or using the graph paper and the snap cubes. In any event, I need a picture and I need a number sentence. One thing that is important is you're telling me how many *packages* I have to open. How many *packages*, not how many pencils did I give everyone. How many packages did the teacher open? We're basing it on *how* many children in the class?

Several children: Twenty-one.

Claire: Twenty-one.

By now Claire has passed out a paper with the questions for today's work, graph paper, and calculators. Next she puts out the snap cubes. The children get to work on these problems: Some are building with snap cubes, some are drawing on the graph paper. Claire circulates. She comments in our after-class interview about this point in the class, about her feelings on passing out the snap cubes.

I was wondering how they were going to use them. / / And my temptation was to say "No, look, build four boxes, will you? Please build four boxes. (laughs) And each one's a pencil." That was my temptation, (Claire, second interview, March 17, 1997)

Claire's feelings now are similar to those she expressed in December. It is still difficult for her to watch the children engage in their own struggle with a mathematical problem. It is still a temptation to offer her wisdom in the form of a ready-made solution. In December, that solution was skip counting on a calculator. In March, she is tempted to tell children how to use the snap cubes to represent four boxes of pencils. However now in March, Claire resists that temptation and takes a different action to address her mathematical goals for the children. She encourages and supports the children's attempts to represent the problem in a way that makes sense to them—in a way that Claire trusts they will learn from if she supports and encourages a careful exploration of these representations.

We see this in Claire's work with Luis. She comes to Luis asking questions about the meaning of his work. In doing so, she gains some understanding of his approach, and *his* connection to the meaning of his representation is, if anything, strengthened as both he and Claire put it into words.

Claire: How are you working it?

Luis: (with pairs of snap cubes on the table in front of him) Two snap-its.

Claire: What do these two mean?

Luis: These are two pencils for each kids.

Claire: So do these mean two pencils? These are two for Enrique, two for Carmen, two for Samuel . . .

Luis nods yes in answer to Claire's questions. As she stands back to watch and listen a little more, Luis begins to give classmates' names to each of the pairs of cubes in front of him. He soon shifts to *counting* the pairs, each pair being a "one," and is satisfied when he reaches "twenty-one" pairs of cubes that he has the correct number.

He now begins to stack these pairs of cubes into towers of 12. He composes the first tower, counting by twos as he adds each pair of cubes: "two, four, six, eight, ten, twelve." Luis recounts the stack of 12, this time by ones, and lays the tower down, patting it and now counting the whole stack as "one." He continues in this same way composing two more packages of 12, then stacks the remaining six cubes, counting: "one, two, three, four, five, six." Luis, now sure he has solved this problem, calls to Claire who is across the room: "I know the answer."

By his actions, we see that Luis has not only arrived at an answer, but has taken the opportunity in his counting and recounting of the same cubes to explore, a little, the relationships among single pencils, the 2 pencils per child of the problem, and the 12 pencils per package. It is this nesting of groups within groups, it is the *multiplication* of this problem, that makes it complicated and worth the hard work that Luis invests.

Pablo, who has worked on this problem similarly, seems to have a good understanding of the general structure of this problem, but he miscounts. Here Claire faces a situation that is reminiscent of the miscounts in the December class, but it plays out differently now. Claire focuses, along with Pablo, on *his* representation. Together they take a careful look at how he has structured and represented the problem. In doing so, Pablo is able to solve the problem.

Claire: Pablo, any solutions?
Pablo: Yes. Four packages, but with seven left over.
Luis: Six.
Pablo: No. Seven.
Claire: Can you show me? Can you show me the packages?

With this question, Claire shows her own willingness to examine Pablo's representation of the problem and invites Pablo to be even more explicit about his representation. In doing so, she does not disengage from her sense of the mathematics, but now with Pablo, as with Luis, she uses her mathematical understanding differently than she did in December. Pablo accepts Claire's invitation and uses the cubes in front of him to build 3 towers of 12 cubes each. He composes each of pairs, counting by twos to 12. At reaching the first 12, Pablo says "one package." He continues until he has before him 3 packages and a stack of 5 cubes. Claire asks him a question that I am unable to hear, and in response Pablo begins to pull the packages apart into their component pairs. He counts 6 pairs in the first package. Claire also counts 6 and then points to the second package and says "six more." Pablo pulls this package apart into its 6 pairs and does the same with the third package, counting.

Claire: Eighteen.

Pablo: (pulling the 5 cubes into 2 pairs and a singleton, and counting) Nineteen (one pair), twenty (the second pair), twenty-one (the singleton).

Claire, picking up the singleton that Pablo has counted as "twenty-one," looks at Pablo and smiles. A broad grin spreads across his face as well, as he picks up one more cube to complete that pair. He needs one more cube, and he understands exactly why.

Now in March, Claire creates for Pablo, Luis, and all of her students an opportunity to represent what they understand about this problem. As we see with Pablo and Luis, Claire's choice to provide children with the materials and the opportunity to represent what they understand allows them to solve the problem and to address errors. Within these representations, the children capture the structure of this multiplicative situation. They capture the complicated relationships among children, pairs of pencils, and packages of pencils. In doing so, they work toward understanding more than just *this* problem, but problems of this kind. Claire has invited the children to represent their own thinking, their own understandings about a problem, as a way to build on their knowledge.

Larger Data Set as Context for Claire's Classroom Story

Portfolio writing from 17 of the 23 teachers in the seminars suggests classroom practice changes of the kind or direction that Claire's story illustrates. Two examples follow. In the first example, a teacher describes her interaction with a preschool student. The child had shown the teacher evidence of an ability to count to at least 13 and to reason about the relative quantities of numbers into the teens. When the child later exclaims that 10 and 10 is 5, the teacher responds in a way reminiscent of Claire's teaching in March—by offering the child materials with which to model the situation.

The third child, Evie, is a child who shows pretty good skills overall. She counted carefully to 13. She was able to tell me which stack had more cubes over several trials. She also could tell me which number was more, 16 or 3, 12 or 2, 5 or 9.

She then said, "I know what 10 and 10 is. It's 5." She was excited by this and so was I! Because of the work we have done in the seminar, I think I reacted to her answer in a very different way. In Sept., I probably would have taken the cubes, made two ten stack[s] and helped her to count to twenty so she could get the right answer. Instead I asked her if she could use the cubes to show 10 and 10. (Preschool teacher and special education resource teacher K–6, Portfolio Assignment 2.1, February 4, 1997)

This teacher, like Claire, has changed her practice so that she and her students ground their work in the children's explicitly represented thoughts. The teacher quoted next speaks of a similar focus in her teaching, and the story she tells also points up some of the delicacy of this kind of work.

Valentine's Day needs prompted my presentation of the following problem to my first grade class:

> I want to buy enough heart stickers so that each child in first grade has 3. If we have 13 children in our class, how many stickers do I need to buy?

I have been working this year to help my students expand the ways they have both to solve problems and to represent their thinking. Most of the students in my class are now comfortable pursuing a solution to problems of this type, and will make choices of manipulatives, drawn pictures, or a combination of the two to support their verbal explanations of their thinking as well as their answers.

. . .

One of the boys who had originally wanted me to just get on with it by buying two packages of stickers had worked independently, using the yellow jewels, which are strings of three. He counted out 14 strands, then counted each individual jewel, to get 42 for the number of stickers I would need to buy. He said he had 13 strands for the 13 kids in the class. I suggested that we count the strands to check and when we arrived at 14, he seemed deflated. To try to keep him focused, because he often struggles and I could see he had worked hard, I asked him why he had chosen the manipulative he was working with. I lost the moment with him because he answered "Because everyone likes yellow." I'll never know if he had seen the potential for considering both 1 child and 3 stickers together by using this manipulative, although I suspect that he did because his original answer was so close. I asked him how we could figure the answer using 13 strands and he said that he didn't know—the moment had passed for him. I felt very frustrated because I couldn't help him work through his feeling of "being wrong" to see what was right in his solution. The class had begun to drift, so only a few kids were still focused enough to build on his thinking, and answer my questions about how using this particular manipulative gave us a unique perspective on the problem. (Grade 1 teacher, Portfolio Assignment 2.2, February 26, 1997)

Although in the particular moments that this teacher describes for us, this child is unable to articulate his thinking, and the teacher chooses to let it go for the time being, it is clear from the teacher's writing that in this class there will be other opportunities to build on these thoughts. Like Claire, this teacher has taken the stance in her teaching that she will encourage students to explicitly represent their understandings and to reflect on them as a means to work through complicated mathematics. In Claire's class in March, and in both the jewels and stacks of 10 vignettes, we see classrooms in which the students' struggle to make sense of some piece of mathematics is brought out into the open so it can be better understood.

The importance of this—opening up for inspection ideas that are still ill-formed, of bringing to light one's understandings, however strong or weak at the moment—is something that some of the seminar participants spoke about learning from their seminar work on fractions. Tamar, a preschool teacher in one of the DMI seminars, is articulate about her own experience of struggling with the division and multiplication of fractions, and that it changed her response to her students' intellectual struggles in class. In an interview in June of the seminar year, Tamar says:

> Well, I don't know if it's something I've been thinking a lot about, but I enjoyed, or I should say I got a lot out of the work we did on, / (laughs) / on the divisions . . . on the division of fractions / /, and multiplication of fractions. Um, . . . just because I think I was really *challenged* to look at *numbers* in a different way. And um, . . . you know, I had learned how to *solve* them, and I was pretty *confident* that I was doing it correctly, / / but it had always been hard for me to look at those kind of problems in context. You know, if I ever had to, um, you know, in a real life situation, um, come up with some kind of solution to those problems, I would be *lost*. / / Um, but I think diagramming, um, the problems the way we did, you know, different pie slices or you know, bolts of cloth or whatever, and um, looking at the problems as *word* problems, and also we went back . . . , I think it was [the seminar facilitator] who suggested to one of my small groups one day to um, go back and think of the problems as a whole number problem / / and think about what you're actually doing. Um, you know, instead of three fourths and one sixteenth, / / you know, times one sixteenth, you know, think of a whole number and think about what multiplication is actually *doing* to those numbers. / / And I think it just gave me a, a greater understanding of math, one that I've . . . or of these operations, one that I've never *had* before. And, you know, it's just um . . . , it's just kind of *empowering*, you know, you're, . . . *I'm not a dummy*. / (Laughs). / You know, I can really do this. If somebody had taught me the right way, um, you know, I could have been a mathematician. You know, it was like a really good feeling about yourself and um, you know, it, it, I think it also helped me to empathize, . . . , with the kids, and sort of see how they're feeling when they struggle with ideas. Um, and I, when I did it I really wanted to get it, I really wanted to understand it, but there's also times when, you know, "We're running out of time, we only have two more minutes," and, you know, and you're like "Oh, I know I'm going to get it if I could just," and so a lot of that was, was helping me understand, you know, what kids are sort of *facing* in their math classes.

SC: So did it change how you feel about watching kids struggle? I mean, does it,

Tamar: It did. I think it did.

SC: What does it make you want to do about the struggles you see kids go through?

Tamar: Well, it makes me, um . . . , want to . . . , I mean, I wish there were, there were ways that I could be like [my facilitator], and just come over and give them, like, "Well, think about it in terms of whole numbers," // and you know, just help their understanding with just like a little phrase like that. Um, but also, um . . . , you know, to give them *time* to struggle with ideas, and give them *opportunities* to talk about it, talk with *friends* about it. I mean, we worked on those in *whole* groups, and um, a lot of understanding comes from different people explaining it at different times of your, you know, struggle. Um, so that, you know, kids that can talk about it with peers and, um, you know, talk about it in class, and you know, all those kind of things.

SC: Is that different from how you used to, I mean, did you used to have more patience with the struggle, less patience with it, avoid it?

Tamar: I used to have *so* much less //, um, patience, you mean, with kids?

SC: Yeah, as you watch kids struggle, I mean, more tolerance for their struggle, or a different value for it or something.

Tamar: No. I, I don't think I *understood* what they were doing. I would just, you know, they would have some problem or whatever and I would just go over and give them the answer. You know, and, you know, "That will be it. That's enough. We have to end snack now and you know, let's move on to something else." You know, just *give* them the answer, um, move on quickly, . . .

Both Tamar and Claire place new value on student struggle or engagement with ideas. Neither teacher is now content with offering her students a ready-made solution. Each of them believes that something important happens when a person has the opportunity to represent a problem in his or her own terms—terms that make sense to him or her—and then reflect on that representation for what it holds mathematically. Neither Tamar nor Claire wants to short-circuit this process now.

ORCHESTRATING CLASSROOM INTERACTION AROUND DIFFERENT REPRESENTATIONS OF DIFFERENT IDEAS

In the next story, Liz's story, we see a teacher who supports her students' explorations of their own ideas. Liz, like Ella and Claire from the first two stories, encourages her students to hold their ideas still long enough that they can describe or represent them. Like Claire, Liz makes deliberate use of children's representations to solve and illuminate problems. Yet in Liz we also see a teacher who asks children to consider one anothers' representations, consider their conflicting points of view, and work both independently and jointly at building a better understanding of the mathematical topic. Ideas in this classroom are held by individuals, of course, but they are also shared and worked on by the class as a whole. Each child's beliefs, questions, uncertainties, and points of view help enrich the representation that evolves as the class works together. Through it all, Liz has a complicated set of mathematical issues to sort through. Through it all, Liz orchestrates.

Liz's Classroom Story: Working Together to Build New Representations

Liz begins math class on a Monday in May by reminding her fourth graders that on Friday they had been considering the fractions 5/3 and 6/5: what those fractions might look like if you drew them, and which one was the larger fraction. In Friday's class, Liz noticed there was a good deal of confusion about these numbers, and so she brings the issues up with the class again. She reports that on Friday some children thought that 5/3 was the bigger number, others thought that 6/5 was the bigger number, and there were different thoughts about what a drawing of these numbers might look like. Liz puts out for consideration four student drawings that she copied from the blackboard after their Friday discussion. Today she asks the children to respond to these, first in their journals and then in class discussion.

Liz turns on the overhead projector to show the class the four student drawings she would like them to consider (Figs. 4.2, 4.3, 4.4, and 4.5).

Liz: Kayla told us that she thought five thirds was the bigger fraction, and her way of representing five thirds was to show this picture. . . .

FIG. 4.2.   Liz's presentation of Kayla's representation of 5/3.

Ben told us that he thought five thirds was represented in this way.

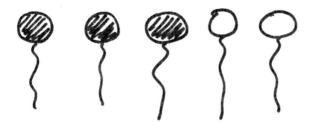

FIG. 4.3.   Liz's presentation of Ben's representation of 5/3.

Evan told us that he felt that six fifths was bigger and that it was represented with this kind of a picture.

FIG. 4.4.   Liz's presentation of Evan's representation of 6/5.

Maggie told us that six fifths was larger and she said that *this* is what six fifths looked like.

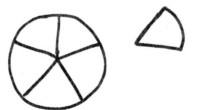

FIG. 4.5.   Liz's presentation of Maggie's representation of 6/5.

So, what I'd like you to do is pick *someone's* thinking this morning, and I would like you to tell us *again*, which one of the people's thinking do you most agree with? Talk about what does six fifths look like, if it looks like one of these, or what does five thirds look like. And if you want to, tell us what you think is the answer to which is bigger, six fifths or five thirds.

So you're going to have a journal entry this morning that will tell us about your thinking. And you can pick a question here, or you can pick an idea that you see from someone's work.

With this, Liz has invited the children to consider their own and their fellow students' ideas and provided some time for each student to gather his own thoughts and privately express them before joining a larger discussion of the issues the drawings raise. Liz tells the children they will work at this for 6 or 7 minutes, sets a timer, and begins to circulate. The children are working independently writing at their desks. Liz's interactions at this point are to help students focus on a question to write about and to consider the student work on the overhead. The following is a sample interaction with a girl who, when Liz passes by her desk, is looking around not yet writing.

Liz: Did you choose a question to answer?
Jill: Yeah.
Liz: Can you just tell me what your gonna uh . . . talk about from up there?
Jill: I think "What does six fifths look like?"
Liz: What does six fifths look like? So you're gonna answer that question. And does one of your classmates have a good answer that helps you?
Jill: Yeah.
Liz: So, . . . you might talk about how, then . . .

After about 7 minutes, Liz invites those students who feel ready to come form a circle on the floor by the chart paper where they will begin the discussion. Liz also offers to those who are still working on their ideas that they can finish up and join the circle as they become ready. Six children come to the chart paper area at this point. Liz asks whether anyone would like to go first in sharing their ideas. Vanessa volunteers. She is the first to speak in a discussion that continues for about 40 minutes.

Vanessa says that she agrees with Maggie that 6/5 is larger than 5/3, but she disagrees with Maggie's drawing. Vanessa believes that Maggie's drawing shows too small a quantity, and she begins to draw what she believes the number 6/5 refers to. Her first drawing consists of six circles each divided into fifths (Fig. 4.6).

FIG. 4.6. Vanessa's first representation of 6/5.

Over the course of the next few minutes, Vanessa alters this representation by taking the five fifths of the sixth circle and passing them out to each of the other five circles. She now draws a diagram just beneath her first one that looks like five iterations of Maggie's drawing (Fig. 4.7).

FIG. 4.7. Vanessa's second representation of 6/5.

Then on considering this representation, Vanessa decides that if she is going to have six pieces in each grouping, she should have drawn five circles, each divided into sixths. She draws Fig. 4.8 beneath her first two representations.

FIG. 4.8. Vanessa's third representation of 6/5.

Vanessa does not articulate any more of her thinking than this at this time. Yet we might, for a minute, consider her representations and the mathematical strengths and weaknesses each embodies. Initially, Vanessa's drawing of six wholes, each divided into fifths, may seem a curious representation of 6/5. Yet consider the number 1/2. One way that we can imagine this number is that it is one whole divided into two equal pieces; from the whole we then take one of the two pieces and that piece is 1/2. Similarly, we can consider 6/5 to be six wholes each divided into five pieces, and from each whole we take one 1/5 size piece to get 6/5. Vanessa's initial drawing creates six wholes each divided into fifths. What she has not done is take out only one fifth from each whole to yield 6/5.

In Vanessa's second drawing, she distributes the pieces of the sixth whole so that she now has five correct drawings of 6/5. We do not know what Vanessa's intentions are here. Could she be taking six wholes, distributing them so as to make five equal-size portions, and so carrying out the division—6 divided by 5? The slippery idea here is that 6/5 refers both to the division, which she has carried out, and the result of the division—one portion. It is this part that is missing from Vanessa's second representation. Yet one strength of this representation worth noting is Vanessa's understanding that we can take pieces of a whole and discuss those. We need not stick only with whole numbers. This is necessary if she is to compose the quantity 6/5. Her representation allows for the creation of fractional numbers larger than one while preserving the 1/5-ness of each slice.

As Vanessa continues to consider her drawings and changes her drawing into five wholes, each divided into sixths, she recognizes that each group of six 1/5-sized slices could be thought of as forming their own whole. That is, Vanessa now shifts to seeing the quantity of 6/5 as the whole and it has six parts, and this she sees as the defining property of sixths. If you take six 1/5-size portions, you have six portions, which raises the question: Do you then have sixths? She is confused about the difference between one whole *pie* (or whatever her circle represents), which might also be called 5/5 or 6/6, depending on the partitioning, and the whole *quantity* 6/5.

Vanessa's drawings hold much to consider—for Vanessa, for her classmates, and for her teacher. So far in the class little of this has been put into words. The drawings remain up, however, and now Liz invites Maggie to respond to Vanessa and explain her own thinking about 6/5.

Liz: Maggie do you wanna talk to Vanessa? Do you wanna go up and help Vanessa . . . or help other people get their questions answered? (Maggie goes to the chart paper.) Because people, I think, are still questioning your idea and Vanessa's got, she has *several* different ideas now since she started with her thinking. . . .

(Maggie at the chart)

Liz: If other people are ready to join the group, bring your chairs up to the outside of the group and to the back there, so you can see and hear them. Maggie?

Maggie: Well what I was trying to show was six fifths.

Liz: OK, do you wanna give us a little demonstration to help us out?

Recognizing that the children need Maggie to be more explicit than this if they are to understand how she sees her drawing as capturing 6/5, Liz encourages Maggie to say more, maybe even draw more.

(Maggie begins drawing next to Vanessa's drawing. She makes a circle.)

Liz: You know what Maggie, just to keep things clear, if you could draw a line under Vanessa's work, and put yours below that, that would be helpful. (Maggie draws a line across the chart paper under Vanessa's work.) Just put "VS" in that circle up there that you just drew. We'll know that's Vanessa's work. (Maggie writes "VS" in the circle.) Great.

In asking Maggie to keep her work and Vanessa's work separate, Liz helps maintain the integrity and clarity of each representation or thought.

(Maggie writes her own initials under the line and begins to draw) (see Fig. 4.9).

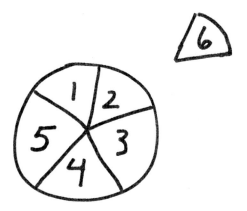

FIG. 4.9.   Maggie's representation of 6/5.

Liz: Ben what's your question?

Ben: (referring to Maggie's and Evan's drawings on the overhead that children considered at the start of class) Like Evan's and Maggie's and Jan's are like the same. Just Maggie took out the piece that, that like eaten

Liz: Maggie took out the piece and Evan left it in so you see those as being the same picture?

Liz paraphrases Ben's comment and, by her tone of voice, asks for more information. Ben and Evan make this thought a little more explicit.

Ben: Yeah. Yeah like hers, if she colored um . . . if you take the five right there, are the five that Evan colored in and the one right there is the one that he didn't color in that hasn't been eaten yet.

Evan: Yeah, she, I mean instead, instead of her coloring them all in she just, like, took *one* out.

For Ben and Evan, Maggie's drawing is the same as Evan's because each shows a group of five pieces and a sixth piece that is somehow separated from these five. They equate the 5/5 of Maggie's drawing with the shaded in 5/6 portion of Evan's drawing. They also equate the 1/5 outside of Maggie's circle with the unshaded 1/6 piece of Evan's drawing. This would, in fact, be sensible if the area of the shaded 5/6 of Evan's circle was equal to the area of Maggie's whole circle. Evan would have just drawn a differently shaped 5/5. This is not a part of this conversation, however. Nor is this the usual assumption made by these children as they draw circles to represent wholes.

However, the idea that Ben and Evan come close to articulating is similar to one that was implicit in Vanessa's transition from her second to her third drawing. If we have six pieces, then we have sixths. Maggie addresses this question shortly:

Child: Well I thought it was supposed to be when you *made* it, when you made it out of the oven.

Liz: Let's see what Maggie has to say. Maggie just . . . these two boys are having a conversation. They think yours and Evan's are the same.

Maggie: Well Evan's, to me shows sixthses. And then there's six.

For Maggie it is clear. If you divide one whole into six parts, that is different from one whole into five parts plus one more part.

Boy: (correcting her pronunciation) Sixths.

Evan: (addressing Maggie's comment that his drawing shows 6ths) Yeah, but I colored five in.

Jacob: So does *yours*. So does yours. It has six.

Jacob agrees with Evan, Ben, and Vanessa. He sees Maggie's drawing as representing sixths.

Liz: Let's . . . Can Maggie finish her statement please? And then, because Maggie, Evan, you're talking about something right here, let's have, let's *listen* to what they're trying to talk about. Maggie, what did you say to Evan just now? You think . . .

Maggie: The picture looks like it's more like groups of sixthses.

Liz: Why do you think it shows sixths, Maggie?

Maggie: Because there are six pieces in one circle.

Liz: And you don't think yours is the same as his?

(Maggie shakes her head "no.")

Liz: Why not?

Maggie: Because, um, I took one piece out and I left five in one circle. It makes six fifths.

Liz: So how is yours different from Evan's, if Evan's is sixths? (Long pause.)

Liz asks Maggie to put into words the difference between her representation of 6/5 and Evan's representation that Maggie has just said is sixths. But Maggie does not have an answer yet.

Liz: What do you think yours shows Maggie? (Pause) What does your big circle show?

Maggie: It shows a group of five.

Liz: A group of five. What do you call groups of five?

Maggie: Fifths.

Liz: So could you count those groups of five for us so we can kind of hear what they sound like?

Maggie: (pointing to the numbered sections of her circle) One, two, three, four, five.

Liz: Are they pieces?

(Maggie nods "yes.")

Liz: Do ... if ... Are they pieces of *one* whole?

(Maggie nods "yes.")

Liz: Is there another name for those pieces?

Maggie: Five fifths.

Liz: Five fifths. Could you write that, write something down about that? Five fifths. How would that look in writing, Maggie?

Maggie looks for several seconds and then writes "5/5" to the left of the circle partitioned into five pieces that she has drawn.

Liz: And where are those five fifths Maggie?

Maggie: (Pointing with her finger at the circle that she has drawn and circumnavigating it several times) Right in there.

Liz: So that part that you have called number one, how is that related to five fifths?

Maggie: Well it's just for counting the pieces.

Liz: OK. Is there another name for that number one?

Maggie: *One* fifth?

Liz: One *fifth*? What do people think about that? Number one stands for one fifth. Justin, do you agree?

Liz, having probed to get Maggie to make explicit some of the assumptions that underlie her understanding that the drawing she has made represents 6/5, now asks the other children to assess Maggie's claim that her segment labeled "1" equals 1/5. Not only does Maggie have a chance to put more of her thoughts into words, but Liz solicits other opinions about Maggie's idea, encouraging the entire class to consider the proposition that one of Maggie's pieces is equal to 1/5.

Several children disagree.

(Justin shakes his head "no.")

Liz: Jacob, do you agree with that number one standing for one fifth?
Jacob: No, it stands for one sixth. BUT! I think . . . I don't think it's . . . the
            problem can work.

Jacob has now made the claim that was more implicit in Vanessa's, Ben's,
and Evan's earlier comments. If there are six pieces, we have sixths. Further, he believes that the problem is flawed.

Liz: OK, I'll . . . before we go to the way that you *don't* think it can
            work, I want to give Maggie time to walk through her problem.
            And you can keep your *idea*, I'd just like to see a little bit more
            about Maggie's idea up here before we move along.

Liz promises Jacob that his idea—that this problem cannot work—will
be taken up. She also works to keep the class focused for now on the question of what quantity Maggie's drawing represents.

Liz: Maggie, is there anything else you can tell us about your picture?
            (Long pause.) What does five fifths in your picture stand for again
            Maggie?
Maggie: Five.
Liz: Where is that?
(Maggie points to her circle partitioned into five pieces.)
Liz: What does number six stand for?
Maggie: That's the sixth fifth.
Liz: That's . . . Is *that* six fifths right there, that number six piece?
Maggie: Not by itself.
Liz: Not by itself? What is it by itself?
Maggie: One fifth.
Liz: That number six is *one* fifth? Could you draw an arrow or some-
            thing to that and write one fifth there? 'Cause I want to think
            about that a little bit. That piece of six equals one fifth, she said.

Liz invites the class to consider this idea that the piece outside the circle, the one labeled "6," equals 1/5. She issues the invitation by modeling—expressing her own interest in Maggie's thought. It is an interest that
grows from her understanding of the mathematics at issue. Liz continues
to hold the focus on the idea that each of Maggie's pieces, even the number 6 outside the circle, is 1/5.

(Maggie writes "1/5" and draws an arrow connecting it to the wedge-
shaped piece she has drawn and labeled "6.")
Liz: OK, anything else you want to say Maggie?

(Maggie nods "no.")

Liz: You sure?

(Maggie nods "yes.")

Liz: Are you convinced your picture shows six fifths?

(Maggie nods "yes.")

. . .

Liz: OK, Vanessa's got a question for you. Then we're gonna let Evan talk to you about his idea.

Vanessa: Well, Maggie said that that (the piece labeled "6") was one fifth, that really just doesn't make . . . I don't see . . . I kinda don't really think that that's true because

Vanessa takes up Liz's invitation to express an opinion about Maggie's point. She respectfully takes issue with Maggie's position.

Liz: Nice and loud Vanessa. I can't hear well on Mondays.

Vanessa: Because there's . . . these are in the circle, there's five pieces but . . . if you . . . and then if you have . . . that circle was never part of that circle altogether in a whole. Maggie said that's one fifth, but it was never in the circle with fifth pieces . . . with the five pieces in it, so it sounds more like it's one sixth, cause all the other ones it is five plus one is six. And . . . I just think it's one sixth and not one fifth.

Vanessa has now articulated more clearly her position that was implicit before, and that Evan, Jacob, and Ben have also been expressing. Vanessa's idea is that the piece labeled "6" in Maggie's drawing cannot be a fifth if it was never part of a whole divided into five parts. Vanessa, looking at Maggie's drawing, sees the whole as the set of six pieces that Maggie has drawn. Because the piece labeled "6" is 1/6 of what Maggie has drawn, Vanessa believes that it represents the quantity 1/6. In contrast, for Maggie it is the sixth 1/5 of a circle. Vanessa confuses the whole of Maggie's drawing with the whole of one circle.

Evan, like Vanessa, focuses on the importance of there being six pieces involved in a representation of 6/5. Based on his observation that in both Maggie's representation and his own there are these six pieces, five of which are grouped together in some way, Evan believes that Maggie's representation and his representation are equivalent. He goes to the chart paper, draws a line separating Maggie's work from the space at the bottom of the page, and draws the same drawing he had drawn on Friday (a circle divided into sixths with five of the six pieces shaded). The chart paper in front of the class now looks like Fig. 4.10.

Evan begins to speak about how he sees his drawing and Maggie's as being the same.

FIG. 4.10.   Vanessa's, Maggie's, and Evan's representations of 6/5 as arranged on the chart paper.

Evan: Like, Maggie, she's got five in this circle and she took one out of
          another circle, but I just put six in my circle. And then, and then,
          instead of taking one out of . . . I just colored in, she has five and
          then I left one blank, she left one blank *out* of the group.

Daniel: I think the same thing that Evan said because the thing that's . . .
          Maggie's the one that's out, the six, if she just put it in, it would
          make the same thing as Evan's.

Liz: Do you think if she put that one fifth in, back into the pie, that both
          of those would be the same size?

Daniel: Yeah.

. . .

Liz: What do you think Maggie, would you be willing to put that number
          six back in the circle? (Maggie shakes her head "no.")

For Maggie, these drawings do not represent the same quantities. A few more comments are exchanged, and then Liz asks a question that draws attention to an aspect of the problem the children have not yet addressed. Liz, attending to both the *children's* understandings and *her own*, now introduces the question of the relative sizes of the pieces the children are considering. As Liz listens to her students, she recognizes this issue of size as an important aspect of the problem that has been missing from the children's discussion so far.

Liz: I guess I'm confused about why you want Maggie to put her part back in, and one of the things that I would ask myself, if I were looking at that—If I were . . . I wonder what's bigger.

Evan: Well they're both the same.

Daniel: (offering his thought about the conditions under which Evan's statement is true) If you put that one *in*. If you put *that* one in.

Liz: I don't see them that way though. I see . . . I see Maggie's pieces as *bigger* than Evan's pieces so I'd rather have one of Maggie's.

Evan: If she got hers (the wedge labeled "6") out of this one (the circle partitioned into fifths) they're the same, but if she got this one (the wedge labeled "6") out of another *piece* then it's bigger.

Evan has now made an important observation. He makes this observation explicit and public, and it represents a change from his thinking a few moments before when he assumed that Maggie's sixth piece came from a second circle, but was nonetheless the same as his drawing. He now makes a new point. If the sixth piece of Maggie's drawing originally came from within the circle that now has five pieces in it—in other words, if the circle was originally divided into sixths—then Maggie's and Evan's drawings are equivalent, and each of the six pieces in each of their drawings are equivalent in size. However, if Maggie has gotten her sixth piece from a different whole, then Maggie's pieces are bigger than his are.

There is a little more conversation, and then Liz goes to the chart. At this point, she decides to offer something more for the children to consider.

Liz: I just have some questions that I want people to think about. Jacob?

Jacob: I don't think the fraction works.

Liz: Jacob says AGAIN, "I don't think the fraction works." I'm not going to let that go. Um . . . (Liz draws two circles on a fresh piece of chart paper and asks the children whether they are "equal in size." The children say that they are not, and Liz draws a third circle, now asking of this one and the circle that is directly above it) Are these two equal in size?

Class: Yeah.

Evan: They look the same.

Sam: How do you get six out of five?

Liz: "How do you get six out of five?" is one of the questions that some-
         one is raising. (Liz writes this question at the top of the chart page.)

Jacob: Because you can't. It's only a fraction.

Sam has elaborated another piece of why 6/5 is a difficult number and
why some of the children are shifting to view the six pieces as the whole:
They hold the belief that fractional numbers are less than one. So as Sam
asks, "How do you get six out of five?"

Liz continues drawing. She divides her first circle into fifths and says
that this is a pie that she will share with her family. They agree that, with
this pie, each of five people in her family would get one piece. Liz boldly
outlines one of the slices of this pie and asks: "If *this* were my piece, how
much of this pie would I be able to eat?" Several children answer "one
fifth." Liz now labels (aloud, not in writing) each of the pieces of this pie
with the name of one of the people in her family. She then divides the next
circle into sixths. "If everybody in my family has a piece of *this* pie, will
there be enough pie for us?" Liz and the children together label five of the
six slices of this pie with Liz's family members' initials, as if serving up the
slices. The children say there would be enough for everyone to get one
piece and there would be one piece left over. To Liz's question about how
much of the pie would be left over, a couple of children offer "one sixth."

Liz and her class go on to establish that the whole of the pie divided
into five slices would be eaten by five people each taking one slice, and
that that whole can also be called 5/5. Further, the class labels the portion
of the second pie that would be eaten by five people each taking one slice
as 5/6. Liz, pointing to a boldly outlined slice from each of her pies, now
asks the children which piece of pie they think she would prefer. A few
children say that the 1/5 size portion would be the better one because she
would have more to eat—it is bigger.

At this point in the conversation, Liz's diagram on the chart paper
looks like Fig. 4.11.

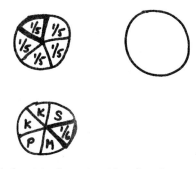

FIG. 4.11.   Liz's drawing of one pie cut into five pieces and a second pie cut
into six pieces.

Liz: . . . You think I'd want the one fifth cause it would be bigger?
. . .
Daniel: Cause one *sixth* is a bigger number and one *fifth* would have bigger pieces.

Daniel is making a distinction between the 6 of 1/6 being a larger number than the 5 of 1/5, but the quantity represented by 1/5 being larger than the quantity represented by 1/6.

Liz: (writing on chart paper what Daniel is saying) Say that again, Daniel. One fifth is the bigger number . . .
Daniel: One sixth, . . . yeah, yeah because you'd . . . with bigger *pieces*, and one sixth is a . . . a bigger *number*, but you get smaller pieces.
Liz: Smaller pieces.
(There are a few more clarifications as Liz writes Daniel's ideas on the chart.)

Although this basic work comparing 5/5 to 5/6 and 1/5 to 1/6 may provide useful food for thought for the class, it leaves at least one child still wondering about the original question.

Jacob: (unintelligible)
Liz: So Jacob says, "So how does any of *this* prove the question about the six fifths?"
Jacob: It *doesn't*.
Sam: But Maggie had another piece.
Liz: (nodding) Maggie had another piece. (There are a few seconds of low voice comments, all on top of one another.) Can anybody think of a way that Maggie could get another piece . . . of *fifth*?
Boy: Well, uh, I don't think . . .
Liz: Is there a way to get another piece that equals one fifth?
Evan: Make another pie. Take one from that.
. . .
Liz: I'm gonna use, . . . I'd like to use Evan's idea. Now Evan said, "Make another pie, get a piece from that."

Liz repeats Evan's thought and the idea is met by objections from both Sam and Jacob to the notion of using only a piece of a whole pie and leaving some of the pieces unused.

Sam: You'd still have a whole other pie.
Jacob: Yeah, you'd still have all the other pieces.
Sam: So you'd have to make another pie.

Jacob: Yeah.

Sam: And take another one from there . . .

While Sam and Jacob are concerned about the validity of any method that leaves some portion of the pie unused, Liz suggests at least trying Evan's idea.

Liz: (draws another circle and says) Well let me try what Evan is suggesting. He said "There is a way I could get six of those slices." He said "Make another pie like Maggie did . . . and take a piece." So I'm gonna try it. (Liz now divides the new circle into fifths.) So I made another pie like Maggie did. (Liz draws an arrow from the new circle to the first pie in fifths, and Sam once again brings up his thought that you can't have this other pie. Liz continues.) Take away one. (She now writes "1/5" in the slice of the newest pie that is connected to the arrow. Then, to Sam) Well wait a minute, you're like *running* with me Sam. I need to understand Evan's thought here first. (Liz boldly outlines the slice labeled "1/5" from the new pie. Liz's drawing now looks like Fig. 4.12.)

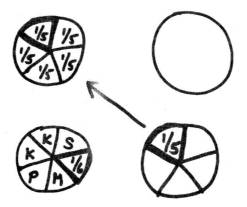

FIG. 4.12.   Liz's drawing in which there are now two pies each cut into five pieces.

So how much do I have here? If I . . . Evan said "Make another pie, and take another piece out . . ."

Child: (unintelligible)

Liz: But I asked how is it possible to get six fifths pieces? So Evan, how . . . did "make another pie and take a piece out" answer that question for you?

Evan: Well, if you got a fifth here (pointing to the new pie) and fifths here (pointing to the original pie in fifths), then you have one fifth, two fifths, three fifths, four fifths, five fifths, and then five fifths right

> there (pointing at the original circle and moving his finger in a circular pattern across the drawing), and then you want right here (points to the piece of the new circle labeled "1/5"), six fifths.

Evan has now articulated the logic behind Maggie's original drawing.

Liz: Evan said, let me see if I can say what you just said, I wanna make sure I've got this . . .

Liz paraphrases Evan's statement and adds orally and in writing that she wonders whether "$5/5 + 1/5 = 6/5$" captures his meaning. Evan is not sure whether it does, but Liz's question is an important one for the class to ponder given the ideas with which they are grappling. Although they have run out of time for now, Liz ends the class with this invitation:

Liz: It's our lunch time. I know (a few children stand up)—hold on for a minute—I know people have a lot of questions. We have a homework assignment tonight that's a little bit different than the assignment that we're working on in terms of—well *what is* six fifths and is it bigger than five thirds? Which . . . we didn't answer that question. But I *would* like people to take some time and think about the work that's here (points to her chart paper page) and here (flips back to the page with Vanessa's, Maggie's, and Evan's drawings) and if you have *questions*, I'd like you to write the questions *here* (points to some blank space on the Vanessa, Maggie, and Evan chart page) during the day, or by math class tomorrow. If you come up with some questions about the work that's here, feel free to take a marker and come up and write down those questions.
> And I really want to thank you because you did a good job of working together this morning.

Liz thanks the children for their hard work in thinking about one anothers' ideas this morning. Liz too has been working hard. She works hard to make sense of the ideas that she hears the children express and to analyze the mathematics for ideas that they are not expressing. She works to promote the discussion and conversation among them, uncovering assumptions and bringing differences out into the open to be sorted out and considered by the group. She works hard to keep the children involved and connected as the complicated and evolving ideas emerge. By issuing invitations to further discussion, like the one she ends this class time with, she works at maintaining a mathematical focus for the class that goes beyond the math period for any given day. These children in this class are involved in an ongoing exploration of the meaning of fractions. This was today's topic, but any topic that lies just outside the children's current grasp would provide fertile ground.

What if Liz had instead chosen to begin today's class by telling her children, clearly and directly, how to represent 6/5? What if, for instance, Liz had told her class that Maggie's representation was correct and the children should represent the number 6/5 that way? Given the discussion that actually took place and the questions and beliefs that surfaced in it, it is unlikely that Liz's hypothetical telling would have met with any greater success than Claire's telling did in the Boxes of 200 lesson that opens her story.

Instead, in today's class, by following the logic of the children's thoughts, Liz and her students have considered a variety of questions concerning fractions larger than one. For at least some of the students, a first question raised by this study was, is it possible to have a fractional quantity greater than 1? How might this be possible? Most of the class time was spent explicitly considering whether 6/5 is such a number? How is it composed? In what units is it measured? If 6/5 is composed of six pieces, can it still be built of fifths or is it sixths? What is the meaning of fifths when there are more than five pieces? What is the meaning of one whole with quantities greater than 1? How are the six pieces of 6/6 and the six pieces of 6/5 similar and how are they different? Most, if not all, of these questions are questions on which most, if not all, of the children are still working. Given this, of course, the original question of which is larger, 6/5 or 5/3, is a piece of mathematical analysis that lies ahead. With this day's class, however, the children in this classroom have begun to tackle these complex ideas, wrestling with the limits and strengths of their own understandings and those of their classmates.

In thinking about the mathematical work Liz has had to engage in in this one class period, we might think back to the stories from chapter 3. These stories—of in-seminar, whole-group work on fractions, and of Tamar's out-of-seminar work on counting—offer glimpses of the kind of practice and training that help a teacher deal well with on-the-spot mathematical work of the kind that Liz is called on to do.

Although we might think about the origins of Liz's mathematical preparedness to teach the class we have just been reading about, we can also think about the origins of her pedagogical preparedness. The kind of teaching and learning we see in Liz's story are related in important ways to the changes in teaching and learning that Ella's and Claire's stories illustrate. Further (and we return to this point in the concluding chapter), all bear strong resemblance to the core aspects of the DMI seminar. In Ella's story, we saw a teacher and her class change their classroom conversations. The children and the teacher came to expect, encourage, and listen to children's expressions of mathematical thoughts. Without similar expectations and classroom practices, the segment of Liz's class that we have just read would not be possible. Similarly, in Claire's story, we were seeing the development of another piece of teaching practice essential to the kind of teaching and learning that take place in Liz's story. In Claire's story, we saw that the children and teacher come to expect that the children's ideas about mathematical problems and their models of these problems would be good starting places in building new understandings. For Liz to orchestrate the group consideration of ideas as she does, she must share Ella's and Claire's convictions that her students have ideas, and that their ideas and models are good starting places for the work of coming to greater understandings. In addition, Liz brings her own ability to understand the tangle of mathematical ideas that her students are working on as she enables their work of joining together to hold these ideas up for examination.

It is the extent to which Liz holds up ideas for this joint examination—the extent to which she expects, supports, and helps the class to build on one anothers' ideas—that makes Liz's story really stand out. She works hard to get children to make their thoughts public; once a thought is made public, Liz continues to work hard at sustaining it as the focus of joint attention and reasoning. The children are the richer for it. The payoff is in the depth and solidity of the mathematics that the children articulate.

Larger Data Set as Context for Liz's Classroom Story

Liz's story is a good example of a teacher and children who engage with the substantive mathematical ideas they find in one anothers' represented thoughts. Although these practices are connected in many ways to those we saw in Ella's and Claire's stories, still Liz's teaching is not typical of the seminar participants' classroom practices after 1 year of DMI. The segment of Liz's teaching that we have just seen conveys a strong belief that student expressions of their understandings create the terrain in which teacher and students work, and Liz maintains a strong presence to do that work. The writing of the other seminar participants suggests that this is not yet a common stance.

In March of the seminar year, the seminar participants were asked to write a response to these questions:

In many of the cases you have been reading, the teacher/authors have been presenting the conversations of their students in detail. In the seminar, we have used these student discussions to analyze the mathematical ideas with which these students are working.

Turning from the seminar to thinking about teaching, what do you learn from, and how can you use your students' thinking? Describe one or two instances in which student ideas were important to your teaching.

In addition, what might be the importance or usefulness to the students of expressing their own and their peers' mathematical ideas in class? Please use one or two examples from the seminar cases, videos, your own seminar experiences, or from your own classroom to illustrate what you mean.

Of the 23 seminar participants, only 2 wrote that student expression of ideas was important to *her as a teacher* because these representations are the materials for the joint work of the teacher and students. Four more teachers wrote that the opening for student progress in students expressing their ideas came not so much in the joint examination of the idea, not so much in the back-and-forth discussion we see in Liz's story, but in the opportunity for self-correction they anticipated from children making their own ideas explicit.

These numbers are low. They are likely to be low for several reasons. First, the writing was done in March, which is still mid-year in the seminar and prior to the fractions work from which teachers learned a great deal about their own mathematical learning. Second, developing the teaching practice and articulating one's thoughts about it are two different things. In all likelihood, these teachers' practices will change prior to their being able to explicitly describe the changes and the reasons for them. In other words, although Liz's story emerges from observing her practice and is implicit in her practice, it may not be until a later time that Liz would explicitly describe the kind of thinking that makes these practices possible. Finally, it is also likely that Liz's teaching *was* unusual, and that developing this kind of teaching practice typically takes more time and support than was offered in this 1-year DMI seminar.

What was more common in the teachers' written responses to the questions posed in March were statements to the effect that student expression of ideas was important to *teachers* so they could come to know more about what their students understand which, in turn, could help them in planning for future lessons. Teachers more commonly wrote that student expression of ideas was important to *students* because it bolstered their self-esteem, built their confidence as contributing members of the classroom community, or because classmates' ideas were likely to make more sense to other children than were the teacher's ideas. All are valid points, and some are issues we look at more carefully in the concluding chapter.

A focus on joint exploration of a thought or an idea, a focus on classroom conversation as an opportunity for the building of new and stronger understandings, is one that is still growing in this group of teachers. However, although Liz's story may not be typical, neither does it stand entirely alone. Her story represents a direction of change that is shared in this group of teachers. We have already seen some connection between Liz's teaching and the kinds of change in practice in Ella's and Claire's stories. Beyond this, there is evidence from the portfolio writing that other teachers were also considering some of the issues raised by this kind of teaching. We end with one example.

Allowing kids to express their ideas helps the teacher know where they are and where to go with them. If you simply knew that they didn't get an answer, you wouldn't know why or what the problem was. Did they have a good strategy and just miscalculate? Did they lose track half way through? Did they have no idea what to do from the beginning? Listening to kids' ideas lets them tell you what the problem is.

This leads to the next step in teaching very naturally. Instead of using a set format, step by step, the next lesson is decided by the kids' needs and their expression of why they can't do it or which way they can do it. Being flexible and going with their thoughts allows them to work through their strategies and develop a better understanding.

When a child explains his math to peers there is a great deal involved. The child must be reading and interpreting his written work in front of him, thinking about and holding it in his head, speaking verbally in terms he hopes others to understand, demonstrating with manipulatives, diagrams, and/or numbers, and calculating all while keeping the end goal in sight. The other children are in a much more comfortable position. They simply need to listen and think about the ideas being presented. It is much easier to see the whole picture and keep the goal in mind. This is a nice position to be in—to be relieved of all the other duties and look at the big picture—to get meaning from or understand what is being presented. This makes me think of the reader who struggles so sounding out every word that he loses the meaning of what he has read. The listener may also be a child with the same difficulty but because he is relieved of those duties, is able to sit back and listen to the story and fill in words from the context. He gets meaning from the big picture that can be lost when getting bogged down with details.

Certainly being able to express ideas clearly is an admirable skill, although no[t] always an easy one to accomplish. Being able to sit back and interpret what is being presented allows one to think about the process without being encumbered by all the other duties. It allows the child to say "Oh, I see . . ." and follow along with an understanding. (Substitute teacher, Portfolio Assignment 2.3, March 12, 1997)

Although this teacher says little about what role she sees the teacher playing in all of this, she clearly finds it important for a teacher to develop detailed images of what children do and do not understand. This is a belief shared with Liz. She also points nicely to different roles of speaker and listener in classroom conversation and the different demands these roles place on a student. Her description makes clear the potential for listening students to sharpen their understandings, but she stops short of articulating the potential for contribution to the class discussion of a student who was listening and might next speak. She stops a bit short of explicitly outlining the potential for jointly holding and building ideas, the kind of potential we see realized in Liz's teaching. What is present in this teacher's writing are many of the building blocks she will need for moving (or continuing to move) her teaching practices in the direction we have seen Liz and others take. What we as readers might consider is what kind of support is most likely to help this teacher and others to continue to build on this challenging work already begun.

5

Conclusion

PART 1: BENEFITS TO CHILDREN

As teachers' classroom practices evolved across the seminar year, many teachers spoke and wrote in their portfolios about the changes that they were noticing in their classrooms. In the next several pages, we consider what these teachers said and what they wrote, using their reports as a source of evidence about the benefits students receive as their teachers' practices change in the direction of Ella's, Claire's, and Liz's stories from the previous chapter.

Teachers make these points. Children began to experience themselves, the subject matter, and the classroom community differently. The teachers see increased student engagement in the classroom, and it shows up in four ways: (a) The students enjoy mathematics, (b) they feel like they can do it, (c) they go further and more deeply into the subject matter than their teachers had thought was possible, and (d) a new kind of community is built.

They Like It

Teachers report that their students now enjoy mathematics. For some, this is in sharp contrast with previous years' experience. Children enjoying their study of mathematics is surely a beneficial experience, one from which they might learn not only to enjoy mathematics, but perhaps more broadly to enjoy thinking, building understandings, or, even more broadly, to enjoy themselves.

Abby, the teacher of a mixed-grade special education class who we encountered in Strand 1, comments in an interview at the end of the school year that "Everybody liked math":

Abby: You know what, [. . .] it's the first time in a long time where kids, everybody liked math this year. *Everybody* liked math. And, to see it in that,

SC: Including you?

Abby: Including me. That probably has something to do with the whole thing. But you know, I can remember a number of times where I'm looking at the clock, saying I'm going to have to tell them to knock it off now, I got to . . . , I'd be going around distributing coats on the backs of their chair. They did not want to go home at the end of the day. . . . (Abby, interview, June 9, 1997)

She continues, later in the interview, pointing out that her students not only did not want to go home if it meant interrupting their math work, but that during this year they began to concentrate on mathematics for much longer periods of time. This is a fact that surprises, pleases, and impresses her.

What I'm going to do next year is I'm starting [the day] with math and I'm starting *with* the problem, // I'm starting with a problem that needs to be solved. And what I found out this past year is that my students, when we used to do math at the end of the day, I don't know if you saw it on one of the videotapes or not, [. . .] they don't want to go home at the end of the day. //They weren't *finished* with the problem yet. They were really invested in it. We're talking about going over forty-five minutes for kids who are . . . , that I write in their ed plan fifteen minutes is their max time attention to task. I mean, they weren't totally on task that [whole] time, they need to be brought . . . but their investment, in terms of solving the problem. . . . I mean, it's understandable, because I felt the same, . . . I mean, I think everyone in the seminar felt the same way. "No, let's get the answer to that problem. We're not going any further . . ." [we said] to [the facilitators] a couple of times. (Abby, interview, June 9, 1997)

It is interesting that Abby not only comments on her students' investment in the mathematical work they are doing in class, and on their enjoyment of this work, but also draws on her own experiences in the seminar in doing so. She knows first hand the feeling of engagement with a mathematical question and the importance to a problem solver of seeing his or her work through to a satisfying conclusion.

The following examples of teacher writing also point to children's increasing enjoyment of their mathematical work:

I am enjoying the mental math activities and have been implementing mental math more and more into my mathematics curriculum. Students do enjoy this and are becoming stronger in this area. I have also been able to watch my students become more efficient at expressing their math processes in words. By integrating this skill into their daily mathematics, they have become much more comfortable with and accepting of this strategy. (Grade 4 teacher, Portfolio Assignment 1.5, November 20, 1996)

I have realized that there is a "wonder" about numbers which is abstract and difficult to conceptualize at times, although I thought I had a thorough understanding. I am continually amazed at the students' variation in levels of understanding which become so apparent in this program (as opposed to a more regimented, old-fashioned way of presenting mathematics). I really think the students feel as I do, and that many are making new number discoveries on a daily basis. These discoveries are building a new or renewed comfort with numbers for many students in my class, who, at the start of the year, said that they didn't like math. Now they are saying it is fun.

I am, and continue to be amazed at the seemingly inexhaustible array of strategies for mathematical problem solving. What has impressed me the most is the (what seems to be) innate comfort level of some students in solving problems their way, and the fact that these ways work!!

I must say that I am enjoying math more than ever before, and I am hearing more positive feedback from the general student population. The majority of students are challenged with the material, and are enjoying it. . . . (Grade 6 teacher, Portfolio Assignment 1.3, October 23, 1996)

The changes taking place in these classrooms are leading to noticeable differences in children's engagement with and enjoyment of their mathematical studies.

They Feel Like They Can Do It

The kinds of changes engendered by the strands lead to classrooms in which children not only enjoy mathematics, but also feel they can think mathematically. As the stories of Strand 3 show us, they can. As children have opportunities to experience themselves as people who can make sense of something that feels, at first, beyond them, it is not surprising that they come to see themselves as mathematically able and, perhaps more generally, feel a sense of pride and empowerment, confidence and self-esteem.

When the students are taking risks in the classroom and sharing with their classmates, I see their confidence increasing knowing that more than one procedure is "acceptable" when solving problems. A particular example that comes to mind that was important to my teaching occurred when children were sharing various responses for a problem. Several strategies were utilized to represent how the problem could have been solved. This had now become a common activity that was relatively new to students. [. . .] I had been using the "exploring" of strategies for some time and had been wondering how much the students were valuing the experience. After one particular day, a student was so enthralled by what had occurred during math he could not resist continuing to discuss his interest. We were working in a different subject area, but he was so eager to share his strategy in math, he continuously asked me if the group could continue the activity the next day. Assured that this indeed would take place, he replied, "Oh good, I love this sharing time. This is so fun!" This idea, although not directly showing me a particular unique strategy, reinforced the importance of this type of mathematical exploration. This type of feedback is so important to my teaching because it shows the comfort level and confidence building in students. . . . (Grade 4 teacher, Portfolio Assignment 2.3, March 12, 1997)

Although this child makes his enjoyment explicit—"I love this sharing time. This is so fun!"—it is in action, through his desire to offer up his ideas, through his tenacious connection to the subject matter, that the teacher reads his confidence. It is also her sense that he is not alone in the class in having these new feelings.

From other teachers we hear:

I have seen quite a change in the attitude of the children about developing alternative strategies. Students who were reluctant to find more than one way to solve a problem, now do so more willingly, and all the children are eager to share strategies with the group. Both in the videos and in my classroom, the satisfaction is evident in children's faces when they have been successful. Each success, in turn, provides the impetus for them to expand their explorations in future mathematical endeavors. (Grade 4 teacher, Portfolio Assignment 2.3, March 12, 1997)

I get a sense that they feel better about themselves. I don't know that, / / but it's just my perception, but they feel better about themselves in math. That *they* feel like if they can say something and it's valid and they have good reason for it and they verbalized it, they seem to pat themselves on the back or feel like . . . I don't know, when have I seen evidence of it? It's an expression they have or the way they carry themselves through the classroom or whatever. The way they do their homework, or come back the next morning and say, "I got it, I got it." Or the way they will offer, "I'll tell her, I'll tell her how to do it." (Claire, interview, May 19, 1997)

In fact, this was a common observation among DMI teacher participants. Several of the teachers in the seminar (7 of the 23) focused on children's increased confidence (or opportunities for improved confidence) when asked in March what the importance might be for students of being in a class in which student ideas are expressed. Sometimes, as in the next quote from Abby, teachers notice that the children's confidence allows them to try out new mathematical terrain. Abby talks about an activity that she does with her students daily. It is an activity that comes from the *Investigations* curriculum materials (TERC, 1998). Each day the children spend a few minutes writing equations for the number of the day. The first day the number is 1; each successive day the children work on the next whole number. In Abby's class, she was finding that children tended to stick to the several methods of generating these equations that had come first to mind and had been discussed in class. Yet when she writes in March, she describes a change she is seeing:

> Like, the [students], who can go beyond twenty-three and say "Well, I'm go-ing to start with thirty and count back, and end up with the twenty-three and I'm going to show her that." Or do a little, or actually do things that we haven't even presented yet, but they're showing that they already know from previous experience. // Before I wasn't getting that with today's num-ber, it was what we've already done, and here it is again, "Aren't I a good student?" // And now I think that, y'know, they feel very confident and very free in being able to do that, . . . (Abby, interview, March 3, 1997)

Abby's students approach their mathematical work with more confi-dence now. Even in this simple example, students are working at making all the sense they can of a mathematical problem before them. They are not limiting themselves to following well-worn paths, but have the confi-dence to consider all that makes sense to them at this point in time. This ability and willingness to take on the work of evaluating what is and is not a valid mathematical argument, or what is and is not a valid mathematical proposition, is an important step in a child's development—mathemati-cally, as well as emotionally.

They Go Further

> In my wildest dreams I would never imagine to be down and having, and having a child write a number line that went to a hundred in pre-school, you know? (Laughter) You know? Or that we would be doing these kinds of things. It's incredible. It's really, it's really incredible how driven they are to do it. How much they love it. How excited they get about concepts of math and // and just like, we're doing subtraction, and they're all, like they were like, (laughter) "I can do subtraction. I guess I can. Yes." (Tamar, preschool special education teacher, interview, June 6, 1997)

In this quote, we hear Tamar's amazement at what she was able to work on with her young students, and she points to the role of the children's enjoyment and confidence in allowing for this progress. For Tamar, the fact that she is supporting her young students' investigations of counting numbers, written number, and subtraction stands out from their work in previous years. Her expectations from previous years are being readjusted as she sees that even young children can and do seriously entertain complicated mathematical topics.

We hear something similar from a first-grade teacher. She notes that for the first time in her teaching experience, this year the children in her first grade have an understanding of fractions. It is this teacher's belief that her seminar experiences played an important role in this.

> We have been working with fractions in our first grade class for the past couple of weeks. Because of my work with fractions I am better able to guide the students as they explore and discover what fractions are. I am also better able to develop activities and questions which have led students to develop an understanding of fractions. For example, when I asked them to use different color unifix cubes to make a tower that shows 1/2, 1/3, 1/4 etc. . . . they have no trouble constructing it and explaining it. The same is true if I construct one and ask them to tell me what fraction of the tower is a given color. The students are also able to explain what 1/2 means. They are able to tell me that the 1 means one of two equal pieces and the 2 means it's been divided into two equal pieces. The same is true when I ask them about other fractions such as 2/3, 3/4, 4/6 etc. . . . This is the first time working with first graders that I can honestly say the students truly understand what fractions are. I do not know if this would have happened had I not participated in this seminar and experienced it firsthand as a learner. (Grade 1 teacher, Portfolio Assignment 2.8, May 1997)

The changes that the seminar enabled for this teacher, in her estimation, made it possible for her to support her own students in a way she had not been able to before. She finds that she can use her new knowledge of fractions to guide her students toward a greater understanding of this topic than she has seen among first graders before. They have gone further. Children who study a subject matter deeply, who look into the more complex issues of a topic, have the chance to experience themselves as *able* to deeply understand something and spend more than a moment entertaining ideas. Not only are the children learning more of a subject matter, mathematics in this case, but this too is likely to support a child's view of him or herself as intellectually able.

These anecdotal reports match well with findings by Cohen and Hill (2001), Gearhart et al. (1999), Brown et al. (1996), and Sconiers et al. (2003) that standardized test scores improve among students in classrooms where teachers have received professional development and/or curricular materials that (like DMI) help them focus more on mathematical understanding.

From Ella's writing there is the suggestion that this greater progress rests in part on the new kinds of relationships that the children in her classroom have formed with one another.

> My math program has changed during the course of the year due in part to the comfort level of my students working with one another and gaining ideas from one another. They respect each other and their mathematical abilities. My students have pushed the boundaries of their learning and have gone "places" in math that I have often been astounded at. I have learned so much from my can-do students. They have given me the encouragement to continue to push those boundaries in learning. What a gift and a privilege it is to be an educator. (Ella, Portfolio Assignment 2.8, May 1997)

As the students' respect for each other grows, as they look more carefully at each other's ideas, they are able to go "places in math" that have surprised and pleased Ella. She tells us that she and her students "continue to push" beyond what she previously assumed were boundaries. Ella sees all of this as having become possible, at least in part, because of the new kind of community she sees forming in her classroom. It is this community-building that we look at next.

A New Kind of Community Is Built

The strands of teacher learning that fill this book, the changes in teaching practice that fill the previous chapter, lay the groundwork for a shifting in relationships. Children's relationships to the subject matter change. Children's relationships with one another change. Children's relationships with their teacher change. There is a shift in the goals of the classroom toward greater understanding of the subject matter and of each other's thoughts about the subject matter. The community built in the process stands out to the teachers as something richer, more connected, and more respectful than the community it replaces. From the stories of chapter 4, we get a sense of these new communities. The following quotes give us the teachers' own descriptions of the changes they are seeing.

Some teachers, like the one quoted next, comment on the changes they hear in classroom discussion:

> Even the children seem to be more comfortable in raising their hand if they did a problem another way. At first I think they felt because they didn't do the problem the same way the first child who had it correct "they were wrong." The class seems to be more open to different ways to attack a prob-

lem. There is more discussion going on now. The children are definitely learning from each other. (Grade 3–4 loop teacher, Portfolio Assignment 1.6, December 18, 1996)

The kinds of interaction this teacher is noticing in her classroom have changed. She senses a shift in the children's openness to new ideas, in their willingness to discuss these ideas. She senses a shift too in what the children get from their interactions with one another. It seems likely that it is the teacher's own shifts—made possible by the seminar community— that have made the changes in the children possible.

In the next quote, Abby comments on how the changes in her teaching are changing the children's interactions with each other. She gives us one example of what she has noticed. The children's conversational style is changing as the community values shift. In the example Abby offers, the class has been studying geometric solids. Abby asks the children to categorize the solids by the number of faces each has. She has given each child a paper on which to record his or her answers. After working individually for awhile, the children are asked to find a partner and discuss their results with each other. Abby talks about what she heard children saying when they disagreed with each other and how that differs from what she used to hear.

Abby: . . . and the other child, instead of just saying "It doesn't belong there," would say, "Show me how you counted the sides." So that they're now picking up from me, um, ways to ask questions of their less able peers. // And *that* was pleasing. So all of my . . .

SC: [. . .] you were noticing in listening to your children that they were listening to each other or asking questions of each other that they didn't used to ask.

Abby: Yeah. Tremendously so. (Abby, interview, January 8, 1997)

The children in Abby's class were beginning to interact differently with one another. In some instances, Abby began to see that children were inquiring about each other's reasoning. They were providing both themselves and each other with opportunities to examine a thought to learn from it.

Finally, a Grade 1 teacher articulates the importance to her of this engaged classroom community and the importance she believes membership in it holds for the children. She also notes, with both interest and pleasure, that the children are beginning to have the same kind of respectful, reflective discussions in other subject matter areas. The new community they are building is not limited to mathematics.

Creating a classroom where students are encouraged to express their thought[s] and explore their thought processes is essential for learning. I am amazed by what I can learn from my students about who they are, how they think, and how much more easy it is for me to help them to the next step in their learning when I listen to the "why" of their answers. That there is so much information to be shared and responded to is sometimes overwhelming, but I feel energized by the dialogues we have as we explore mathematics. I am also fascinated to see similar discussions pursued by the children across subject areas—they recognize the need to integrate rather than segregate topics as they explore their world.

. . . It is important for all children, but especially young children, to begin to reflect on other people's ideas, to see how those ideas fit with their notions of the world.

. . . Part of the questioning process for me when my students share their ideas is that we see ourselves as a community of learners, and see each member of that community as a resource and an individual with ideas to share that will enrich our community. This is easier said than done. It is a slow process because of individual needs. But taking the time to listen to how and why a child is thinking about something keeps me involved in the process of their learning and keeps me learning, too. (Grade 1 teacher, Portfolio Assignment 2.3, March 12, 1997)

To this teacher, each member of the community, as well as each thought they offer, enriches the community they are building. The students in this class have the opportunity to be heard and the opportunity to hear their peers. They have the opportunity to experience their teacher as respectful and to experience themselves and their peers as respectful. They have the opportunity to experience community as a joining together for mutual benefit.

PART 2: PARALLELS BETWEEN THE CHANGES
FOR TEACHERS AND THE CHANGES
FOR THE CHILDREN THEY TEACH

This is, in fact, the kind of community that the *teachers* have been part of in the DMI seminar. As it turns out, the broad outlines of the changes that teachers describe in their classrooms among their students parallel the broad outlines of the changes we have seen among the teachers in the stories of the past three chapters.

This is no coincidence. Just as the seminar provided teachers with a learning environment that supported their growth—their development of a new relationship with the subject matter, with ideas, with colleagues—

we saw in chapter 4 that seminar participants began to change their classrooms. They moved toward the subject matter rigor and toward the family of pedagogies enacted by seminar facilitators and portrayed in the seminar cases, providing new learning environments for their students. That these new classroom environments supported the same general kinds of change among these children—altering their connection with the subject matter, with ideas, and with each other—as the seminar supported among teachers is therefore not coincidental. Indeed this was one of our hopes and intentions in designing DMI as we did.

In Part 4 of this chapter, we look at how the seminar supports these changes. For now, we stay with the teachers' characterizations of the changes they saw among their students and lay them out next to the strand structure I have used to describe the changes among the teachers. The broad categories of change described by each closely resemble one another.

The most obvious difference is in the first category of teachers' descriptions of the benefits for their students: "They like it." The teachers wrote about a change in their students' feelings about mathematics. The strands do not label this change among teachers, yet teachers participating in DMI came to enjoy mathematics, just as we have seen that their elementary school students did.

We need only look to the teacher reports from the "They like it" section of Part 1. Each of the teachers quoted in that section reports not only that her students were enjoying mathematics, but that she too, during the seminar year, came to enjoy mathematical work.

> Abby: *Everybody* liked math. . . .
> SC: Including you?
> Abby: Including me. (Abby, interview, June 9, 1997)

> I am enjoying the mental math activities and have been implementing mental math more and more into my mathematics curriculum. (Grade 4 teacher, Portfolio Assignment 1.5, November 20, 1996)

> I must say that I am enjoying math more than ever before . . . (Grade 6 teacher, Portfolio Assignment 1.3, October 23, 1996)

Further, in chapter 3, both Liz and Rose write about their enjoyment of the mathematical work they were doing in the seminar:

> Math activities made me have ♥ palpitations all over again! I had to work hard! I felt like quitting! I <u>loved</u> working with partners because I trusted that I wouldn't leave without learning something I couldn't see before. (Liz,

course evaluation, rating "math activities" 4+ on a scale of 1 to 4, May 28, 1997)

Somewhat less passionately, but no less clearly, Rose writes:

I especially enjoyed learning how and why multiplying a fraction by its reciprocal works. The mathematics activities and discussions for these sections were fun as well as useful. (Rose, DMI course evaluation)

In addition to these quotes, we might also take the level of engagement apparent in the stories from each of the strands as an index of teachers' enjoyment. The remaining benefits for students reported by teachers find easy parallels with the strands of teacher learning.

"They feel like they can do it." Teachers describe this change among their elementary students, and in Strand 1 we saw this same shift among the teachers. The seminar participants came to believe that they could have mathematical ideas. Ella offers us a strong example as she shifts from looking to others when unsure about the mathematics to looking to herself to build the understandings she needs. As we saw, she was not alone in this shift.

"They go further." As we saw with Strand 2, in both the fractions story and in Tamar's story, the DMI participants, like their students, were going further—deepening their mathematical understandings.

"A new kind of community is built." Participants in DMI were learning to be part of a strong intellectual community and learning to support the development of this kind of community. In the fractions story of Strand 2, we see evidence of teachers participating in this kind of community within the seminar. In the stories of Strand 3, we see Ella, Claire, and Liz work toward building these communities in their classrooms, learning to listen to their own and others' ideas, and to support the same among their students.

To draw these parallels is not to say that the children and their teachers learned the same things. Nor do these general characteristics capture all that the stories of the previous chapters reveal about teacher learning in the professional development seminar.

In the next sections of this chapter, we look back across the stories and evidence from earlier chapters. We look back across them twice. In Part 3, we revisit the strands, considering what DMI seminar participants learned, what they learned more quickly, and what came more slowly. In Part 4, we focus on the features of professional development using the data presented in the book to take up the questions posed in chapter 1 about the three core aspects of DMI.

PART 3: THE STRANDS REVISITED

Together the three strands (and the stories that illustrate them) describe a direction of change. We have seen teachers come to appreciate their own and their students' ability to have mathematical ideas. We have seen teachers exploring the sense that their students and that they themselves make of the subject matter of their curriculum. We have seen teachers building teaching practices in which student thought is articulated, held up for examination, and moved forward in classrooms.

So far we have considered each of the strands and each aspect of each strand individually as it contributes to this direction of change. Now we look back across all three strands and the evidence of chapters 2, 3, and 4 for an overview of what teachers were learning in the seminar and over roughly what time period they were learning it. What came relatively quickly and what took a longer time? The more fully we can answer these questions, the more ably we can shape effective professional development.

The following three bulleted points highlight interesting comparisons in timing that emerge from the data of the previous chapters. Although each bullet makes its own point, like the strands, these three findings are related and not entirely separable from each other.

- **Although teachers fairly quickly expressed the general understanding that children have mathematical ideas, it was a slower process for teachers to appreciate the mathematical place and importance of these ideas, and a slower process also to develop ways to encourage students to express and reflect on their ideas.**

Teachers fairly quickly came to express the general notion of Strand 1: that ordinary people—children and teachers—can and do have mathematical ideas, make mathematical conjectures, and pursue mathematical truths. With respect to children, this belief shows up in nearly all of the participants' portfolios by the sixth seminar session, and with respect to the teachers, virtually all write about this belief by the end of the seminar year after the difficult work with fractions. However, it is a more protracted process to (a) develop the substantial body of mathematical knowledge, and (b) develop the new understandings about teaching that together make it possible for teachers to see the potential in each idea children express.

The previous paragraph holds three important observations. We can separate them from each other and consider each in turn.

1. *DMI participants came to see children as havers of mathematical ideas before having changed their teaching practices enough to reliably elicit children's ideas or build with them.*

By the sixth seminar session (typically in late November or early December), 20 of the 23 seminar participants had come to see children as capable of having mathematical ideas and had come generally to a vision of teaching that puts these ideas center stage. However, participants were, at this same time, very much in the middle of reforming their teaching practices. We saw this in the stories and portfolio quotations from chapter 4. Teachers were learning how to focus classroom conversation on children's ideas. They were learning how to make use of represented ideas. They were learning how to make productive use of the variety of understandings that their students held. Each of these is a significant undertaking.

That DMI participants were midstream in this pedagogical work is a substantial accomplishment. Any teacher who has worked to improve her practice, any teacher educator who has worked with teachers toward improved practice, or any researcher in the field can vouch for this. Yet as we think about how to support teachers' professional growth over time, it is important to keep in mind how much of a work in progress this was. Coming to see children as people with mathematical ideas is a good beginning, and we would do well to stay equally mindful that it is both "good" and that it is a "beginning." Changes in practice develop slowly over a long period of time.

2. *DMI participants came to see children as havers of mathematical ideas before having enough mathematical knowledge to reliably and productively guide them in working with their students' thoughts.*

Although across the seminar year DMI participants had all changed their views about themselves and children as mathematical thinkers, the data suggest that it is a more protracted process to develop a body of mathematical knowledge substantial enough so that it consistently provides context and guidance to teachers considering students' mathematical ideas. We heard from teachers in chapter 3 that, by the end of 16 three-hour seminar sessions spread across 1 school year, they felt they had learned a great deal of mathematics. We also heard that they felt ready to learn more mathematics, rather than feeling they had learned all of the mathematics they needed. We saw in chapter 4 the complexity of the mathematical thinking that classroom teaching calls for—a complexity great enough that for most teachers 1 year of intensive seminar work in elementary mathematics left them very much midstream in developing the knowledge they needed.

As with the pedagogical work, the fact that seminar participants were midstream in this kind of mathematical learning is a substantial accomplishment. Yet as with the pedagogy, as we think about supporting teachers' long-term professional growth, it is important to keep in mind both (a) that 1 year offers a good beginning, and (b) even after 1 year of a rigorous seminar such as DMI, this building of subject matter knowledge was work to be continued.

This is likely to be due to both the complexity of learning to think deeply about any mathematical topic and the multitude of mathematical topics that are part of the elementary curriculum. The seminar work that the teachers of this book participated in focused on the topics of number and operations. No doubt there is more to learn about these topics, but there are also many other topics in elementary mathematics (e.g., data analysis, measurement, geometry, algebraic thinking) for future study.

3. *DMI participants came to see children as havers of mathematical ideas before seeing themselves in this way.*

In the course of the year's work in DMI, seminar participants reliably made two basic and powerful discoveries about classroom members as mathematical thinkers: Children have mathematical ideas and they themselves have mathematical ideas. Teachers first articulated their excitement about children's mathematical power. By the sixth seminar session, 20 of the 23 seminar participants had begun to write that children can and do have mathematical ideas. It was not until the end of the seminar year, after the challenging work with the multiplication and division of fractions, that 20 of the 23 participants wrote with equal power of coming to see themselves in this way. Earlier in the seminar year, of course, participants worked with their own mathematical ideas, coming to new understandings and gaining comfort and skill in following their own sense of a mathematical problem. Yet the excited declarations about teachers' own ability to build mathematical ideas—declarations that parallel the ones they make earlier about children—come after the seminar work on fractions.

It is interesting to note that for teachers coming to see children as capable of having mathematical ideas was not sufficient for changing their views of themselves. Teachers changed their views of their own mathematical power as they gained direct experience of themselves as mathematically powerful.

Although teachers came to see their own mathematical power and that of children at different times during the seminar, this difference in timing is likely to be more malleable than the other differences we have discussed (e.g., coming to see children as havers of mathematical ideas more quickly than building the new teaching practices needed to elicit and work with these ideas). For instance, we can imagine a DMI-like course that is designed in such a way that teachers first work on mathematics for themselves and only in a second-semester work through classroom cases and student work. Teachers in a course that was structured in this way would, I suspect, first come to know and believe in themselves as mathematical thinkers and would later come to see the same potential for children. Of course, we do not have data on this or, more interesting, on what different effect, if any, it might have on teachers' changing practices to come more quickly to see themselves as mathematical thinkers and perhaps a bit more slowly to seeing children in this way. However, these might be interesting issues to learn more about in the future.

• **Within the seminar itself, teachers quickly became more engaged and active mathematical thinkers. Yet it was usually a later development for individual teachers, outside of the seminar sessions, to carry out mathematical analyses of similar complexity and duration.**

During seminar sessions early in the seminar year, teachers came to engage in mathematical work with interest, confidence, and persistence. In the fractions story of chapter 3, we saw one group working in this way to understand why "invert and multiply" is a valid procedure for dividing by a fraction. Although this story took place late in the seminar year, this kind of engaged, thoughtful, and persistent mathematical work began to take place during seminar sessions that occurred much earlier in the year. For individual teachers to engage in similarly complex and sustained mathematical investigations outside of the seminar setting, however, took a longer time.

Put another way, by the end of the seminar year, teachers in the seminar sessions were regularly participating in and jointly creating mathematical discussions such as the one in the fractions story. However, at this same point in time, we saw that Tamar's story (involving an analysis of the mathematics of counting and its development in children) and Liz's story (involving complicated, on-the-spot analysis of a variety of partial understandings of fractional quantities), although they occurred, were not yet universal, nor even typical.

This comparison exposes complicated questions. It exposes questions about the role that the seminar group plays, the role that the seminar materials play, and the role that the facilitator plays in sustaining the mathematical explorations of teachers during seminar meetings. The comparison also exposes questions about individual differences among seminar participants. Is it that all teachers are first able to engage in sustained mathematical exploration in the more supported group setting of the seminar, and only after some time and experience able to pursue similar investigations on their own? And/or is the seminar work resting on the shoulders of a core group of participants who are also able, at roughly this same point in time, to do similar work in their classrooms, while others are doing it neither in the seminar nor in their classrooms?

From the stories and portfolio pieces of this book, we cannot yet tell to what extent the finding reflects each of these possibilities. A more detailed explanation of this finding awaits future research. In such an explanation, both the supports of the seminar and individual differences are likely to have roles to play. For all teachers, it is likely that the structures and social supports of the seminar allow each participant to work at the edge of her ability. Seminar facilitators, the cases and focus questions, the mathematical problems posed, and the contributions of colleagues are all likely sources of both emotional and mathematical support, allowing teachers to take their work further than they might outside of this context. At the same time, there are likely to be individual differences among teachers both with respect to their mathematical engagement within the seminar and in the speed with which they re-create that engagement in situations beyond the time and place of the seminar sessions.

- **Teachers' classroom practices changed more quickly to support children's articulation of their thoughts than they did to include productive teacher moves in response to the thoughts the children express.**

Over the course of the seminar year, teachers' classroom practices changed in ways that supported more articulation of children's mathematical thoughts. This change was relatively quick and universal. Yet it was a more protracted process—indeed a process that extends beyond 1 year's work—for teachers to develop classroom practices that consistently and productively used children's thoughts, once expressed, as the basis for the joint work of building new and stronger understandings.

If we look at each of the stories of changing practice in chapter 4 and the counts of seminar participants whose portfolio writing indicates similar change, the data are clear. Relatively early in the seminar year (by February), 19 of the 23 teachers are writing in their portfolios about the kind of change we saw in Ella's story. At this point, teachers are reporting that they and their students are increasingly focusing on children's thinking, children's ideas, and that representing these ideas in the classroom is becoming increasingly central to classroom culture. By the end of the seminar year, all of the participants had written about this in their portfolios.

If we next look at the kind of change represented in Claire's story—teachers coming to use, within the classroom, children's representations of a problem as the starting place of that child's work on understanding something new about the problem—this appears somewhat later in teachers' writing. By February, roughly one half of the teachers (11 of 23) had written about this kind of change in their practices. By the end of the seminar year, 17 of the 23 teachers reported this kind of change. This is a large majority of the participants making an important shift in their classroom practices. It is also later than and not quite the universal shift we saw related to the changes of Ella's story.

In Claire's story, the use of children's representations was primarily an individual effort or a joint effort of one child and the teacher. Liz's story takes the process a bit further. We see several different representations being considered by individuals and then by the whole class. Attempts are made to understand each representation and, in doing so, to reconcile the differences and better understand the underlying mathematics. We do not see the same widespread evidence of this kind of teacher change—at least not by March and not in teachers' written reflections about practice. At that time, only 2 of 23 participants write in their portfolios that student-represented ideas are important to them as teachers because these representations shape the mathematical terrain that they explore with their students. Even by the end of the seminar year, in my direct observations of the six mathematics classes, practice of this kind was rare.

It is interesting to consider these findings next to Lee Shulman's (2000) one-sentence summary of the dominant view of teaching and learning among education scholars. Shulman writes: "In a simple, yet deep sense, that is the essence of pedagogy: putting the inside out, working on it together while it is out, then putting the outside back in" (p. 133).

In Shulman's terms, what we have seen in the stories and teacher writing of this book is that seminar participants more quickly change their teaching practices in ways that support bringing the inside out and even getting it back in in a way that has progressed beyond the initially expressed thought. We can see this in Ella's and Claire's stories, where children's ideas are made explicit and even worked on some (often individually or in one-on-one exchanges with the teacher) so that they are differently understood when "put back in." Yet we have also seen (in Liz's story and supporting data) that it is a later change for teachers to become skilled at supporting the joint work of a group of students on an idea as it is understood and made explicit by the various members of the class. Thus, "working on it together while it is out" involves changes in practice that come more slowly. It is these changes that eventually support greater change to the initially expressed ideas—that is, greater learning.

Of course it is not really that simple. The processes are neither entirely separate from one another nor from the subject-matter knowledge that this pedagogy requires. As one piece moves forward, the others shift and benefit as well. Getting the inside out is earlier in the process—early enough that by the end of 1 seminar year teachers are reliably making this change in their classroom practices. The work that is slower to develop is seeing in the thoughts represented by children what there is to work on, figuring out how to work on it, providing opportunities for making the new work explicit, and, therefore, making it more amenable to being put back in in a new form. From a comparison of the classroom stories of Claire and Liz and from the related portfolio writing, I wonder if other teachers, like Claire, might work at these aspects of practice one-on-one with students at first. Perhaps this one-on-one work serves as a stepping stone to orchestrating a group consideration of a variety of representations for what each alone holds and for what, as a group, the represented thoughts might offer.

The three bulleted points just considered are not entirely separable from one another. Each set of observations overlaps with and is related to the others. Yet each also focuses on a particular comparison worth our attention. The strands of teacher learning that the bullets refer to are similarly an overlapping, intertwined set. They are neither logically nor in the actual work of teachers independent from one another.

The three strands work *together* to enable the changes we have seen—the changes that come more quickly as well as those that come more slowly. Progress in each strand supports greater progress in the others. Consider the ways that Strand 1 gains support gains in the other two strands. The Strand 1 discoveries illustrated by Abby's and Ella's stories—discovering their students' and their own abilities to have mathematical ideas—make it more likely and possible for teachers to deepen their own mathematical understandings (Strand 2). The more a person sees herself as a mathematical thinker, not just a receiver of mathematical dogma, the more fully she might participate in work such as that described in the fractions story of Strand 2, and the more likely it is that she will engage in the kind of mathematical analysis that Tamar showed us in her analyses of her students' counting. Similarly, the kind of changes in thinking that we found with Abby and Ella in Strand 1 surfaced again as we looked at teachers' changing practices in Strand 3.

Teachers who have the expectation that they and their students have mathematical thoughts are more likely to engage with and analyze the mathematical content of student offerings, during and after class, and to change their teaching practices in ways that encourage both the articulation of ideas and the joint consideration of the strengths and weaknesses of student understandings.

Progress along Strand 2, such as we saw in the fractions story and in Tamar's story, is also a likely support of progress in the other strands. The deeper and broader a teacher's knowledge of mathematics, the more likely it will be that she will recognize mathematical ideas in others and in herself (Strand 1), and the more effectively she is likely to be able to work with her students on moving their understandings forward (Strand 3).

Changes in teaching practice of the kind described in chapter 4 are also likely to support progress in the other two strands. The more that Ella's, Claire's, and Liz's teaching came to support student expression of ideas, the more their students revealed themselves as thinkers and offered opportunities for teachers to deepen their Strand 1 understandings. These same changes in teaching practice, as we could see in Liz's story especially, also provide teachers with rich opportunities for learning more mathematics within the classroom (Strand 2).

In addition to some of these logical connections among the strands, we can see the interweaving of the strands within and across the teachers' stories. For example, it is easy to find in the stories examples of the same work feeding multiple strands of learning for a given teacher.

If we think back to Abby's story and the changes set in motion by the facilitator's question to her—"Why would 60 be too much?"—we can see that this experience fed all three strands. It helped Abby to articulate her new view of children as people with mathematical ideas (Strand 1). It helped her to move forward in her mathematical investigation of division during that seminar session (Strand 2). Further, Abby was able to use this experience as an opportunity to reconsider her classroom practices (Strand 3). She draws from her own feelings in response to the seminar facilitator's question an initial vision for how she might interact differently with her students and with their ideas, and she begins to enact this vision.

Similarly, if we think of Tamar's story from Strand 2, her work with the number line fed her mathematical understanding of the relationship between the order of counting numbers and their value (Strand 2). It also fueled a reconsideration of classroom practices (Strand 3).

Finally, we might remember Ella's stories from Strands 1 and 3. Ella takes from her seminar work on fractions a changed sense of herself as a mathematical thinker (Strand 1), new mathematical knowledge (Strand 2), and increased engagement with the mathematical ideas expressed by children as she teaches in her own classroom (Strand 3).

In the last several paragraphs, we have focused on the ways in which progress in one strand supports progress in the others. By similar logic and evidence, the converse is also true. Lack of progress along one strand may impede or limit a teacher's growth in the others. Without addressing all the possible combinations here, one example may make the point. It may seem obvious that limited understanding of the mathematics of the elementary curriculum will limit what a teacher can do in her classroom when faced with student ideas. Similarly, a teacher who is strong in the mathematics she is teaching may be limited if she has only rudimentary skill at eliciting student ideas. For it is through an exploration of these student ideas that the teacher will gain access to some of the mathematics that is relevant to the topic under study (Schifter, 2001), but that may remain invisible to her, just as some of the mathematics underlying counting was invisible to Tamar until she looked more carefully at student work.

Finally, although the strands are interwoven, the stories of this book make each strand visible. In the picture that emerges, one further point stands out. The strands of this book separate out teachers' recognition that we have mathematical ideas from teachers' knowledge of those ideas and from teachers' knowledge of how those ideas develop in children. We have watched as teachers came to appreciate that ordinary people are havers of ideas, and we saw that this discovery happens, to some extent, separately from developing a deep understanding of the ideas or their developmental trajectory. The notion that teachers differ from one another in the extent to which they believe in people (or children at least) as capable of generating mathematical ideas is not new (e.g., Franke, Carpenter, Levi, & Fennema, 2001; Schifter & Simon, 1992). Yet what the stories of this book reveal about the construction of this belief, and how it is situated with respect to teachers' other developing mathematical and pedagogical understandings, is new. The relative ease and speed with which this Strand 1 discovery appears highlights its potential as leverage in building other aspects of teachers' knowledge and practice.

PART 4: THE SEMINAR AS THE HUB OF TEACHERS' PROFESSIONAL DEVELOPMENT—THE CORE ASPECTS REVISITED

If we are to create, offer, and participate in effective professional development for teachers, we must not only consider these strands of teacher learning, but we must also consider how the features of the seminar help to bring about these changes.

A first, and perhaps obvious, point is that the DMI seminars and the culture that the facilitators work to establish within them provide a safe and supportive community in which to do the hard work we have been reading about: articulating and reflecting on mathematics and on one's teaching practices. The seminar offered participants colleagues with whom to laugh and/or cry and/or celebrate, as they felt frustrated or uncertain or wrong or triumphant or proud in the course of tackling this demanding work. It offered community members—participants, facilitators, and case writers—who could serve as models and fellow explorers of mathematics and pedagogy. This kind of seminar community is the hub of the teachers' professional world.

The character of a DMI seminar community—its supportiveness, agenda, and rigor—owes a good deal to the three core aspects of the seminar set out in chapter 1: (a) the solidity and complexity of the mathematics, (b) the concurrent study of teachers' and students' mathematics, and (c) the parallel between the seminar's pedagogy and envisioned elementary classroom pedagogy. In that first chapter, I raised a number of questions about these aspects of the seminar. In the pages that follow, we return to those questions. What can we learn from the stories of this book about the features of professional development that are foregrounded in the DMI seminars?

A. Solidity and Complexity of the Mathematics

What do the stories reveal about the mathematics that teachers are learning and the ways in which they are using their mathematical knowledge and experience?

All of the DMI activities—the mathematical work designed for teacher investigations, the work with the print and video cases representing student thinking on particular mathematical topics, the focus questions for the discussion of readings, the research highlights essays, and their discussion—are designed to strengthen the seminar participants' understanding of the mathematical topics that comprise the elementary mathematics curriculum. Each is designed to offer opportunities for teachers to further investigate what, at some level, are familiar mathematical topics, this time, however, in a context that aims at teachers coming to understand the underlying ideas, not simply memorizing standard algorithms. The seminar work also aims at providing teachers with opportunities to make mathematical arguments and assess the validity of these arguments and other mathematical propositions. The fractions story is one example of this.

So what was the impact of these experiences on teachers? One approach to this question would be to catalog the specific mathematical knowledge gained during the seminar year. This study was not designed to provide a complete catalog of the mathematical knowledge that teachers gained from their DMI experience. We still have a lot to learn about the particular mathematics that teachers learned in DMI and perhaps also what they did not learn. This is a job for future research.

However, this study does show us that teachers were learning mathematics from their seminar work, and that the mathematics they were learning was able to support their work as teachers outside of the seminar. The stories and teacher writing contained in this book show us that (a) there is a good deal for adults to learn about elementary mathematics. This is evident in numerous places: among them, the fractions story and teacher portfolio writing about it, Tamar's reflections on counting, Abby's work during the seminar to understand a child's division algorithm, and Ella's comments about her work on the "birthday" problem and the multiplication and division of fractions. It is also clear from these same stories (among others) that (b) given the opportunities available in the DMI seminar, teachers were learning mathematics. Further, we know that by the end of 1 year, (c) teachers were bringing this new mathematical knowledge into their planning (Tamar's story offers an example of this), and (d) into their classrooms. As we saw teachers' practices changing, it was toward more productive engagement with the mathematics in their classrooms.

Although it may be obvious that a seminar such as DMI—one that offers the solid, complex study of elementary mathematics—would be important to teachers in building the subject matter knowledge necessary for teaching, another set of outcomes of this rigorous study of mathematics may have been less predictable. From the DMI participants, we learn that the study of complex mathematical ideas, in the teaching and learning environment offered by DMI, has important pedagogical implications as well. The fractions work played a central role. In this work, teachers built understandings that felt entirely new to them. They were not elaborating on or deepening their understanding of a topic they felt they already understood. In coming to understand the multiplication and division of fractions, teachers also changed their views of themselves as mathematical thinkers, changed their willingness to engage with mathematical ideas that are initially unfamiliar, and changed their conviction that new knowledge could be built in this way. These changes, which came about as teachers joined together to work on solid and complex mathematics, affected the stance that teachers took within their own classrooms.

Because the work of coming to understand the multiplication and division of fractions was as rigorous as it was, and because the seminar pedagogy was as it was, teachers also came to understand that learning often involves frustration. They learned that persistence brings rewards, and that frustration is neither something that can nor should be avoided. Rather, they found that exploring errors can be fruitful, and that frustrating moments can be valuable ones.

Teachers' own experiences with rigorous subject matter study led to still other discoveries about learning. Teachers wrote and spoke about learning that understandings can come and go. Just because an idea is clear at one moment, there is no guarantee that it will stay clear. Understanding is not an all or nothing proposition. Ideas may often need to be rebuilt.

Further, teachers' own work at building a new and complex mathematical understanding supported their growing sense that knowing how to perform a calculation is different from understanding a mathematical idea, and that the former is not sufficient. We know from Abby's story, and the writing of other teachers, that this was a conviction that grew in part from watching children in the seminar's print and video cases engage in solid mathematical work. Yet we also saw in teacher writing after the fractions work that teachers' own engagement with complex mathematical ideas that were new to them contributed to their growing knowledge of and focus on sense-making as a teaching objective.

Thus, teachers' experience with challenging, rigorous mathematical investigations in the seminar resulted in new mathematical understandings, a new engagement with mathematics, and new insights into the process and experience of learning. All of these served the participants well both in and out of the seminar sessions.

B. Concurrent Study of Teacher and Student Mathematics

Do teachers draw on their own experiences as mathematics learners to inform their work with children? Do they draw on their experiences of children's mathematical thinking to enrich their own work in mathematics? If so, how? In what kinds of situations?

In DMI seminars, teachers are concurrently studying student work for the mathematical strengths and needs it reveals and doing their own mathematical work on the same general topic. We can look to the stories and teacher writing of this book for information about how separate or intermingled these two kinds of work are for teachers. What teachers know about mathematics and what they know about children learning mathematics *could* be held quite separately. Indeed the literature offers terms that might apply separately to each—content knowledge and pedagogical content knowledge (Shulman, 1986, 1987), pedagogical content knowledge being "that special amalgam of content and pedagogy that is uniquely the province of teachers" (Shulman, 1986, p. 8) and including, among other things, teachers' understanding of how children come to learn particular topics. Although it behooves us to be aware of the importance of both kinds of knowledge, in practice the boundary between the two is not so clearly drawn.

Throughout the book, it is interesting to note the ways in which teachers move back and forth between their own experiences learning mathematics in the seminar and their observations of children's mathematical work. When they reflect on the children's work, it is sometimes to shed light on children's work and sometimes to better understand their own work pedagogically or mathematically. Similarly, when the teachers reflect on their own mathematical learning, it is sometimes to better understand their own processes and sometimes to better understand children and their needs.

Each of the stories contained in the book offers its own set of examples of this movement between the world of children's mathematical experiences and the teacher's own mathematical experiences. We can take Abby's story as illustrative of the dance between the two. Abby's story begins in the seminar where Abby is working to understand and carry out a strategy used by a child in one of the cases for solving a multidigit division problem. Here the seminar makes the child's mathematical work into a mathematically engaging problem for the teacher. The teacher, Abby, takes up this problem and encounters in it her own mathematical issues. As Abby works through her issues—aided by the facilitator's question "I'm confused, why would 60 be too much?"—she comes to better understand the mathematics, the child's strategy for dividing, and her own learning. Further, Abby uses her own experience of this mathematical inquiry and the facilitator's question to think more about the mathematical experiences of her students. She thinks about the important role that the facilitator's question played in her mathematical work, and she moves easily from there to consider the kinds of experiences she offers to the children whom she teaches. As we know from the story, Abby becomes dissatisfied with the learning environment she is creating. Abby's own experience learning mathematics is not the only springboard for her reconsideration of her students' mathematical experiences. She also draws on her careful study of the seminar's print and video cases—of hearing children "explain what they're thinking . . . coming up with ways of solving problems that necessarily isn't the most expedient, but *that they understand*, and they're building a foundation" (Abby, interview, January 8, 1997)—in reconsidering the work of her own students.

This thumbnail sketch of Abby's story offers a sample of the ease and fluidity with which teachers reason back and forth about their own mathematical work and that of the children whom they teach. We can see in it that one teacher's focus on her own mathematical work informs both her own further work and her sense of her students' work. We can also see that this same teacher, in focusing on student work, uses what she learns to inform both her sense of the student work and her work as a teacher. Each of the stories of this book offers similar examples. If we break each story down into smaller parts, we can pull from the stories examples of each of these kinds of reasoning.

Sometimes teachers make use of their reflections on children's work to better understand just that—children's mathematical work. As just noted, for Abby (chap. 2), the more she observed children who were working to make mathematical sense, the more she came to believe that her students could engage with mathematics in these same ways. Abby's study of children's mathematical work as portrayed in the cases led her to reconsider her own students' mathematical experiences—what these experiences had been and what she wished they might be. As we know, Abby went on to consider how she might encourage her students to further express and reflect on their mathematical ideas. We get a glimpse of this as she reconsiders what changes she might like to make in the lesson concerning geometric solids and counting the faces of a solid.

In Tamar's story (chap. 3), we see another example of a teacher who, in carefully considering student work, comes to better understand that student work. As Tamar reflects on her students' counting, their judgments about the order and value of counting numbers, and their representation of number on the number line, she comes to understand more about her young students' ideas about counting and how they develop over time. Observing her students, Tamar comes to believe that they are working at (a) remembering a rote string of number names, (b) consciously reasoning about the order inherent in the counting numbers, and (c) understanding the quantitative relationships among counting numbers.

Perhaps less predictably, teachers' reflections on children's work sometimes helped teachers shed light on their own mathematical work. Abby's and Tamar's stories again provide examples. As Tamar studied her students' counting and representations of number, as she studied the ideas that they appeared to have and to be working on, she built for herself a better understanding of the mathematics of counting. Similarly, Abby's seminar work to understand a child's algorithm for division led to new mathematical understanding for Abby. In carrying out the child's algorithm, Abby learned something more about the structure of division situations and the importance and difficulty of holding in mind the number of groups, the number of items in a group, and the whole being divided.

Teachers' reflections on their own mathematical work, like their reflections on children's work, served multiple purposes. The whole of the fractions story (chap. 3) is an example of teachers reflecting on their own mathematical work to further their own mathematical work. In addition, the portfolio writing reveals the impact of the fractions experiences not only on teachers' understanding of fractions, but also on teachers' thoughts and feelings about themselves as mathematical thinkers. The last paragraphs of Section A of Part 4 of this chapter bear this out. Further, teachers' reflections on their own mathematical work were sometimes used to shed light on children's mathematical work. Ella's story (chap. 2) provides examples. When Ella was faced with the birthday problem in the seminar, she solved the problem in a way that she soon decided was "completely wrong."

> ... and I left feeling, "But don't leave me like this. Because I don't know how to figure this out." // Um, ... and that was enlightening for me because I thought "I wonder if I do that to any of my students." We don't get to it, so.... I mean, we worked at something, but we don't get to it ..., and we don't, we don't even get back to it, at least I hope, but you never know. In their minds, I could think I've covered it all and everyone's clear, but there could be one student that I didn't get to, that wasn't vocal, and do they ever leave math thinking, "But, wait a minute, wait a minute. I didn't get it." You know? (Ella, interview, February 10, 1997)

Ella reports a similar experience in October of the seminar year as she works through some of the mental calculations she is asked to perform in the seminar. Here again while Ella begins with a focus on her own mathematical work, she moves freely to consider the potential applicability of what she learns about her own mathematical thinking to the mathematical work of the children she teaches.

> ... it had me really thinking about strategies and the one strategy that I tend to rely on, and why do I do that? And so I was trying to explore other ways that I was learning. And I think that that has really helped me in the classroom with realizing that sometimes these kids really are stuck. // They can't always think of some new way to come to things. And maybe that's really very difficult for them. // It was very difficult for me.... (Ella, interview, October 28, 1996)

All of this supports a view of teachers' mathematical knowledge and teachers' knowledge of children's mathematical understanding that is blended in some way. The particular blends and entwinements of subject matter and pedagogical knowledge that teachers call on in their classroom practices has received considerable attention recently (Ball, 2000; Ball & Bass, 2000; Ball, Lubienski, & Mewborn, 2001; Ma, 1999; Schifter, 1998, 2001; Sherin, 2002; Wilson, Floden, & Ferrini-Mundy, 2002). The evidence from the work of DMI teachers may show us some of the ways in which teachers build their knowledge for teaching. They make use of their opportunities to study mathematics and children's mathematical thinking to build a joined and integrated pool of knowledge that has relevance to their work as teachers. The two kinds of knowledge do not appear to be held separately by teachers, at least not when that knowledge is gained in the context of a seminar designed around the three core aspects that describe DMI.

C. Parallel Pedagogy

What do the stories reveal about the ways in which teachers draw on seminar pedagogy in their changing beliefs and practices? Which aspects of the pedagogy are most salient to participants? Which are least salient?

In what ways does the DMI seminar provide opportunities for participants to articulate pedagogical ideas and questions? When? By whom? What is the impact of choices like these on teachers' changing practices?

All of the stories of changing teaching practice in chapter 4 move in the direction of the seminar pedagogy, and this is not a coincidence. The seminar offered participants two sources of pedagogical models—those in print and video cases, and those instantiated in the seminar facilitator's own pedagogical practices within the seminar. Not only were these pedagogical models available, but the evidence—classroom observations, interviews, and teacher portfolio writing—indicate that participants were drawing on these models.

Ella writes about the cases as a source of pedagogical borrowing—borrowing that helped her focus classroom conversation on children's reasoning and on representing it (Ella's story, chap. 4).

> There have been many ideas that I have gotten from both the readings and the videos that I have implemented in my classroom. [. . .] In the very first video that we viewed, the teacher had the students explain their strategies for solving an addition problem. I was so moved by this video that the very next day I imitated a reproduction with my students. I was so impressed by the outcome that I have since used this same method many times and I will continue to do so. (Ella, Portfolio Assignment 1.6, December 1996)

It is with this case-inspired image in mind, and with her own firmer connection to mathematical ideas (developed in the course of the seminar), that Ella begins to explore with her students the variety of ways they conceive of 35 × 5, for instance.

Another teacher writes in her portfolio (chap. 4) about a rule of thumb she has distilled from several cases. She writes:

> The seminar has also helped me to see that figuring out how a person solved a problem is an important step to understanding their thinking. Much of my work in both the Preschool and the upper grades is with children who have

difficulty with either expressive and or receptive language. Explaining their thoughts is not an easy thing for many of these children. This step can be difficult to get at with young children who lack the language necessary to talk about their ideas or for older children whose language skills are weak. One of the lessons which I have been reminded about from the readings is to have children show what they did to solve a problem. This can serve as a catalyst for conversation about their work. (Preschool special needs and K–6 resource teacher, Portfolio Assignment 1.6, December 3, 1996)

Teachers not only borrowed from seminar cases, they also drew on seminar pedagogy as they experienced it from their own mathematical work in the seminar. Ella makes this point in her course evaluation written in June:

In doing the "mental math" activities in the seminar, I was afforded the opportunity to listen to my peers strategies on problem solving. This contributed to the importance that I place in my students' opportunity to share their strategies with one another. I cannot emphasize enough how useful this information is to me as a facilitator of math instruction. (Ella, course evaluation, June 2, 1997)

In this passage, Ella highlights her experience of the mathematics and of the interactions among teachers in the seminar. Of course these experiences were possible, in part, because of the structure of the seminar and the pedagogical choices of the facilitator.

Some of the stories in previous chapters speak directly to participants borrowing from the sense they made of the *facilitator's* work during the seminar sessions. Recall the prominent role that the facilitator's question played for Abby as she considered fundamental questions related to her own pedagogy. The facilitator's question—"I'm confused. Why would 60 be too much?"—and the question's impact on Abby helped her think more deeply about a number of issues. As a teacher, what role did she accord to student ideas? To her own ideas? What roles did she wish to accord to them? In her first attempts at envisioning answers to these questions, Abby's exchange with the seminar facilitator loomed large. It seemed to offer a rich piece of experience that she would then spend a good deal of time and thought to better understand. How did it differ from her own practice at the time? Why had it been helpful to her own learning? How might she draw on it in her own work with children?

Similarly, in chapter 4, Tamar speaks about the importance of a facilitator's question that was posed during her exploration of the multiplication and division of fractions. The facilitator suggested to Tamar's small group that they might think about the problem first as a whole number problem to better understand what each operation is accomplishing. Tamar is interested in how helpful this suggestion was, in better understanding the teaching stance it represents, and in bringing this stance into her own teaching.

> I think it was [the seminar facilitator] who suggested to one of my small groups one day to um, go back and think of the problems as a whole number problem // and think about what you're actually doing. Um, you know, instead of three fourths and one sixteenth, // you know, times one sixteenth, you know, think of a whole number and think about what multiplication is actually *doing* to those numbers. // And I think it just gave me a, a greater understanding of math [. . .] or of these operations, one that I've never *had* before. And, you know, [. . .] it's just kind of *empowering*, you know, you're, . . . *I'm not a dummy.* / (Laughs). / You know, I can really do this. [. . .] I think it also helped me to empathize, . . . , with the kids, and sort of see how they're feeling when they struggle with ideas.
> [. . .]
> I wish there were, there were ways that I could be like [my facilitator], and just come over and give them, like, "Well, think about it in terms of whole numbers," // and you know, just help their understanding with just like a little phrase like that. Um, but also, um . . . , you know, to give them *time* to struggle with ideas, and give them *opportunities* to talk about it, talk with *friends* about it. I mean, we worked on those in *whole* groups, and um, a lot of understanding comes from different people explaining it at different times of your, you know, struggle. Um, so that, you know, kids that can talk about it with peers and [. . .] talk about it in class, and you know, all those kind of things. (Tamar, interview, June 1997)

Tamar, like Abby, draws on the facilitator's work, along with her own learning and her own feelings in those moments. The moments become emblematic. They provide a rich representation of some of the complex interactions among teacher, student, and subject matter that Tamar, as a teacher, is working to use to her preschool classroom community's advantage.

These emblematic moments—whether they come from the seminar's print and video cases or from the participants' own experiences of the mathematical teaching and learning facilitated by the seminar leader—are in a particularly rich and available format. They are vivid and detailed, and we know that vividly imaginable detail contributes to the ease with which a memory is called on in making judgments (e.g., Tversky & Kahneman, 1974).[9] So to the extent that these emblematic moments hold valuable pedagogical and/or subject matter lessons, their vividness increases the likelihood that teachers will make use of them.

---

[9]Although this principle is most often invoked to explain deviations from purely probabilistic reasoning, the more general point—that memory for vivid case example is strong—also applies when the information held in these memories is appropriate to invoke.

Yet what do these emblematic moments hold for teachers' use? What information do they contain? The various parallel pedagogies that are available in the seminar context offer participants access to different aspects of the teaching practices portrayed. In all instances—written cases, video cases, and facilitators' practices—participants see the *teachers' actions, their interactions with students, and students' actions*. Further, in most of the written cases and in some of the video cases, participants also have access to some of the *teachers' thinking*: their reflections on their teaching moves, their questions about past or future teaching moves, and, in some cases, their stated agendas or intentions for their classes.

However, as participants experience the seminar facilitator's practice, the aspects of practice they do and do not have access to are different. As with the cases, participants see the facilitator's interactions with her students, but in the context of the facilitator's practice, because the participants are the students, participants have access to *students' thoughts and feelings* in these moments. As we saw through the example of teacher writing about their fractions experience (Section A, Part 4 of this chapter), this was a powerful source of information about learning. Yet the flip side of this coin is that participants experiencing the facilitator's practice do not get direct evidence about the issues, questions, and agendas that drive the facilitator's practice within the seminar.

For example, Abby is aware that the facilitator directs her (Abby's) attention back to her own reasoning, and she is aware of the flood of thoughts and feelings that ensue for her. Similarly, Tamar is aware that the facilitator poses a mathematical question that proves helpful as she works to better understand the multiplication of fractions. Yet neither Abby nor Tamar is privy to the facilitator's concerns and reasoning in making these choices.

Recognizing this variety in the kinds of pedagogical information available to seminar participants raises questions about the place and function of each of these windows on pedagogy for teachers who are working at developing their practices. How might each be best used? To what extent, in what ways, and when are samples of practice that are relatively unanalyzed with respect to the teachers' thoughts and intentions useful to teachers who are building or changing their teaching practices? To what extent, in what ways, and when is it important for teachers who are working on strengthening their practices to engage in precisely that analysis of a *teacher's* thoughts and intentions as she interacts with her class? To what extent, in what ways, and when is it important for teachers to experience and reflect on the feelings and the thoughts they have as *students* within this kind of pedagogy?

Surely all are important, and opportunities for all of these exist within the DMI seminars. However, in considering what kinds of pedagogical explorations might be most useful at what points in practice, it may be helpful to recall which aspects of practice were most salient and which least salient to participants after 1 year of DMI. We have seen that it is a beginning step—and not a trivial one—for teachers to teach in such a way that children's ideas are represented in the classroom. As teachers enact these first, most salient aspects of the teaching and learning they are experiencing in the DMI seminar, they are, like Ella, Claire, and Liz, face to face with questions and issues about how to use the representations for which they are now making a place. Yet how groups work together to create new understandings out of represented beginnings is a complicated matter. We saw this in Claire's and Liz's stories. Perhaps it is at these junctures that explicit study of teaching moves and their outcomes might be most helpful.

We have also seen that it is a later, more slowly developing step (or set of steps) for teachers to build practices that work productively with children's represented ideas. The kind of practice that we see in Liz's story requires of teachers that they (a) engage more deeply with the subject matter ideas, (b) develop a stronger sense of the functions of represented ideas in teaching and learning, and (c) develop ways to make fuller use of the classroom community and the variety of ideas held by community members.

The mathematical and pedagogical work accomplished in DMI plays an important role, as we have seen. Yet we might consider what comes next for the teachers we have been reading about or teachers who reach places these teachers have reached. I wonder what would happen if, for instance, after working through *Building a System of Tens* and *Making Meaning for Operations*—after establishing norms around subject matter engagement and depth of thinking, after having come to make changes in practice like those we saw in Ella's story—these teachers had professional development opportunities to explore more carefully moment-to-moment classroom interactions and their effects on the building of ideas. What would happen if, following participation in a DMI seminar, teachers had opportunities to focus on the teaching and learning issues that are as structured and carefully crafted as their opportunities to study mathematics in DMI are?

Certainly there are myriad questions about how this might be accomplished. Issues of timing are complicated. In addition, what kinds of sample practice might be useful ones? Might teachers examine samples of practice from a seminar session (in which they are the students), from a teacher's own elementary classroom teaching (in which at least one participant is the teacher), from observations of a peer's practice, from video or print cases, and/or perhaps from working through written cases such as those in chapter 4 of this book?

How and when we offer opportunities for teachers to make their pedagogical questions and understandings explicit, represent them, work on and with them, and represent them again are important questions for all of us. They are questions that we can begin to address as we learn in more detail about the various big ideas that come up for teachers as they work to build new, more powerful teaching practices that align with national standards and visions for strong teaching. It is my hope that the stories and analyses of this book are helpful in this regard.

CODA

DMI and the genre of professional development for teachers that it belongs to hold great promise. Professional development seminars such as these are vibrant, rigorous, and respectful intellectual communities that support teacher learning in all of its complexity. They also open up for our further study teacher learning in all of its complexity. For me, the stories of this book raise questions about finding a balance that includes subject matter work as well as a focus on the pedagogical interactions—the structure of classroom interchanges. It is my sense that the most profound changes happen when professional development is able to hold teachers' and teacher educators' focus on both interactional and subject matter issues. Although for now some of the details about how, in what balance, and at what times along the way may still be somewhat fuzzy, the general direction and its effectiveness are not fuzzy at all. As a community of educators, if we can be as reflective about teacher learning as we hope that teachers will be about children's learning, we will no doubt get better and better at supporting teachers as they develop practices that hold great promise for individual children and communities of children. As teachers, teacher educators, researchers, and subject matter specialists, we will no doubt get better and better at bringing both children's and teachers' understandings to light—both in teacher seminars and in elementary classrooms.

Yet as tall an order as this is, there is more to accomplish than learning how to nurture the development of powerful teaching practices. We also need the community vision and support to make schools and teaching what we know they can be. I hope that the portrayals of teachers at work in the stories of this book help to build that vision and to rally that support—for that is perhaps our greatest challenge.

APPENDIX A
Mathematical Topics, Agendas, and Written Assignments for DMI

Topic	Agenda	Portfolio Assignment (Paraphrased) Due at Next Session
	Building a System of Tens	
		Choose three pieces of student work, one strong, two less strong. What satisfies you in the strong piece? Why? What is your analysis of the others? What are your learning goals for each student? (PA 1.1)
Session 1 Children's algorithms for adding and subtracting two-digit numbers	• Orientation • Sharing and discussion of PA 1.1 • Mental math: addition and subtraction of two-digit numbers, and sharing methods • Case discussions • Math activity working with addition of two-digit numbers	What are your expectations for the seminar? How did the first session compare with your expectations? (PA 1.2)

(Continued)

Topic	Agenda	*Portfolio Assignment (Paraphrased) Due at Next Session*
Session 2	Recognizing and keeping track of groups of 10 while operating	• Video of children in classrooms solving two-digit addition and subtraction problems • Case discussions • Reflections on case discussions and establishing group norms for them • Mental math: two- and three-digit addition and subtraction with discussion of strategy	What ideas about number and number systems have been highlighted for you in this seminar? What questions do you have? (PA 1.3)
Session 3	Written numerals and the structure of tens and ones	• Case discussion • Video of math interview with child—viewed twice, once focusing on the mathematics, and a second time focusing on the questions asked • Math interview preparation	Math interview with a child (PA 1.4)
Session 4	More on addition and subtraction of two-digit numbers	• Discussion of interviews • Case discussion (including a discussion of the role of the historically taught algorithms) • Video case discussion • Mental math activity involving addition, subtraction, and multiplication, with a sharing of methods	What are you learning? Write about your questions, doubts, feelings. (PA 1.5)
Session 5	Multiplication of multidigit numbers	• Discussion of PA 1.5 • Math activity on multiplication • Case discussion • Mental math activity involving multiplication and division	Have there been any shifts in your teaching practice and/or in what you are thinking as you work with your students? If so, what have they been? Have you gotten any ideas from the cases that you are trying in your classroom? (PA 1.6)

Topic	Agenda	*Portfolio Assignment (Paraphrased) Due at Next Session*
Session 6 Division of multidigit numbers	• Discussion of PA 1.6 • Case discussion • Mental math: 159 ÷ 13, writing word problems that would be solved by this calculation, and then calculating mentally and sharing methods • Videotape case discussion: The video shows children solving the problem 159 ÷ 13	Pick a case that had a particular impact on you. Describe that impact. What is interesting to you about this case? What makes it useful? (PA 1.7)
Session 7 Decimal numbers	• Math activity: rules for ordering numbers, including nonwhole numbers • Case discussion • Discussion of PA 1.7	(a) Write a case. (b) Write about a point of agreement with the research article and a point about which you wonder or that does not match your experience. (c) Choose one piece from your portfolio—a piece that you'd like to share. (PA 1.8)
Session 8 Highlights of related research	• Sharing cases • Discussion of *Highlights of related research* • View and discuss video already seen in session 4 • Portfolio discussion— sharing of the pieces selected	Choose 3 pieces of student work, one strong, two less strong. What satisfies you in the strong piece? Why? What is your analysis of the others? What are your learning goals for each student? How does your response to this PA compare with your response to this assignment for the first session? In what ways has your thinking changed, in what ways has it remained consistent? (PA 2.1)

(Continued)

Topics	Agenda	Portfolio Assignment (Paraphrased) Due at Next Session
	Making Meaning for Operations	
Session 9 — Counting up, counting back, and counting by	• Discussion of PA 2.1 • Math activity: figuring out the time between two dates in days, months, years • Case discussion	Write a case. (PA 2.2)
Session 10 — Addition and subtraction as models	• Math activity on the nature of subtraction and the variety of situations it models • Case discussion • Discussion of participant written cases	What do you learn from and how can you use student thinking? Why is it important to have students express their own and their peers' mathematical ideas in class? (PA 2.3)
Session 11 — What is multiplication? What is division?	• Case discussion • Viewing and discussing videotape cases showing classroom scenes of children solving problems involving ideas of multiplication and division • Math activity: 32 ÷ 5, story problems that could be solved by dividing 5 into 32, and the variety of answers one might arrive at depending on the situation of the story. Similar work with 5 ÷ 32.	Make a list of questions or tasks you might use for math interview with a child. (PA 2.4)
Session 12 — • When dividing gives an answer less than 1	• Case discussion • Math activity centering around fractions, the wholes to which fractions refer, and addition of fractions • Planning interview #2	Math interview with a child. (PA 2.5)

(Continued)

Topics	Agenda	*Portfolio Assignment (Paraphrased) Due at Next Session*
Session 13 Combining shares or adding fractions	• Discuss interviews • Case discussion • Math activity involving the multiplication and division of fractions	Describe your own mathematical learning about fractions from the past few seminar sessions. What are you still working on? What has this experience been like for you? (PA 2.6)
Session 14 Taking portions of portions, or multiplying fractions	• Discuss PA 2.6 • Case discussion • Math activity focusing on the division of fractions	Choose three pieces of student work, one strong, two less strong. What satisfies you in the strong piece? Why? What is your analysis of the others? What are your learning goals for each student? How does your response to this PA compare with your response to this assignment before? In what ways has your thinking changed, in what ways has it remained consistent? (PA 2.7)
Session 15 Expanding ideas about division in the context of fractions	• Discuss PA 2.7, student work samples • Case discussion • Discussion about which case had an impact	Reflection: Choose a portfolio piece that reflects your own development during this seminar and write about it. (PA 2.8)
Session 16 Highlights of related research	• Discuss *Highlights of related research* • Discuss portfolio review (PA 2.8) • Complete evaluation forms • Closing	

Note. PA = Portfolio Assignment.

References

Abdal-Haqq, I. (1995). *Making time for teacher professional development* (Digest 95-4). Washington, DC: ERIC Clearinghouse on Teaching and Teacher Education.

Ball, D. L. (1990). Prospective elementary and secondary teachers' understanding of division. *Journal for Research in Mathematics Education, 21*(2), 132–144.

Ball, D. L. (1993). With an eye on the mathematical horizon: Dilemmas of teaching elementary school mathematics. *Elementary School Journal, 93*, 373–397.

Ball, D. L. (1994). Developing mathematics reform: What *don't* we know about teacher learning—But would make good working hypotheses? *Paper prepared for conference on Teacher Enhancement in Mathematics K–6*, Arlington, VA.

Ball, D. L. (1996). Teacher learning and the mathematics reforms: What we think we know and what we need to learn. *Phi Delta Kappan, 77*(7), 500–508.

Ball, D. L. (2000). Bridging practices: Intertwining content and pedagogy in teaching and learning to teach. *Journal of Teacher Education, 51*(3), 241–247.

Ball, D. L., & Bass, H. (2000). Interweaving content and pedagogy in teaching and learning to teach: Knowing and using mathematics. In J. Boaler (Ed.), *Multiple perspectives on the teaching and learning of mathematics* (pp. 83–104). Westport, CT: Ablex.

Ball, D. L., Lubienski, S., & Mewborn, D. (2001). Research on teaching mathematics: The unsolved problem of teachers' mathematical knowledge. In V. Richardson (Ed.), *Handbook of research on teaching* (4th ed., pp. 433–456). New York: Macmillan.

Barnett, C., Goldenstein, D., & Jackson, B. (Eds.). (1994). *Fractions, decimals, ratios, and percents: Hard to teach and hard to learn?* Portsmouth, NH: Heinemann.

Bastable, V., Schifter, D., & Russell, S. J., with Lester, J. (2001a). *Examining features of shape, facilitator's guide.* Parsippany, NJ: Dale Seymour.

Bastable, V., Schifter, D., & Russell, S. J., with Harrington, D., & Reynolds, M. (2001b). *Examining features of shape, casebook.* Parsippany, NJ: Dale Seymour.

Borko, H., Eisenhart, M., Brown, C. A., Underhill, R. G., Jones, D., & Agard, P. C. (1992). Learning to teach hard mathematics: Do novice teachers and their instructors give up too easily? *Journal for Research in Mathematics Education, 23*(3), 194–222.

Brown, C. A., Stein, M. K., & Forman, E. A. (1996). Assisting teachers and students to reform the mathematics classroom. *Educational Studies in Mathematics, 31*, 63–93.

176

Calkins, L. M., & Harwayne, S. (1987). *The writing workshop/A world of difference: A guide for staff development.* Portsmouth, NH: Heinemann.

Carpenter, T. P., Ansell, E., & Levi, L. (2001). An alternative conception of teaching for understanding: Case studies of two first-grade mathematics classes. In T. Wood, B. S. Nelson, & J. Warfield (Eds.), *Beyond classical pedagogy: Teaching elementary school mathematics* (pp. 27–46). Mahwah, NJ: Lawrence Erlbaum Associates.

Carpenter, T. P., Fennema, E., Franke, M. L., Empson, S. B., & Levi, L. W. (1999). *Children's mathematics: Cognitively guided instruction.* Portsmouth, NH: Heinemann.

Carpenter, T. P., Fennema, E., Peterson, P. L., Chiang, C. P., & Loef, M. (1989). Using knowledge of children's mathematics thinking in classroom teaching: An experimental study. *American Educational Research Journal, 26,* 499–531.

Carroll, D., & Carini, P. (1991). Tapping teachers' knowledge. In V. Perrone (Ed.), *Expanding student assessment* (pp. 40–46). Reston, VA: ASCD.

Cohen, D. K., & Hill, H. C. (2001). *Learning policy: When state education reform works.* New Haven, CT: Yale University Press.

Cohen, S. (1999). Highlights of related research. In D. Schifter, V. Bastable, S. J. Russell, with S. Cohen, J. B. Lester, & L. Yaffee, *Building a system of tens: Casebook* (pp. 125–151). Parsippany, NJ: Dale Seymour.

Conference Board of the Mathematical Sciences. (2001). *The mathematical education of teachers: Part 1.* Washington, DC: Mathematical Association of America.

Cox, H. (1975). Foreword. In R. Frost, *You come too* (pp. 6–10). New York: Holt & Company.

Duckworth, E. (1987). *"The having of wonderful ideas" and other essays on teaching and learning.* New York: Teachers College Press.

Duckworth, E. (Ed.). (2001). *"Tell me more": Listening to learners explain.* New York: Teachers College Press.

Featherstone, H., Pfeiffer, L., & Smith, S. P. (1993). *Learning in good company: Report on a pilot study* (Research Report 93-2). East Lansing: National Center for Research on Teacher Learning, Michigan State University.

Fernandez, C., Ertle, B., Chokshi, S., Tam, P., Allison, C., Appel, J., & Schafer, C. (2002). *A lesson study initiative aimed at exploring how to promote critical thinking: Findings, process, and reflections.* Paper presented at the Research Presession for the annual meeting of the National Council of Teachers of Mathematics, Las Vegas, NV.

Franke, M. L., Carpenter, T. P., Fennema, E., Ansell, E., & Behrend, J. (1998). Understanding teachers' self-sustaining, generative change in the context of professional development. *International Journal of Teaching and Teacher Education, 14,* 67–80.

Franke, M. L., Carpenter, T. P., Levi, L., & Fennema, E. (2001). Capturing teachers' generative change: A follow-up study of professional development in mathematics. *American Educational Research Journal, 38*(3), 653–689.

Franke, M. L., & Kazemi, E. (2001). Teaching as learning within a community of practice: Characterizing generative growth. In T. Wood, B. S. Nelson, & J. Warfield (Eds.), *Beyond classical pedagogy: Teaching elementary school mathematics* (pp. 47–74). Mahwah, NJ: Lawrence Erlbaum Associates.

Gearhart, M., Saxe, G., Selzer, M., Schlackman, J., Ching, C., Nasir, N., Fall, R., Bennett, T., Rhine, S., & Sloan, T. (1999). Opportunities to learn fractions in elementary mathematics classrooms. *Journal for Research in Mathematics Education, 30*(3), 286–315.

Goldsmith, L., Mark, J., & Kantrov, I. (2000). *Choosing a standards-based mathematics curriculum.* Portsmouth, NH: Heinemann.

Graves, D. (1989–1992). *Reading/writing teacher's companion.* Portsmouth, NH: Heinemann.

Graves, D. (1994). *A fresh look at writing.* Portsmouth, NH: Heinemann.

Grossman, P. L., Wilson, S. M., & Shulman, L. S. (1989). Teachers of substance: Subject matter knowledge for teaching. In M. Reynolds (Ed.), *Knowledge base for the beginning teacher* (pp. 23–36). New York: Pergamon.

Grossman, P. L., Wineburg, S., & Woolworth, S. (1998). *But what did we learn? Understanding changes in a community of teacher learners*. Unpublished manuscript, University of Washington.

Hammer, D. (1997). Discovery learning and discovery teaching. *Cognition and Instruction, 15*(4), 485–529.

Hammer, D. (1999). *Teacher inquiry*. Newton, MA: Center for the Development of Teaching, Education Development Center.

Heaton, R., & Lewis, J. (2001). *Strengthening the mathematics education of elementary school teachers: A partnership between the Teachers College and the Department of Mathematics and Statistics at the University of Nebraska Lincoln* [Abstract]. Paper presented at the Conference Board of the Mathematical Sciences' National Summit on the Mathematical Education of Teachers: Meeting the Demand for High Quality Mathematics Education in America. Retrieved October 31, 2001, from http://www.maa.org/cbms/NationalSummit/workinggroups.htm.

Karmiloff-Smith, A. (1979). Micro- and macro-developmental changes in language acquisition and other representational systems. *Cognitive Science, 3*(2), 91–118.

Karmiloff-Smith, A. (1981). Getting developmental differences or studying child development? *Cognition, 10*, 151–158.

Karmiloff-Smith, A. (1986). From meta-processes to conscious access: Evidence from children's metalinguistic and repair data. *Cognition, 23*, 95–147.

Karmiloff-Smith, A. (1992a). Beyond modularity: Innate constraints and developmental change. In S. Carey & R. Gelman (Eds.), *The epigenesis of mind* (pp. 171–197). Hillsdale, NJ: Lawrence Erlbaum Associates.

Karmiloff-Smith, A. (1992b). *Beyond modularity*. Cambridge, MA: MIT Press.

Lampert, M., & Ball, D. L. (1998). *Teaching, multimedia, and mathematics: Investigations of real practice*. New York: Teachers College Press.

Lehrer, R., Schauble, L., Carpenter, S., & Penner, D. (2000). The interrelated development of inscriptions and conceptual understanding. In P. Cobb, E. Yackel, & K. McClain (Eds.), *Symbolizing and communicating in mathematics classrooms: Perspectives on discourse, tools, and instructional design* (pp. 325–360). Mahwah, NJ: Lawrence Erlbaum Associates.

Lewis, C. (2002). *Does lesson study have a future in the United States?* Paper presented at the Research Presession for the annual meeting of the National Council of Teachers of Mathematics, Las Vegas, NV.

Lord, B. (1994). Teachers' professional development: Critical colleagueship and the role of professional communities. In N. Cobb (Ed.), *The future of education: Perspectives on national standards in education* (pp. 175–204). New York: College Entrance Examination Board.

Ma, L. (1999). *Knowing and teaching mathematics: Teachers' understanding of fundamental mathematics in China and the United States*. Mahwah, NJ: Lawrence Erlbaum Associates.

Mokros, J., Russell, S. J., & Economopoulos, K. (1995). *Beyond arithmetic: Changing mathematics in the elementary classroom*. Palo Alto, CA: Dale Seymour.

Morse, A., & Wagner, P. (1998). Learning to listen: Lessons from a mathematics seminar for parents. *Teaching Children Mathematics, 4*(6), 360–364, 375.

National Council of Teachers of Mathematics. (2000). *Principles and standards for school mathematics*. Reston, VA: Author.

Piaget, J. (1975). *L'équilibration des structures cognitives: Problème central du développement*. Paris: Presses Universitaire de France.

Piaget, J., & Inhelder, B. (1969). *The psychology of the child*. New York: Basic Books.

Putnam, R. T., & Borko, H. (1997). Teacher learning: Implications of the new view of cognition. In B. J. Biddle, T. L. Good, & I. F. Goodson (Eds.), *The international handbook of teachers and teaching* (Vol. II, pp. 1223–1296). Dordrecht, Netherlands: Kluwer.

Root, R. L., Jr., & Steinberg, M. (1996). *Those who do, can: Teachers writing, writers teaching*. Urbana, IL/Berkeley, CA: National Council of Teachers of English/National Writing Project.

Rosebery, A. S., & Puttick, G. M. (1997). *Teacher professional development as situated inquiry: A case study in science education*. Newton, MA: Center for the Development of Teaching Paper Series, Education Development Center.

Russell, S. J. (1998, November). *Classroom teachers becoming teacher educators: "Just facilitators or active agents?"* Paper presented at the annual meeting of the North American Chapter of the International Group for the Psychology of Mathematics Education.

Russell, S. J., Schifter, D., & Bastable, V., with Konold, C., & Higgins, T. (2002a). *Working with data, casebook*. Parsippany, NJ: Dale Seymour.

Russell, S. J., Schifter, D., & Bastable, V., with Lester, J. (2002b). *Working with data, facilitator's guide*. Parsippany, NJ: Dale Seymour.

Russell, S. J., Schifter, D., Bastable, V., Yaffee, L., Lester, J. B., & Cohen, S. (1995). Learning mathematics while teaching. In B. S. Nelson (Ed.), *Inquiry and the development of teaching: Issues in the transformation of mathematics teaching* (pp. 9–16). Newton, MA: Center of the Development of Teaching, Education Development Center.

Sassi, A., & Goldsmith, L. (1996, April). *Beyond recipes and beyond magic: Mathematics teaching as improvisation*. Paper presented at the 1996 meeting of the American Educational Research Association, New York.

Schifter, D. (1995). Teachers' changing conceptions of the nature of mathematics: Enactment in the classroom. In B. S. Nelson (Ed.), *Inquiry and the development of teaching: Issues in the transformation of mathematics teaching* (pp. 17–26). Newton, MA: Center of the Development of Teaching, Education Development Center.

Schifter, D. (1997). *Learning mathematics for teaching: Lessons in/from the domain of fractions*. Newton, MA: Center of the Development of Teaching, Education Development Center.

Schifter, D. (1998). Learning mathematics for teaching: From the teachers' seminar to the classroom. *Journal for Mathematics Teacher Education, 1*(1), 55–87.

Schifter, D. (1999). Reasoning about operations: Early algebraic thinking, Grades K through 6. In L. Stiff & F. Curio (Eds.), *Mathematical reasoning, K–12: 1999 NCTM Yearbook* (pp. 62–81). Reston, VA: National Council of Teachers of Mathematics.

Schifter, D. (2001). To see the invisible: What skills and knowledges are needed to engage with students' mathematical ideas? In T. Wood, B. S. Nelson, & J. Warfield (Eds.), *Beyond classical pedagogy: Teaching elementary school mathematics* (pp. 109–134). Hillsdale, NJ: Lawrence Erlbaum Associates.

Schifter, D., Bastable, V., Russell, S. J., with Cohen, S., Lester, J. B., & Yaffee, L. (1999a). *Building a system of tens, casebook*. Parsippany, NJ: Dale Seymour.

Schifter, D., Bastable, V., Russell, S. J., with Lester, J. B., Davenport, L. R., Yaffee, L., & Cohen, S. (1999b). *Building a system of tens, facilitator's guide*. Parsippany, NJ: Dale Seymour.

Schifter, D., Bastable, V., Russell, S. J., with Yaffee, L., Lester, J. B., & Cohen, S. (1999c). *Making meaning for operations, casebook*. Parsippany, NJ: Dale Seymour.

Schifter, D., Bastable, V., Russell, S. J., with Lester, J. B., Davenport, L. R., Yaffee, L., & Cohen, S. (1999d). *Making meaning for operations, facilitator's guide*. Parsippany, NJ: Dale Seymour.

Schifter, D., Bastable, V., & Russell, S. J., with Woleck, K. (2001a). *Measuring space in one, two, and three dimensions, casebook*. Parsippany, NJ: Dale Seymour.

Schifter, D., Bastable, V., & Russell, S. J., with Lester, J. (2001b). *Measuring space in one, two, and three dimensions, facilitator's guide*. Parsippany, NJ: Dale Seymour.

Schoenfeld, A. H. (1985). *Mathematical problem solving*. Orlando, FL: Academic Press.

Schifter, D., & Simon, M. A. (1992). Assessing teachers' development of a constructivist view of mathematics learning. *Teaching and Teacher Education, 8*(2), 187–197.

Sconiers, S., Isaacs, A., Higgins, T., McBride, J., & Kelso, C. R. (2003). *The ARC Center tri-state student achievement study: A report of the ARC Center at the Consortium for Mathematics and its Applications (COMAP)*. Lexington, MA: COMAP.

Sherin, M. G. (2002). When teaching becomes learning. *Cognition and Instruction, 20*(2), 119–150.

Shulman, L. S. (1986). Those who understand: Knowledge growth in teaching. *Educational Researcher, 15,* 4–14.

Shulman, L. S. (1987). Knowledge and teaching: Foundations of the new reform. *Harvard Educational Review, 57,* 1–22.

Shulman, L. S. (2000). Teacher development: Roles of domain expertise and pedagogical knowledge. *Journal of Applied Developmental Psychology, 21*(1), 129–135.

Silver, E. A. (1996). Moving beyond learning alone and in silence: Observations from the QUASAR project concerning communication in mathematics classrooms. In L. Schauble & R. Glaser (Eds.), *Innovations in learning: New environments for education* (pp. 127–159). Hillsdale, NJ: Lawrence Erlbaum Associates.

Sowder, J. (2001). *The role of understanding children's thinking in convincing teachers that they must develop a profound understanding of the mathematics they teach* [Abstract]. Paper presented at the Conference Board of the Mathematical Sciences' National Summit on the Mathematical Education of Teachers. Meeting the Demand for High Quality Mathematics Education in America. Retrieved October 31, 2001, from http://www.maa.org/cbms/NationalSummit/workinggroups.htm.

Stein, M. K., Smith, M. S., Henningsen, M. A., & Silver, E. A. (2000). *Implementing standards-based mathematics instruction: A casebook for professional development.* New York: Teachers College Press.

Stein, M. K., Smith, M. S., & Silver, E. A. (1999). The development of professional developers: Learning to assist teachers in new settings in new ways. *Harvard Educational Review, 69*(3), 237–269.

Stigler, J. W., & Hiebert, J. (1999). *The teaching gap: Best ideas from the world's teachers for improving education in the classroom.* New York: The Free Press.

TERC. (1998). *Investigations in number, data, and space.* Parsippany, NJ: Dale Seymour.

Tversky, A., & Kahneman, D. (1974). Judgment under uncertainty: Heuristics and biases. *Science, 185,* 1124–1131.

Warren, B., & Ogonowski, M. (1998). *From knowledge to knowing: An inquiry into teacher learning in science.* Newton, MA: Center for the Development of Teaching, Education Development Center, Inc.

Wilson, S. M. (1991). Parades of facts, stories of the past: What do novice history teachers need to know? In M. Kennedy (Ed.), *Teaching academic subjects to diverse learners* (pp. 99–116). New York: Teachers College Press.

Wilson, S. M., & Berne, J. (1999). Teacher learning and the acquisition of professional knowledge: An examination of research on contemporary professional development. In A. Iran-Nejad & P. D. Pearson (Eds.), *Review of research in education* (Vol. 24). Washington, DC: American Educational Research Foundation.

Wilson, S. M., Floden, R. E., & Ferrini-Mundy, J. (2002). Teacher preparation research: An insider's view from the outside. *Journal of Teacher Education, 53*(3), 190–204.

Wineburg, S., & Grossman, P. L. (2000). Scenes from a courtship: Some theoretical and practical implications of interdisciplinary humanities curricula in the comprehensive high school. In S. Wineburg & P. L. Grossman (Eds.), *Interdisciplinary curriculum: Challenges to implementation* (pp. 57–73). New York: Teachers College Press.

Yaffee, L. (1999). Highlights of related research. In D. Schifter, V. Bastable, S. J. Russell, with L. Yaffee, J. B. Lester, & S. Cohen, *Making meaning for operations: Casebook* (pp. 127–149). Parsippany, NJ: Dale Seymour.

Author Index

A

Abdal-Haqq, I., 3
Agard, P. C., 11
Allison, C., 6
Ansell, E., 3
Appel, J., 6

B

Ball, D. L., 2, 3, 5, 11, 12, 48, 164
Barnett, C., 3
Bass, H., 164
Bastable, V., 9, 11, 12
Behrend, J., 3
Bennett, T., 7, 144
Berne, J., 3
Borko, H., 3, 11
Brown, C. A., 7, 11, 144

C

Calkins, L., 2, 3, 4
Carni, P., 3
Carpenter, S., 16
Carpenter, T. P., 3, 5, 158

Carroll, D., 3
Chiang, C. P., 5
Ching, C., 7, 144
Chokshi, S., 6
Cohen, D. K., 3, 6, 7, 8, 144
Cohen, S., 9, 11, 12
Conference Board of the Mathematical Sciences, 2, 3, 8
Cox, H., 21, 25

D

Davenport, L. R., 9, 11, 12
Duckwork, E., 3, 14, 16

E

Economopoulos, K., 25
Eisenhart, M., 11
Empson, S. B., 3
Ertle, B., 6

F

Fall, R., 7, 144

Subject Index